THE MAN WHO SOLD AMERICA

Also by Joy-Ann Reid

Fracture

THE MAN WHO SOLD AMERICA

Trump and the Unraveling
of the American Story

JOY-ANN REID

WILLIAM MORROW
An Imprint of HarperCollins*Publishers*

A hardcover edition of this book was published in 2019 by William Morrow, an imprint of HarperCollns Publishers.

FIRST WILLIAM MORROW PAPERBACK EDITION PUBLISHED 2020.

Library of Congress Cataloging-in-Publication Data has been applied for.

ISBN 978-0-06-288011-6

20 21 22 23 24   DIX/LSC   10 9 8 7 6 5 4 3 2 1

To the stars of my show:
Jason, Winsome, Jmar, and Miles

CONTENTS

THE MAN WHO SOLD AMERICA

INTRODUCTION

Welcome to Gotham

Introduce a little anarchy. Upset the established order and everything becomes chaos.
    I'm an agent of chaos.

—The Joker, from *The Dark Knight*

TO TRULY UNDERSTAND DONALD TRUMP, YOU NEED TO HAVE lived in New York City in the 1980s and 1990s, when his business and marital escapades were a tabloid staple. Or maybe you just need to have grown up on Batman.

Gotham City—which the brooding billionaire Bruce Wayne polices as his vigilante alter ego—is an exaggerated, dystopian send-up of old New York. It's filled with over-the-top villains who, like Batman, possess no actual superpowers but get by on their cleverness, their ostentatious wealth, and their ability to wreak havoc on the urban landscape.

Donald Trump seems ripped right out of that comic book supervillain universe. With his cantilever hairstyle, weirdly long signature neckties, bizarre syntax, and penchant for slapping his surname on everything he's connected with—from buildings and golf courses to bottled water, board games, and, for a time, a sham "university" that promised anyone could learn to be just like "The Donald"—Trump and the cast of characters surrounding him could fit right in with Joker, Riddler, Penguin, and Lex Luthor.

Trump has existed on the outskirts of American celebrity and popular culture for the life spans of most Americans under the age of forty. He made cameos in movies like *Home Alone 2: Lost in New York* and on TV shows such as *The Fresh Prince of Bel-Air*. He sat in the guest chair on *The Phil Donahue Show* and *The Oprah Winfrey Show*. And he performed mock-fights with World Wrestling Entertainment chairman Vince McMahon on multiple episodes of WrestleMania. (He even pretended to buy WWE's lucrative *Monday Night Raw* franchise in an elaborate ruse in 2009, which tanked the entertainment company's stock price, prompting Trump to quickly pretend to sell it back for twice the price.)

Despite his history of alleged housing discrimination against black tenants and his full-page ad in the 1980s calling for the return of the death penalty in the face of black and brown teenagers being accused of a gang rape they didn't commit, Trump managed to work his way into mainstream popular culture. Early on, he was a "tabloid-friendly rogue" and celebrity hanger-on, and later, the king of the "B-list" stars who jockeyed for his approval on *The Celebrity Apprentice*.

Had he not signed on to the racist "birther" conspiracy, claiming that America's first black president, Barack Obama, was not born in the United States,[1] and plunged headfirst into the morass of anti-immigrant xenophobia that helped win him the presidency, the old Donald Trump might have carried on. He may have remained a cultural gadfly—that peculiar brand of celebrity whose views on everything from geopolitics to the Oscars are sought out for no particular reason other than that he is famous and "quotable."

But Donald Trump did become president—and so, here we are.

As a candidate, Trump offered Republicans the taste of the celebrity status that Ronald Reagan had given them; something normally reserved for Democrats. That's what attracted Sam Nunberg, the thirty-eight-year-old political adviser who toiled on Trump's warm-up attempts at presidential runs and on the real presidential deal until he lost a war with Trump campaign manager Cory Lewandowski and was fired in the summer of 2015. (Nunberg says Lewandowski saw to it that old, racist posts on his Facebook page surfaced; he later apologized for those posts.) And though Nunberg readily says that Trump "screwed him," he claims he would vote for him again in 2020, because Trump has delivered on Republican policies and judicial nominations.

"I knew our campaign was doing well when I went into a restaurant after he announced," Nunberg said. "The TV was on CNN, and he was on, and people were watching. These were people who probably normally wouldn't give a shit. But they were watching *him*."

Trump wasn't just another politician doing a TV hit. "He was an American mogul, an entertainer," Nunberg said. "And he wasn't rich from making microchips or selling stocks. It was from building. Construction. It was this image of success; of him being rich and he can make you rich. We were the WWE–Fox News version of the Obama campaign in the beginning, and I mean that as a compliment. It was aspirational. It was, 'we can fight the system.'"

Nunberg was raised on the Upper East Side of Manhattan and nurtured on conservative talk radio, strident support for Israel, and suspicion of "the Middle East." After volunteering for Mitt Romney's 2008 campaign, he worked for right-wing lawyer Jay Sekulow during the 2010 fight to prevent the construction of a mosque near the "ground zero" site of the September 11 terrorist attacks in Manhattan. (He says Trump wrote a "bullshit" letter at the time, offering to buy the land where the mosque was to be built, but the offer was just a PR stunt.) Nunberg's parents were lawyers, and he became one, too. His father had worked for a law firm that Trump and his father had used for real estate deals. But Nunberg didn't meet Trump in person until he was introduced to him in 2010 by yet another Gotham City character: Roger Stone—the villain with the Richard Nixon tattoo on his back.

"I wanted to win a national election and thought Trump could win," Nunberg says of his eagerness to sign on. "I thought it was cool that Obama went on the late-night shows. I thought the [John] McCain ad showing Obama speaking to millions of people and showing Paris Hilton and slamming him as a Hollywood celebrity was the dumbest fucking thing I've ever seen." He said he all but screamed at the time: "You just won him millions of votes!"

Nunberg thought his party was living in the 1950s. And though Trump was his own version of the *Mad Men* era, to Nunberg, he was a Mad Man for the twenty-first century. He and Trump share a sensibility he likens to a retired New York City firefighter or cop who mainlines Fox News, plus Rush Limbaugh and Mike Levin on talk radio and thinks to himself, "this country has gone to shit, and we need a guy in the White House who's willing to punch a few holes in the wall to make it like it was when I was coming up."

Trump seems like "one of *them* who made it." He grabbed the brass ring and the trophy wives and the all-gold penthouse. Even if his Horatio Alger story was a lie—he inherited millions from his dad and never needed to pull himself up by his own bootstraps—Trump's fans appreciated that he was hated by the Chamber of Commerce crowd and the fancy set in Manhattan. They liked that because they felt those "elites" hated them, too. If Gotham needs a Batman, it also needs a Joker. And Trump was their Joker, sowing chaos on their behalf and taking the whole Injustice League with him to the White House.

The trouble is, he didn't seem to actually want to be president. What he did want was to put on the greatest presidential campaign show of all time.

When he glided down the Trump Tower escalator on June 16, 2015, to announce that he was a candidate, wife Melania was smiling and waving silently beside him in a white sleeveless dress with a bare neckline. Neil Young's "Rockin' in the Free World" was blaring on loudspeakers. Crowds lined up along the upper floor railing, watching the couple descend, hooted and cheered. The woman chosen to introduce him, daughter Ivanka Trump, one floor below and also in white sleeveless, was clapping along to the music, standing beside a makeshift podium in front of a backdrop of blue curtains and a row of huge American flags with gold eagles on top. All the Trump children, from Barron up to Donald Jr., were there, waiting in the wings. Emblazoned on the podium was the campaign's slogan: "TRUMP: MAKE AMERICA GREAT AGAIN."

Trump poured it on. "That is *some* group of people— *thousands!*" he exclaimed, marveling at the crowd behind the phalanx of media and photographers. Nunberg recalls the crowd consisting of a couple *hundred* people, including some hired extras paid $50 apiece to cheer Trump on and wave premade signs. They had been hired by Extra Mile, a subcontractor of a company called Gotham Government Relations. When *The Hollywood Reporter* revealed that fact, via emails its reporter obtained,[2] Lewandowski issued what would become a familiar Trumpian denial. "Mr. Trump draws record crowds at almost every venue at which he is a featured speaker," he deadpanned to *The Hollywood Reporter*. "The crowds are large, often record-setting and enthusiastic, often with standing ovations. Mr. Trump's message is, 'Make America Great Again.'"[3] The FEC later dismissed a complaint about the whole affair.[4] But the circus had officially come to town, and even the controversy was part of the show.

According to one longtime Republican political operative who knows and supports him, Trump never seriously believed he would be elected president. The Republican field was shaping up to include an armada of heavyweights vying for the jump ball after two terms of President Obama. A bank of current and former governors, including Jeb Bush of Florida, Chris Christie of New Jersey, Scott Walker of Wisconsin, Mike Huckabee of Arkansas, John Kasich of Ohio, and Bobby Jindal of Louisiana, entered the race. So did media favorite Marco Rubio, the junior senator from Florida, South Carolina senator Lindsey Graham, Tea Party favorite Ted Cruz, and libertarian firebrand Rand Paul. Famed neurosurgeon Ben Carson jumped in, too, along with former Hewlett-Packard CEO Carly Fiorina. The entries produced gushing media reviews calling it the finest Republican field in a generation. Surely one of them would take the nomination, and leave the reality show performer behind. Even Trump privately said so.

Trump also told people that every time he had started running for president—in 1988, 2000, and 2012—the money started pouring in. He claimed he'd "made a fortune on the birther stuff," which piqued the interest of billionaire cranks who suddenly took an interest in him. It wasn't clear whether Trump actually believed the conspiracy theory questioning Barack Obama's birthplace, though his antipathy for, and some would say envy of and obsession with, Obama was never in doubt.

During the early months of the campaign, the Republican operative said, Trump told him and a U.S. senator who later became a fellow supporter of the president that his presidential bid would be a marketing boon to his newest hotel, the Trump International Hotel in Washington, D.C. "I'll run for president for a few months and get a bunch of publicity and boost the room rates," the operative says Trump explained. "You can't buy that kind of publicity, and when you run for president, you get it for free."

The property had been the Old Post Office and Clock Tower on Pennsylvania Avenue. The federal government had tried for a dozen years to develop the historic building, with everyone from disgraced lobbyist Jack Abramoff to supporters of a National Women's History Museum offering bids. Trump and his financial partners won out in 2012, with the promise of millions of dollars in rent payments going to federal coffers. Trump even staged his belated admission that Barack Obama was indeed American-born against the backdrop of a soft launch for the hotel, inviting the assembled campaign press on a tour after dropping the admission as a terse one-liner.

The hotel—which one person who has known Trump and his sons professionally since 2003 said was clearly designed under the direction of Ivanka and the Trump sons, and not their father, since its interior is not "all gold"—didn't initially command the luxury rates the family had hoped for, particularly after famed chef José Andrés backed out of a deal to open a restaurant in the hotel, in protest against Trump's anti-immigrant rhetoric. (The Trump Organization sued Andrés for $10 million, and the two sides settled in April 2017.)

The Republican operative describes Trump as a man fixated on his money like no "billionaire" they'd ever met and carrying a "giant chip on his shoulder" inherited from his Queens-developer father, who had felt locked out of the Manhattan real estate market because he wasn't "part of the club"—something Trump made it his mission to rectify. Win or lose, Donald J. Trump for President would make them all pay attention. And it would put tens of millions of dollars into the pockets of a man who may never have had as much of it as he led people to believe.

Nunberg agrees that Trump's 2012 trial balloon was entirely for show. But he says Trump genuinely looked at that 2015 field of standard-issue politicians and thought, "I can beat those guys." And while he admits Trump could have been telling a true believer what he wanted to hear, Nunberg says that at a minimum, Trump wanted to "be number one" in the polls. Trump knew the Clintons, and how formidable they were. After all, during Bill Clinton's tenure, he was a supporter. Nunberg says Trump still believed the Clintons liked him. And he thought winning the White House against a potential first woman president would be harder than stopping the first black president had been. Yet Trump seemingly gave no thought to what actually holding the office of president would entail. According to Nunberg, the weighty issues around what being president of the United States would actually mean simply never came up.

Still, when Trump rode down that escalator in 2015, he had all the trappings of a real campaign: the blue suit, red tie, and flag pin; and a small but dedicated staff, who wrote a speech they knew the candidate would never deliver verbatim. Staffers, including Nunberg, distilled the address into bullet points set in a large typeface, punctuated with phrases like "Mission," "Commitment," "Authentic," and "We have had enough!" in a document marked "Big Day."

Lewandowski red-lined the speech Nunberg wrote, eliminating whole paragraphs and lines that (to Nunberg's annoyance) turned up in Ivanka Trump's introduction speech. Trump was supposed to talk about his rise through the ranks of New York real estate, and how he could translate his success into America's. "Our country needs a comeback," he was meant to say, and politics as usual "has to stop." Trump was to describe how government was failing the American people and that having dealt with politicians all his life, he knew "better than anyone that they are all talk and no action." The theme of the speech was: "it is time"—to change the system and to change Washington. "The American dream is dead!" began the closing line, which Lewandowski added in red. "But, with your help, we can bring it back bigger and better than ever. Together we can make America great again!"

Instead, Trump unleashed a forty-six-minute rant as the cameras rolled. He sneered at the other presidential candidates and their supposed lack of understanding of air-conditioning. They "sweated like dogs" at their announcements, he said. He carped about China and Japan "beating America," about how our country doesn't win anymore and the rest of the world was laughing at us. And he delivered a notorious riff about Mexico "sending" its crime, drugs, and rapists to America. Instead of delivering an inspirational speech that would force the pundit class to take his presidential campaign seriously, "he walked up to that podium and blew himself up," the Republican operative said.

Perhaps Trump was disgorging whatever he had taken in from his favorite channel—Fox News—the night before. Maybe he saw all those people and cameras, and being a natural showman, simply began performing. Maybe all of the resentments and prejudices that had built up inside him over his seventy-plus years just came spilling out. Or perhaps he was exhibiting what political strategists say can happen to any candidate for high office when the reality of what it all means, and the responsibility, really hits them. The pressure can melt a man down, they say, and make him commit the most deviant act he can think of just to relieve the pressure of duty.

But to Trump's surprise—and to the world's—his bill of complaints was exactly what the Republican base wanted to hear.

As HIS IMPROBABLE CANDIDACY BARRELED TOWARD THE WHITE House, Trump had no trouble discarding anyone around him who came up short in his eyes and thus became "a loser." That soon included Nunberg. And it eventually included Trump's longtime lawyer and fixer, Michael Cohen.

Cohen, whose father survived the Holocaust and whose

mother was a nurse, grew up in a New York suburb on Long Island. He started as a personal injury lawyer before veering into real estate law and a taxi medallion business that ultimately crashed along with his legal fortunes. He went to work for the Trump Organization in 2007 after helping him with a recalcitrant condominium board the year before, and soon became Trump's brass-knuckled bruiser. He played the heavy with nosy reporters and once said he would take a bullet for the man whom he, like all Trump employees and associates, called only "boss" or "Mr. Trump"—even after working for him for a decade. When the FBI raided his offices in the spring of 2018, Michael Cohen's journey to turning state's evidence on "the boss," and Trump turning on him, began.

During dramatic, televised testimony in front of the House Committee on Oversight and Reform on February 27, 2019, Cohen told his version of the story behind Trump's decision to run for president. He too said Trump ran for president as an elaborate marketing scheme to promote his hotel business—just not in the United States. In Cohen's telling, after decades of trying and failing to build a Trump Tower in Moscow, Trump hoped that climbing onto the ultimate global stage, as a presidential candidate, would finally put him in position to ink a Russian deal that would "make hundreds of millions of dollars."

"Donald Trump is a man who ran for office to make his brand great, not to make our country great," Cohen said. "He had no desire or intention to lead this nation—only to market himself and to build his wealth and power. Mr. Trump would often say this campaign was going to be the 'greatest infomercial in political history.' He never expected to win the primary. He never expected to win the general election. The campaign—for him—was always a marketing opportunity."

Cohen was describing what could be the longest "long con" in American history.

In testimony that was likened to the 1973 Watergate hearings, when then–White House Counsel John Dean publicly implicated President Richard Nixon in crimes that ultimately led to his resignation under the threat of impeachment, Cohen said he had been "mesmerized" by Trump. So much so that he was "willing to do things for him that [he] knew were absolutely wrong." [5] Among them: arranging payoffs to women—most notably a pornographic actress and a former Playboy playmate—with whom Trump had conducted affairs, to keep their stories from negatively impacting the election. In some instances *The National Enquirer* would buy the lifetime rights to stories that might hurt Trump, in consultation with Cohen and purportedly, the Trump campaign, and then bury the stories instead of publishing them.

Cohen said he made one such $130,000 payment to pornographic star Stephanie Clifford, stage name Stormy Daniels—taking out a home equity loan to do it—and was reimbursed by Trump via $35,000 checks, some affixed with Trump's giant, Magic Marker signature while he was in the Oval Office. Cohen also admitted he lied to Congress about the proposed Moscow tower, when he claimed in an August 2017 letter to the Oversight committee that the negotiations had stopped in January 2016, while Trump was going through the Republican primaries.

The talks actually dragged on at least through June, while Trump, having dispatched the Republican A-team, was on his way to the Republican National Convention. To hear Trump's longtime friend and "TV lawyer" Rudy Giuliani—the bombastic former New York City mayor—tell it, the talks on building a Trump Tower Moscow might have dragged on right through Election Day.

Cohen came to Congress to set the record straight. He had been convicted of tax evasion, financial fraud, and violations of campaign finance laws, including for the $130,000 payment to

Daniels. And Cohen said he not only arranged to pay Daniels and other Trump paramours not to tell their stories but he also lied repeatedly to Melania about the boss's sexual affairs.

The once-brash Cohen came to Congress a humbled man. Months earlier, he had confided to another seminal New York figure, the Reverend Al Sharpton, now the host of MSNBC's *PoliticsNation*, and to his attorney, Lanny Davis, onetime special counsel to President Bill Clinton, that he was prepared to plead guilty without cutting a special deal for himself because he wanted the opportunity to tell the truth and be redeemed. The purge would be public and total. Cohen was headed to prison to serve a three-year sentence after pleading guilty to the U.S. attorney for the Southern District of New York. He had been disbarred. He had gone from the guy who issued Trump's threats to a recipient of them. The thuggish taunts from the president, delivered via social media against the once-trusted lieutenant he now called a "rat," rattled Cohen and his family. So much so, that he asked congressional Democrats for protection prior to his testimony, and even sought to delay it.

In the space of two years, Cohen had gone from deputy finance chair of the Republican National Committee—a position he accepted during the first year of the Trump administration despite being a longtime Democrat—to Public Enemy Number One, for daring to turn on Trump. He faced a relentless barrage of attacks from Trump's über-loyalists on the dais, who appeared to be auditioning to replace Cohen as "Mr. Trump's" new pit bulls.

The day before his testimony, one of those "replacements," Florida congressman Matthew Gaetz, tweeted at Cohen what sounded like a threat of a coming smear. "Hey @Michael Cohen212," Gaetz's tweet read, "do your wife & father-in-law know about your girlfriends? Maybe tonight would be a good time for that chat. I wonder if she'll remain faithful when you're in prison. She's about to learn a lot." Immediate outrage followed, with some calling for Gaetz to be investigated for witness tampering. Florida politicos wondered where a congressman from their state could have gotten alleged dirt—likely invented—about a Trump confidant who lived in New York City. Some openly wondered if it was the latest mischief by Roger Stone, who had been silenced by a gag order as he faced criminal charges of his own, following an indictment by the special counsel investigating Russia's cyberwarfare, hacking, and interference in the election in which Trump became president.

Gaetz soon apologized under pressure from the Democratic House speaker, Nancy Pelosi, and his tweet made him the target of an investigation by the Florida bar. Still, he showed up at the Cohen hearing to sit in the gallery, in what many interpreted as a bid to intimidate the witness with his presence. It was the kind of tough-guy tactic that not long before, might have been pulled by Michael Cohen.

In his testimony, Cohen called Trump an enigma. "He has both good and bad, as do we all," he said in his opening statement. "But the bad far outweighs the good, and since taking office, he has become the worst version of himself. He is capable of behaving kindly, but he is not kind. He is capable of committing acts of generosity, but he is not generous. He is capable of being loyal, but he is fundamentally disloyal."

Cohen went on to describe a man who was virulently racist in his presence. He said Trump told him as they rode through a black neighborhood while Obama was still president, that no decent country had ever been run by a black person, calling all black-run nations "shitholes" and saying black Americans were "too stupid" to vote for him. Cohen says he threatened Trump's former schools on the candidate's behalf, not to release Trump's grades or SAT scores, while Trump publicly demanded that Obama release his. Trump's attempt at proving Obama had been admitted to Columbia University and Harvard Law School on the basis of race, not talent, was a frequent trope among white conservatives who resent the idea of affirmative action, which in their view is nothing more than "reverse racism" against white people. Trump tapped into that resentment.

When a North Carolina Republican congressman, Mark Meadows, who like Trump had trafficked in Obama "birtherism," angrily dismissed Cohen's accounts of Trump's racism by having a black HUD appointee, Lynn Patton—whom he had invited to the hearing—stand up and silently display, with her bodily presence, that Trump could not possibly be racist—Cohen barked back: "You don't know him. I do."

And Cohen said Trump admitted to faking a bone spur injury to obtain deferments and avoid the Vietnam War, dismissing those who did serve or were drafted as suckers. "You think I'm stupid?" Cohen says he told him. "I wasn't going to Vietnam."

As Cohen's testimony dominated the day, Trump was thousands of miles away. He *had* finally made it to Vietnam, his detractors noted wryly. He was openly pitching for a Nobel Peace Prize to match the one Obama received during his first year as president, by meeting for a second time face-to-face with murderous North Korean dictator Kim Jong Un. But the summit was a failure. And Trump found himself staying up overnight in Hanoi to watch as Cohen spilled his secrets.

Cohen spoke of a man whose narcissism and obsession with public perceptions of his wealth and success seemed to consume his life and were now devouring the country. Questioned about his change of heart regarding Trump, he described a crisis of conscience. He said he was driven away from Trump by the president's performance at a summit in Helsinki, Finland, where Trump bowed down to the Russian president, Vladimir Putin, just as he now did with Kim. Citing his family's own escape from the clutches of Nazis in Europe, he spoke of an ugly incident in Charlottesville, Virginia, where Trump proposed a moral equivalence between American Nazi rioters and their victims.

And he spoke of "watching the daily destruction of our civility to one another" under Trump's rule.

Cohen declared himself "responsible" for the goon squad tactics being aimed at him from the dais by Republican members of Congress, saying, "I did the same thing that you're doing now, for ten years."

"I can only warn people," he added, "the more people that follow Mr. Trump, as I did, blindly, [the more] are going to suffer the same consequences that I am suffering."

Cohen had dire warnings for the country, too. "When Mr. Trump turned around, early in the campaign, and said, 'I can shoot somebody on Fifth Avenue and get away with it,' I want to be very clear: he's not joking. He's telling you the truth," he said.

Cohen likened his former boss to a Mafia-like figure. "When he goes on Twitter, and he starts bringing in my in-laws, my parents, my wife, what does he think is gonna happen?" he asked. "He's sending out the message, that he can do whatever he wants; [that] this is *his* country. He's becoming an autocrat." Cohen even voiced his fear that if Trump were to lose reelection, in 2020, "there will never be a peaceful transition of power."

Cohen ended his testimony on a dramatic and cautionary note. "My loyalty to Mr. Trump has cost me everything," he said. "My family's happiness, my friendships, my law license, my company, my livelihood, my honor, my reputation and, soon, my freedom. And I will not sit back, say nothing, and allow him to do the same to the country."

Perhaps it was too late.

Two years into Donald Trump's presidency, all of America was Gotham City. Trump seemed to believe he could treat the federal government like a resistant New York mayor or city councilman, blustering and bullying to get his way. The darkness—of racism and xenophobia and mutual suspicion that he carried with him into the White House—seemed to cover the land.

As old-line Republicans fled, Washington seemed overrun with cartoon villains. There was the Treasury secretary and former Goldman Sachs financier who bankrolled Hollywood movies and posed with his actress wife in front of sheets of money. There was Ms. Patton, the Trump son's wedding planner turned HUD administrator who was used as a human show-and-tell during the Cohen hearings, and who had been handed control of all of East Coast public housing. One of his few media surrogates was the former New Jersey governor, fresh off his own scandal-plagued tenure in office, who had once prosecuted and jailed the father of Trump's son-in-law and current chief White House adviser.

A parade of those discarded by the White House included decorated generals, one of whom left in disgrace, another in ig-nominy, and two unsullied but unable to change the course of the Trump presidency; communications staff who barked osten-tatious lies at an incredulous press corps; a rumpled Rasputin peddling crypto-fascist diktats; and a TV villain turned White House aide who went by the one-word moniker "Omarosa." And those who remained: a young adviser cooking up torments for immigrants and dark dispatches for the president to deliver; a senior adviser whose own husband lathered her boldfaced lies with his public contempt for the president.

Then there's the Family: Trump's beloved, ambitious first daughter and her dictator-courting husband, Trump's raging eldest son, distant younger brood, and mostly silent, mercurial third wife. They presided over the White House like twenty-first-century American Romanovs. And above all, there was the daily descent into chaos at 1600 Pennsylvania Avenue, led by the presi-dent of the United States.

The Trump presidency was a smorgasbord for self-dealers

who were jammed into the cabinet. Government planes became private jets and foreign travel became lavish junkets, all on the taxpayer dime. Corporate executives wined and dined at Trump hotels and golf clubs as they sought the president's favor. Those who earned his ire saw their businesses threatened, or themselves ridiculed by name on his Twitter feed.

The Trump presidency seemed to shatter the old Republican Party and turn it over to the shouting class. All while Trump made his administration a movable feast for the ultimate villain: an autocratic former KGB officer in Russia who found in the untutored and eager forty-fifth president the perfect "apprentice."

Donald Trump sold millions of Americans, and the world, on a raft of lies, that were at once frivolous and dangerous. This book is an attempt to answer two questions: How did he make the sale? And can America undo the damage he has done?

Gotham is awaiting its heroes.

CHAPTER 1

How Trump Happened

"Most people know what it's like for some smug, élite asshole to tell them, 'You can't say that, it's racist, it's bad.' Well, a vote for Trump meant, 'Fuck you, you don't get to tell me what to say.'"

—"Alt-right" provocateur Mike Cernovich, during a November 2016 interview with *The New Yorker*'s Andrew Marantz

MANY AMERICANS AWOKE ON THE MORNING AFTER THE 2016 presidential election to an unthinkable outcome, one that many deemed a mark of cultural decline. Politics often brings unpleasant surprises. But Donald Trump, president of the United States, was one that few—not the pundits, the professional statistical odds-makers, the political press, or the Democratic candidate and her party—came close to anticipating.

Trump, known as a reality TV star, real estate tycoon, and self-declared billionaire with a lot to say about politics but no experience in it, loved to be heard. For decades, he sounded off on everything from Hollywood starlets and movies to politics and foreign policy during TV interviews on daytime talk shows and

on CNN's *Larry King Live*. He burnished his own legend as a billionaire lothario in blind items placed often pseudonymously by
Trump himself in New York tabloids[1] and on the raunchy radio
show hosted by "shock jock" Howard Stern. He had thrice before
threatened to run for president, in 1988 and 2000 (when he was
on the ballot in the California primary) and 2012, but always
pulled his punch.

When he finally dove in for 2016, he was greeted first as a
joke, then as a threat to the seriousness and future of his chosen
political party, the Republicans. South Carolina senator Lindsey
Graham, himself a Republican candidate for president, in February 2016 called Trump a "kook," "crazy," "unfit for office,"
and "the most flawed nominee in the history of the Republican
Party," only to turn around a year later and attack the media
for portraying President Trump in much the same way. Donald
Trump, "kook" or not, had conquered one of America's two
great, historic political parties.

Hillary Clinton, thought to be a potential first woman president since the day she gave the commencement speech at Welles-
ley College in 1969, had run a historic but flawed campaign. Her
data-driven team made assumptions about a map they couldn't
lose, leading them to take for granted the outcomes in states including Wisconsin, Michigan, and Pennsylvania. They failed to
grasp how deeply embedded the hatred was toward the former
first lady, senator, and secretary of state, developed over four decades of Republican prodding, and instilled in parts of the political media. They were surprised by the strength and durability of
the Bernie Sanders campaign, which activated the American left
and young voters hungry for radical change.

When the primary ended, with recriminations against the
Democratic National Committee still deeply felt, some on the
left could barely be roused to pull the lever for Clinton even if
it meant electing Trump. Sanders, the Independent senator and
self-described Democratic Socialist from Vermont who ran on

the Democratic Party line but never signed up for party membership, supported Clinton after she defeated him in the primary but barely hid his lack of enthusiasm.

These mundane political conditions would help doom Hillary Clinton's campaign. She fell short in the partisan Electoral College, with 232 votes to Trump's 306, despite winning the popular vote by some 3 million votes on November 8, 2016. Nearly everything else about the election was unprecedented.

The aggressive, full-throttle voter suppression deployed by Republican secretaries of state in places such as Georgia, Wisconsin, Ohio, and Texas took full advantage of the Supreme Court's gutting of the Voting Rights Act in 2013. The political press's fixation on Clinton's use of a private email server, and the FBI investigation it spawned, consumed the coverage, even as the media, particularly cable television, lapped up "The Trump Show." And there was the barely disguised sexism that crosses ethnic, cultural, and even gender lines to punish women who vie for power.

Clinton performed more poorly than Barack Obama had with men of every ethnic group, exit polls showed. She improved on Obama's 2012 vote share with only one group: white women, and only by one point, as she lost them to Trump by a margin of 43 to 52 percent.[2] Clinton fell short with voters of color overall, underperforming Obama by 5 percent with black men, 2 percent with black women and Latino men, 7 percent with Latinas, and 5 percent with other nonwhite voters, to include Asian- and Native American voters according to exit polls.[3]

Young voters of color seemed to hold Mrs. Clinton responsible for the sins of her husband's administration, including the 1994 crime bill that many blamed for launching an era of mass incarceration that sucked the lives out of a generation of black and brown people. And just eleven days before the election, there was the extraordinary intervention of then–FBI director James Comey, who publicly reopened the Clinton email investigation, only to shutter it again two days before Election Day.[4]

Even more alarmingly, hanging over Trump's election, and ultimately his presidency, was something America had not seen on nearly this scale before: an aggressive, multipronged attack on the American electorate by a hostile foreign power. We have yet to fully uncover the damage the Russians did to our state voting systems, at least thirty-nine of which were breached by cyber-intruders during the election.[5] We do know that many Republican secretaries of state did little to secure their voter rolls against cyber-attack, and that the use of insecure voting technologies was as prevalent as the deployment of fewer, older, and poorly serviced machines in heavily nonwhite areas. We know that Republicans at the national level, led by the Senate majority leader, Mitch McConnell, refused to join the Obama administration in warning the American people about the Russian attack, and that McConnell went further, informing the administration that Republicans would deem any attempt to raise the alarm about Russian interference as a partisan intervention on Clinton's behalf.[6]

The 2016 election saw a surge in third party voting, for Libertarian candidate Gary Johnson and Green Party candidate Jill Stein, who together accounted for 4.3 percent of the votes.[7] Stein, a favorite of Russian state media, chiseled away at Clinton's support among members of the American left. Americans on the right and left were targeted by an extensive Russian disinformation campaign that sought to exploit America's historic racial and political divisions for the benefit of the Trump campaign.

Americans on the far right had their own pro-Trump agenda. Electing him president became a project of the so-called alt-right, a rebranded version of the long-standing white nationalist column in American life. Russian actors, human and robotic, took full advantage, portraying Trump as the savior of White America. And they burrowed into the Facebook feeds of black Americans, too, pressing on the anxieties of those who doubted Clinton's commitment to social justice. Russian intelligence operatives broke into the Democratic National Committee using so-called spear phishing[8] techniques, stealing thousands of emails, including from John Podesta, Clinton's campaign chair, and used WikiLeaks, run by a self-exiled, anti-American anarchist, Julian Assange, to distribute them at key moments in the campaign.

The operation smelled like Watergate, but with burglars based in St. Petersburg. And Trump, ever the star of the show, in July 2016 used a press conference to call on Russia to step up its attack, declaring, "Russia, if you're listening, I hope you're able to find the 30,000 emails that are missing," referring to personal emails not included in the batch turned over to the Clinton investigation. "I think you will probably be rewarded mightily by our press," Trump declared. An indictment of twelve alleged hackers would later note that on the same day Trump issued his call, Russian cyber-intruders indeed went after the servers at Clinton's private office.

With Trump's campaign chairman, son, and son-in-law taking a clandestine June 9, 2016 meeting in Trump Tower with Russians offering to peddle dirt on Hillary Clinton, and then lying about it, and with Trump dictating his son's cover story from Air Force One, many wondered just how in bed with the Russian theft of Democratic emails were members of the Trump campaign. The repeated contacts, and lies about them by numerous Trump campaign advisors, Jared Kushner's attempt to set up a back channel with Russian contacts out of the reach of U.S. intelligence, and the seeming race among Trump campaign aides to set up the "golden meeting" between Trump and Vladimir Putin seemed to be more than just coincidence.

A race seemed to be on, to see who could deliver to "the boss" sufficient dirt on Hillary Clinton, or her deleted emails, in order to sink her campaign. Whether it was just rhetorical, or something more, the behavior of Trump, his family, and aides caught the FBI's attention.

Once Trump fired FBI director James Comey, bragging on television to NBC's Lester Holt that by doing so he had removed the cloud of the "Russia hoax"—a boast he repeated to the Russian foreign minister and ambassador, inside the Oval Office with no American media or aides present—the FBI's attention turned to investigation. The agency's deputy director, Andrew McCabe, opened a counter-intelligence inquiry in May 2017 into Trump's ties to Russia.

A special prosecutor, Robert Mueller, was named to investigate any potentially illegal coordination between the Trump campaign and the Russian agency, which did the hacking; or the distribution of the hacked emails via WikiLeaks, as well as potential obstruction of justice by the president. Then–attorney general, Jeff Sessions— who had endorsed and aided the Trump campaign—recused himself from the Mueller probe.

By year two of the Trump administration, it was revealed that the FBI probe had pondered whether the sitting president was a Russian asset, operating against American interests from inside the White House. That inquiry would remain a mystery even after the Mueller probe seemed resolved.

The country would also be bedeviled by the question of how such a man—a serial business failure, a tax and marriage cheat, and an unrestrained fabulist who ran a campaign of raw xenophobia, misogyny and racism, crude insults and violent rallies— got enough votes to tip the Electoral College.

In the days and weeks after the election, political scientists and pundits, as well as the media, were fascinated by the "Trump voters." Who were they and what had compelled them to vote for him? How could Americans be so susceptible to foreign influence, let alone by a country long thought of as our Cold War enemy? The immediate answer, tossed around during the long months of the campaign and obsessively pursued afterward, was that the typical Trump voter was the "forgotten man," whose skill set had left him marginalized in the modern workforce.

Economic hardship was presumed to have driven these voters into the arms of a wealthy charlatan who promised to put his business savvy to work for them, and to shake up Washington by "draining the swamp" of those who were picking "real Americans'" pockets. Trump promised he would bring back coal. He would revive dying Rust Belt towns and make shuttered steel plants hum to life again.

It was a gauzy fiction—a Norman Rockwell painting of the downtrodden, salt-of-the-earth American falling for the carnival barker who rolled through town with his wagon full of magic elixirs. But since the election, data has emerged that paints a more complicated picture, and in many ways, a more troubling one.

Multiple studies of the 2016 electorate have shown that Trump's voters were motivated more by partisanship, nostalgia, and race-based anxiety than by a sense of being "left behind" by a changing economy. No doubt, the new global economy has exacerbated income inequality and ripped whole industries out of America, as manufacturing and other jobs migrate to countries with workforces who would demand less pay and fewer benefits. That played a role in creating an atmosphere of cynicism and the desire for radical change.

The "Obama-to-Trump voter" indeed existed, though in smaller numbers than many thought. And these voters had jumped party lines before, consistently choosing the more economically populist candidate over the decades. In 2008, they chose Obama over Hillary Clinton in the primary and over John McCain in the general election, seeking a change of direction from the imploding George W. Bush economy. Obama's freshness and charisma, as well as the country's desire to fast-track racial reconciliation, propelled him to a 9.5 million margin of victory in 2008. Obama was able to defeat Mitt Romney in 2012 because as president he had largely done what he said he would do—the economy was out of recession and growing, and under the Affordable Care Act, derisively and shortsightedly labeled "Obamacare" by his Republican opponents, more than 20 million would be added to the health-care rolls.

Obama's intense support from nonwhite voters allowed him to win reelection by nearly 5 million votes, despite losing virtually every cohort of white voters. As journalist Ron Brownstein noted, "In 2012, Obama won a smaller share of white Catholics than any Democrat since Jimmy Carter in 1980; lost groups ranging from white seniors to white women to white married and blue-collar men by the widest margin of any Democrat since Ronald Reagan routed Walter Mondale in 1984; and even lost among Democratic-leaning college-educated women by the widest margin since Michael Dukakis in 1988." And yet, to the consternation and outrage of Republicans, he won.

Trump, in many ways, was the living, breathing backlash. Bishop William Barber, a civil rights activist who was leading a revival of Dr. King's Poor People's Campaign as the Trump era began, likened it to the vicious "redemption" period that halted Reconstruction a decade after the Civil War. That era presaged the nativist rush of the first decades of the twentieth century. It included the rejection of southern European, Asian, and North African immigrants, racial exclusion and lynching in the Jim Crow South, and race riots and violent racial clashes over union jobs up North. If there was going to be an economic race to the bottom in the twenty-first century, some Americans believed it was time to choose ethnic sides.

The emerging data suggests that by 2016 a sense of economic fatalism was growing among many middle-class white voters, particularly regarding the worth of a college degree. This favored Trump, as white working-class voters had over the decades already become more staunchly Republican. And while the data showed that a sense of actual economic doom or struggle tended to produce more votes for Hillary Clinton or nonvotes than votes for Trump, and that his victory truly lay in his support among more affluent white voters, the myth of the broken-down Trump voter persisted.

In the end, the secret to unlocking the outcome of the 2016

campaign was a familiar one, and one few wanted to address: America's perennial bogeyman, race.

A four-year study published in April 2018 in the *Proceedings of the National Academy of Sciences* (or *PNAS*) determined that many Trump voters' concerns about America losing its dominant global economic position were a stand-in for their fears about a loss of white cultural and economic preeminence at home. This anxiety was not set off by any real worsening of their own economic circumstances—white Americans are on average better off financially than nonwhite Americans, whether or not they have a college degree—but rather a sense of *cultural* displacement; the idea that people of other races, ethnicities, national origins, religions, and sexual orientations were achieving a pride of place in American life that was crowding out white Americans, particularly white Christians, cultural conservatives, and those who favor traditional marriages.

In the *PNAS* study, Diana C. Mutz of the Department of Political Science at the University of Pennsylvania noted that "change in financial wellbeing had little impact on candidate preference. Instead, changing preferences were related to changes in the party's positions on issues related to American global dominance and the rise of a majority–minority America: issues that threaten white Americans' sense of dominant group status."[9]

In a joint Public Religion Research Institute (PRRI) study with *The Atlantic* in 2017, Robert P. Jones, who has studied Republican primary and general election voters at length, noted five main drivers of voting behavior in the 2016 presidential election, four of which benefited Trump. The first was identification with the Republican Party. Partisanship in America has become increasingly tribal, and it was inevitable that once Trump was the nominee, he would get the lion's share of those votes, regardless of what he said or did.

Next came fears about cultural displacement, including feeling "like a stranger in their own land," amid the increasing diversity of ethnicities, races, and languages gaining acceptance and power in America. This coincided with a belief that "the U.S. needs protecting against foreign influence," which Trump voters were 3.5 times more likely than non-Trump voters to believe. Third: strong support for "deporting immigrants living in the country illegally," which Trump voters were 3.3 times more likely to favor. And fourth: "economic fatalism," a sense among Trump voters that "college education is a gamble," rather than "an important investment in the future," which Trump voters were nearly twice as likely as non-Trump voters to believe.[10]

The PRRI's fifth variable—the least statistically significant factor in how white Americans voted in 2016—was economic hardship. This was the preferred explanation for white working-class support for Trump in the days and weeks after the election. The survey authors concluded, however, that when it did matter, "being in fair or poor financial shape actually predicted support for Hillary Clinton among white working-class Americans, rather than support for Donald Trump. Those who reported being in fair or poor financial shape were 1.7 times more likely to support Clinton, compared to those who were in better financial shape."[11]

Four in ten white Millennials also voted for Trump, and a December 2017 study by University of Chicago professor Cathy J. Cohen, founder of the GenForward Survey, along with researchers Matthew Fowler and Vladimir E. Medenica, found that "white vulnerability," driven by racial resentment, was the principal factor in their support for Trump's candidacy. Even controlling for economic and employment status, partisanship, religion, educational attainment, and other factors, Cohen, Fowler, and Medenica determined that "when white Millennials scored high on racial resentment, they were 42 percentage points more likely to indicate feelings of vulnerability than those who scored low— and therefore much more likely to vote for Trump."[12]

For some researchers, the origin of Trump's support was the

growing orientation toward authoritarianism on the American right.

A December 2017 report in *Psychology Today* identified five traits dispositive of Trump support: Authoritarian Personality Syndrome, social dominance orientation (exhibiting "a preference for the societal hierarchy of groups, specifically with a structure in which the high-status groups have dominance over the low-status ones"); sparse contact with racial and social groups outside one's own; a sense of being "deprived of something to which one believes they are entitled," also known as "relative deprivation," which the researchers found to be particularly acute in states like Ohio, Michigan, and Pennsylvania; and a tendency toward racial, ethnic or religious prejudice.[13]

But the basis of Trump's increasingly intense hold on the Republican base was also cultural.

Thomas B. Edsall, columnist for the *New York Times*, writes in "The Peculiar Populism of Donald Trump" about the unintended consequences of liberalism's victory in the twentieth-century culture wars. We see in American film and television examples of the forward march of tolerance and liberalism regarding issues of racial, gender, and sexual identity. And yet, Edsall writes, "liberal victory in the cultural revolution of the 1960s and '70s, with its emphasis on so-called post-materialist values—personal fulfillment, openness to new ideas and support for previously marginalized populations—had its costs, which political analysts have been reckoning. Those costs have become particularly evident in the eruption over . . . the Brexit vote in Britain, the increasing power of anti-immigrant parties across Europe and the ascendance of right-wing populism in America."[14]

The theory goes like this: as the West's economies became more stable and prosperous, political parties turned their attention away from economic issues and toward modernizing social values, and that drove a wedge between those parties and their white working-class base. The progressive parties—Democrats in the

United States, the Labour Party in Great Britain, the Socialists in France, and the Social Democratic parties throughout Europe— enjoyed wide popularity for decades in the twentieth century as the architects of their countries' safety net programs, particularly in comparison with the anti-redistributionist conservatives. These progressive parties attracted once-marginalized ethnic and religious groups, as well as in the United States the bulk of the immigrant populations who crowded into urban centers in the Northeast and industrial Midwest. But as those parties' attention shifted from economics to issues related to racial and gender equality, legalized birth control, multilingualism, and nonwhite immigration, some members of the white working class, chafing at their party's lost attention and what they perceived as their own stagnation, began to break away. With their party paying "too much" attention to the black, the brown, the gay, and the foreign, white citizens' lament that "no one is looking out for us" was a golden opportunity for another party to step in and defend them against the forces they perceived to be oppressing them.

Zach Beauchamp, in a January 2017 Vox.com essay, termed this a "white riot,"[15] and noted that the broadly anti-immigrant, xenophobic, anti-Muslim, nationalistic, often racist, and in some instances baldly fascist wave lapped at not just the United States but also Britain, where the Brexit breakaway from the European Union had occurred the year before and which continued to bedevil the United Kingdom in 2019, as the prime minister, Theresa May, struggled to find a way to make the breakaway happen with Parliament's support and without imploding the British economy. This right-wing populist storm nearly devoured France and Germany, which narrowly survived strong election challenges by neo-fascist elements. It had already begun eating away at countries such as Hungary, Italy, and Finland while threatening other parts of Europe.

The Trump voter was not unlike the Brexiteer who believed their vote might reverse the loss of factory jobs in exurban counties like Kent, or who longed for the days when Britain "ruled the waves" as an empire rather than absorbing waves of North Africans and hijab-wearing Muslims into metropolitan London. They echoed the supporter of Geert Wilders in the Netherlands, Marine Le Pen in France, or Viktor Orbán in Hungary, who resented the elasticity of what it means to be Dutch or French or Hungarian in a time of accelerated immigration. They were not unlike the George Wallace voter, the Nixon "law and order" conservative, or those who hewed to Reagan's dire warnings about "welfare queens" or Bill Clinton and Newt Gingrich's parallel vows to "end welfare as we know it" in America in decades past.

Trump voters shared a sense that "being American" used to mean being like them, and now that was changing in a way that they found hard to accept. They were convinced that an amorphous "they" was pouring into America—not to "assimilate" and become American, like *their* forefathers did, but to exploit the good graces of Uncle Sam to steal federal benefits paid for with the hard-earned money of "real" Americans.

For decades it had been an article of faith on the American right that this horde of "line cutters," presumably black and brown Americans or "illegal immigrants," living in the debauched urban ghettos or sneaking over the southern border, were taking without giving to America. "They" don't want to work—"they" just sit around and collect welfare. "They" came to this country "the wrong way." Immigration skeptics saw little symmetry between those teeming at the southern border and turned away from ports of entry by Trump era border patrol agents, and their own forebears, who stowed away on steamships in the 1840s amid the potato famine in Ireland and who arrived in America to find signs on workplace doors reading, "Irish need not apply." They felt no kinship between the Central American migrants picking lettuce in Salinas, California, or selling tamales in border towns in Texas and their own grandfathers who arrived in New

York in the 1920s, illiterate from Italy and pushing a food cart in Manhattan's Bowery district in hopes of building an American life for their families.

There was tremendous irony in Donald Trump being the avatar for this broad rejection of newcomers. Two of his three wives had been immigrants, and Melania's immigration status when she arrived in the United States remained an elusive story to pin down. Her parents and sister joined her in America through the same "chain migration" Trump so vehemently derided. And Trump's own paternal grandfather, Friedrich Drumpf, arrived in the 1890s from Bavaria at sixteen years of age without papers and without speaking English.

Trump family biographer Gwenda Blair wrote that Friedrich failed to find gold in British Columbia, and instead operated a round-the-clock restaurant and brothel servicing the more able prospectors.[16] His son Fred would thrive as a real estate developer in Queens, turning a few small houses into an empire. And Fred's son would become president of the United States. It is the quintessence of the American dream: from immigrant to president in three generations. Yet the Trumps seemed impervious to gratitude for the wondrous luck they had been blessed with. The Trump men evaded military service, Friedrich in Bavaria[17] and his son and grandson in America.

Fred Trump evinced a talent for acquiring wealth, but also a studious avoidance of taxation and a driving antiblack racism, culminating in his arrest at a Klan riot in Queens, New York, in 1927.[18] And a 1973 federal lawsuit accused the company run by Fred and Donald Trump of refusing to rent to black and Puerto Rican tenants.[19] (The Trumps filed a $100 million countersuit accusing the Department of Justice of defamation, but ultimately settled by signing a consent decree that allowed them to avoid admitting wrongdoing.)[20] Far from giving back to the country that made their prosperity possible, Friedrich Drumpf's male descendants pursued aggressive acquisition, and immersed themselves in resentment.

The modern Republican Party, like the old anti-immigrant, anti-Catholic "Know Nothing" Party of the 1850s, promulgators of the Asian exclusion laws of the 1920s, and nativists throughout U.S. history, had become a gathering place for the sons and grandsons of immigrants who were determined to slam the door shut behind them.

Donald Trump was their natural leader.

Many of his followers saw him as a needed shot across the bow of political correctness; a human cudgel against multiculturalism, feminism, Obamaism, secularism, cries of "racism," demands for LGBT rights, and progressive change. In July 2016, I appeared on *Real Time with Bill Maher*, with political writer and filmmaker Michael Moore, as he correctly predicted a Trump win that November. Afterward Moore elaborated on his website that the election would be "The Last Stand of the Angry White Man" who was watching 240 years of his unrivaled place in the American culture beginning to circle the drain.[21]

"There is a sense that the power has slipped out of their hands," Moore wrote. "That their way of doing things is no longer how things are done."[22] Trump made explicit more than forty years of coded racial messaging dating back to Nixon's "southern strategy" and the more humanized vision of white anxiety in the seminal American TV classic *All in the Family*. He broadened and glorified Republican appeals to anxious white suburbanites who looked warily at the moving truck that first brought one, then a second and a third black family to the block. He invited and inspired his base to lean in to their fears, and to let him be the bad guy who was willing to rain down fire on the people they hated and feared.

Trump represented a promise to sweep aside the ritualized shame over slavery and racism and the equivocation over America's role in sometimes setting the world off course. Even if he couldn't refire the coal mines or stop companies from boosting their stock prices by shipping jobs overseas, he could tear up everything Obama put in place: the Iran nuclear deal, the Paris climate accords, the clean air and clean power standards that slowed down American business, the very idea of green energy, a national project to improve public education, and of course, the scourge of Obamacare, which right-wing radio host Rush Limbaugh told his millions of listeners was nothing more than reparations for the descendants of black slaves.

Trump could expose the liberal "lies" of a media that disdained conservative and religious values. He would make sure "his people" were finally taken care of. And he could restore America as a nation bound to Christ—never mind that he evinced no Christian values himself.

Days after questioning the heroism of Arizona senator and former prisoner of war John McCain, Trump traveled to Iowa for the Family Leadership Summit, a gathering of conservative evangelical groups, in July 2015. The campaign had just gotten under way in earnest and Trump was seeking to reassure a key Republican constituency of his fealty to their faith. Yet he told Frank Luntz at the event that he was not sure he had ever asked God for forgiveness. "I think if I do something wrong, I think, I just try and make it right. I don't bring God into that picture," he said.[23] Still, Trump received the blessing of the white conservative Christian establishment, which labeled him a modern-day King David from the Old Testament.

Men like Jerry Falwell Jr., Franklin Graham, Tony Perkins and James Dobson lined up staunchly behind him and never let go. As president, Trump delivered—finally making good on prior, failed Republican promises to hand Christian conservatives real, temporal power. Through his judicial appointments, made straight from the Federalist Society master list, and the help of a Republican-controlled Senate, he would give the religious right sovereignty at last over the courts, the entity that in their view had long been used against them.

For decades, federal judges had ruled against Christian families: stripping the tax exemption from their private, nearly all-white schools, banning public school prayer, and using federal coercion to disrupt racially "pristine" neighborhood schools with forced busing. With Donald Trump in office and unafraid to be politically incorrect, all of that would end. And with the cadre of young, far-right judges Trump was placing on the bench, the Christian right saw a real opportunity to strike a blow against affirmative action, abortion on demand, and other liberal outrages against the "originalist" constitution. These reversions to the past would endure long after the Trump administration was gone, and no matter how much the rest of the culture changed.

When Trump announced that he was "calling for a total and complete shutdown of Muslims entering the United States until our country's representatives can figure out what the hell is going on,"[24] it was met with elation by his base, many of whom believed that former president Obama was a secret Muslim who promoted the spread of "sharia law" in America. Trump may have been an imperfect husband, citizen, and Christian, but in the eyes of many among the Christian right, he was doing more than any previous Republican president to restore this country's character as a white Christian nation.

Perhaps most importantly for his base, Trump was vowing to stop the influx of low-skilled Central American migrants into the United States, who many Republican, and some Democratic, voters were convinced were responsible for lowering their wages and "taking their jobs." Trump, a former campaign adviser said, felt the same outrage that Steve Bannon and other nativists did about this mythical "invasion" from south of the border, having drunk in the rhetoric during his daily hours of Fox News viewing. As the campaign got under way, Roger Stone fed Trump the applause line of building a wall across the southwestern U.S. border to stop the human flow. The line was intended to keep Trump focused on immigration during his freewheeling campaign speeches.[25] It struck at the heart of the resentments Trump shared with his base, and his unique talent for showbiz.

Trump vowed to build a wall of solid concrete. He led his raucous rallies, where protesters were sometimes met with violence, in chants of "build the wall!" Who would pay for it? "Mexico!" It was a call not just for physical separation, but for the humiliation of America's southern neighbor and third-largest trading partner.[26]

Trump had launched his presidential bid with the declaration that Mexico is "sending people that have lots of problems." He famously continued, "They're bringing drugs. They're bringing crime. They're rapists. And some, I assume, are good people."[27] He later claimed the Indiana-born judge hearing the case against his sham Trump University was too biased to hear the case because of his Mexican lineage.[28]

Even less subtle were the nativists with whom Trump was now firmly aligned. They called these fictionalized "invaders" diseased, violent, and, in the words of Iowa congressman Steve King, in a recorded conversation obtained by the conservative *Weekly Standard*, literal "dirt."[29] King had previously slammed Central American migrants as a mass of drug mules with "calves the size of cantaloupes."[30]

Now Trump was taking these views mainstream. His pronouncements delighted readers of anti-immigration, far-right websites like Breitbart and Vdare, and longtime immigration restrictionists like Alabama senator Jeff Sessions, his longtime aide Stephen Miller, both of whom would join his administration, Arkansas senator Tom Cotton, and cable gadflies like Lou Dobbs, Tucker Carlson, and Ann Coulter. Trump was promising mass deportation—going further than Mitt Romney's 2012 call for migrants to "self-deport." He vowed to end the Obama DACA program that shielded from deportation young people brought to the United States as children by undocumented parents. He said he would halt refugee status for migrants from "shithole countries" in Africa and the Caribbean. And rather than treating the "illegals," as the right labeled them, with Obama-like kid gloves or Bush-ian, John McCain–ite calls for a "path to citizenship," he would "round them up, and get them out."

There was no cruelty he wouldn't visit on the teeming masses of brown and non-Christian aliens his base so deeply feared. Unlike the "weak" presidents who preceded him, Trump would put "America first."

America is complicated. Trumpists want it simple. The country is increasingly secular and pluralistic. Trumpists want a return to a white, Christian America. The traditional Republican Party, despite its long history of tapping this same well of grievance, was caught off guard by how powerful those compulsions were among their voting base—by how those fears overrode any fealty to "small government" or low taxes. Trump's campaign, amplified by Russian bots and the American far right media machine, tapped into the fear among some white Americans that they have lost their place atop America's cultural firmament. Trump vowed to give it back to them, to wind back the clock, to hurt the "right people" and rebalance the scales.

That's why he's president.

CHAPTER 2

TWO NATIONS, UNDER TRUMP

"If they don't give you a seat at the table, bring a folding chair."

—Shirley Chisholm

A BIBLICAL DOWNPOUR DRENCHED TALLAHASSEE, FLORIDA, ON election night 2018. The assembled press corps were forced to abandon the media tent, as the rain created a swelling bulge in its center that looked like a water balloon ready to burst. Reporters and producers snapped their laptops shut, pulled phone chargers out of the power strips strewn across the meticulously labeled rows of tables, and fled for the safety of a student recreation building at Florida A&M University, the historically black college where Andrew Gillum's campaign was holding its watch party.

Gillum, the thirty-nine-year-old, African-American mayor of Florida's capital, had been elected to the city council at age twenty-three while he was still enrolled at FAMU as a political science student. As mayor, Gillum had taken on the NRA and its longtime lobbyist Marion Hammer, and now he was running as an unapologetic and charismatic progressive to become the first black governor of Florida. He had emerged from fourth place in the polls during the primary to snatch the nomination from more centrist and better-known candidates, including former congresswoman Gwen Graham, daughter of one-time Florida governor Bob Graham.

His Republican opponent, Ron DeSantis, was nearly a year older, a former Naval Reserve officer and congressman, and, despite his lack of outward polish, a holder of degrees from Harvard and Yale. He had not been the Republican Party's first choice, but he romped to victory in the primary by declaring fealty to Donald Trump and his vision for a nationalist future, including opposition to sanctuary city protections for immigrants and support for the open carrying of firearms in Florida. DeSantis urged Floridians not to "monkey this up" by siding with Gillum, sparking accusations of racism. Gillum in turn pointed out that DeSantis had four times attended and spoken at conferences held by right-wing demagogue David Horowitz, whose views on African-Americans and Muslims ran toward the Byzantine.

DeSantis refused to return campaign donations from a longtime supporter, Steven Alembik, who tweeted that former president Barack Obama was a "fucking Muslim nigger," and justified it to *Politico* by saying, "So somebody like Chris Rock can get up onstage and use the word, and there's no problem? But some white guy says it, and he's a racist? Really? I grew up in New York in the '50s," Alembik said. "We were the kikes. They were the niggers. They were the goyim. And those were the spics." Alembik seemed to have been freed by his party's leader, Donald Trump, to express openly and unapologetically the racism and white supremacy that had been America's private discourse for most of its 242-year history, until the civil rights movement and the martyrdom of Dr. Martin Luther King Jr. made them unpalatable in public.

Trump and his party wrapped their midterm election efforts around a fusillade of aggressive xenophobia, fixating on a few thousand desperate men, women, and children, making their way to the United States on foot from Honduras and other Central American countries racked by the extreme violence that formed part of the runoff of the American drug trade. Stoked by right-wing media, with Fox News in the lead, Republican voters reached a fever pitch over "the caravan."

Two years of Trump had hardened his supporters, but it had done the same to the resistance, sparking historic bids for office by black candidates for governor in three southern states—Florida, Georgia, and Maryland—and for U.S. Senate in Mississippi. A record number of women sought office nationwide, with 234 female candidates seeking House seats (182 of them Democrats), 22 candidates for the U.S. Senate (15 of them Democrats), and a half dozen candidates running in all-women contests nationwide. There were 16 female candidates for governor, 12 of whom were Democrats,[1] and 3,564 female candidates ran for legislative seats.[2] This was 28 percent more women than had run two years earlier, and as with the overall trend, the vast majority were Democrats.[3] Scores of these candidates were women of color—black, Latina, and Asian-American. Two were Native American. Two were Muslim.

In Georgia, home state of Dr. King and of civil rights stalwart John Lewis, Stacey Abrams, the state's former House minority leader, ran an improbable race to become the nation's first black woman governor. She faced Brian Kemp, the sitting secretary of state, whose six-year history of voter suppression directed at black, brown, and Asian-American residents would come to define the second major U.S. election held without the full protections of the Voting Rights Act. In 2013, the Supreme Court, under Chief Justice John Roberts, gutted the landmark law, giving Kemp the ability to cancel more than 1.4 million voter registrations in Georgia from 2012 to 2018,[4] including more than 668,000[5] in 2017 alone. In August, *Rolling Stone* wrote that Abrams "is competing against a rival who is also the referee." In an August op-ed in the *New York Times,* author Carol Anderson labeled Kemp an "enemy of democracy."

In 2014, Abrams had helped found a voter registration organization, the New Georgia Project, with a goal of registering more than 700,000 Georgians of color, Millennials, and unmarried women, whom she called the "new American majority." She had also been fighting Kemp in court and on the legislative battlefield. In the weeks before the election, *Rolling Stone* released audio of Kemp telling donors he was concerned that if all Georgians exercised their right to vote, he could lose the election.

Georgia's population was less than 60 percent white, but Republicans wielded absolute power over statewide and federal offices. Kemp ran on guns, threats against undocumented immigrants, and fervent support for Donald Trump. He was among a handful of secretaries of state to refuse the Department of Homeland Security's assistance to help secure his state's highly vulnerable voting system from foreign hacking.

On the eve of the election, Kemp's office put some 53,000 voter registrations on hold under the state's once court-overturned "exact signature match" system.[6] And he openly cried "fraud" to intimidate groups like the New Georgia Project from registering non-white voters. When a federal court threw out Kemp's "exact match" rule, the Republican Georgia legislature enacted it into law. If Lester Maddox—Georgia's segregationist seventy-fifth governor—could be brought back to life in 2018, he would have a hard time outdoing Brian Kemp.

In Texas, Robert Francis "Beto" O'Rourke, a '90s punk rocker turned El Paso city councilman and Texas congressman, gave Tea Party Republican senator Ted Cruz, Donald Trump's once bitter rival, the race of his life. O'Rourke raised record sums of money from small donors across the country and attracted a fervent following among young and diverse Texans, as well as national comparisons to another "Robert Francis": Bobby Kennedy. He rocketed to national attention with a four-minute, extemporaneous treatise on why he supported the right of black NFL players who kneel during the playing of the National Anthem to protest police violence against black citizens. And for a time, the national media thought he might well snatch Texas from Republican hands.

O'Rourke was on his way to a close finish on Election Night that despite his loss, vaulted him onto the national stage (and eventually, into a 2020 presidential bid). He shared the late RFK's deft touch on issues of race and gun violence, and Barack Obama's ability to electrify a crowd with a message of national unity and commonsense kindness.

Something was happening across the South. The conservative establishment was waging an all-out fight to maintain control, reminiscent of the decades following the Civil War. Despite the Great Migration of blacks to the North, the South was still teeming with black bodies. And the looming question was whether those once relegated to the ranks of the poor and locked out would come to genuinely share power.

As of 2017, of the ten states with the largest African-American populations, eight were in the South, plus the District of Columbia. In 2017, 26.8 percent of Alabama residents were African-American, as were 37.8 percent in Mississippi, 32.5 percent in Louisiana, 31.7 percent in Georgia, 27.6 percent in South Carolina, 22.1 percent in North Carolina, and 30.5 percent in Maryland. The black populations were smaller in states like Florida (16.8 percent) and Texas (12.5 percent), but they were on par with blue states like New York (17.6 percent) and red-trending states like Ohio (12.7 percent).[7] And these states were increasingly home to Latino and Asian-American populations that threatened to tip the balance of political power once those largely young populations came of age and joined the voter rolls.

Republicans responded with some of the most open appeals to racial fear the country had seen in the modern political era. They combined this with flagrant voter suppression, not just in Georgia but also in North Carolina, where the practice had become so notorious a federal judge ruled it was being implemented "with almost surgical precision." In Kansas, then–secretary of state Kris Kobach, who for a time headed Trump's cynical "task force" on alleged voter fraud, was slapped down by a federal judge who threw out the proof-of-citizenship for voting law that Kobach had championed, and ordered him to take a legal course in the rules of evidence in a humiliating sanction,[8] even as he ran for governor (he lost to Democrat Laura Kelly). Meanwhile, in Ohio, Secretary of State Jon Husted, long accused by voting rights activists of aggressive voter suppression, was elected lieutenant governor.

The push to suppress Democratic votes reached well beyond the South. In Wisconsin, Republican governor Scott Walker and the majority-GOP legislature instituted strict voter ID laws that in 2016 may have stripped some 300,000 mostly minority voters of their right to vote, helping Trump eke out a victory in the state by just 22,748 ballots. In North Dakota, Native American voters were disenfranchised en masse in 2018 by a state law requiring them to show IDs with specific street addresses on them, even though many lived on reservations, where street addresses weren't used. Native Americans responded by turning out in historic numbers, but it wasn't enough to reelect Democratic senator Heidi Heitkamp, whose base was largely among the First Nation tribes.

Federal courts were once a bulwark of protection for minority voters, but thanks to Trump and Senate Majority Leader Mitch McConnell, the courts were stocked with judges who rarely intervened on voters' behalf. With Attorney General Jeff Sessions, the former Alabama senator and longtime foe of minority voting rights (who had been vocally opposed by the late Coretta Scott King when he was nominated to the federal bench in the 1980s), in charge of the Justice Department, the midterm elections proceeded with the thinnest federal protection for nonwhite voters since 1965.

In Tallahassee, as the rain dampened the celebratory mood, Gillum walked out onto the makeshift stage just before 11:00 p.m. and conceded the election. He noted the history he had already made and his grandmother's admonitions to him as a child to stand for something, to become something great. The students, staff, and supporters who had braved the rain began to slowly scatter, their disappointment thick and heavy. The same result would occur in Maryland, where former NAACP president Ben Jealous was soundly defeated by the incumbent Republican Larry Hogan, who defied strong anti-Trump sentiment in the deep-blue state to hang on to his office.[9]

In Georgia, Stacey Abrams refused to concede, setting up what would become a bitter recount fight that ultimately saw Kemp prevail. In the minds of many, the theft of tens of thousands of Georgians' right to vote had occurred before Election Day. Democrats surrendered not just the North Dakota Senate seat, but also those they'd held in Missouri and Indiana, a state Barack Obama won in 2008.

Seated in the guest chair on MSNBC, veteran Democratic strategist James Carville declared the "blue wave" a bust. Within hours, as polls closed in the western states, he was proven wrong, and decisively so.

Democrats flipped Jeff Flake's Arizona U.S. Senate seat and also took the seat held by Republican Dean Heller of Nevada, putting two more women into the United States Senate. The Arizona winner, Krysten Sinema, became the state's first woman senator, the nation's first openly bisexual federal lawmaker, and the first Democratic senator from the state since 1988. These races turned largely on Republican threats to gut or repeal the Affordable Care Act, and its protections for Americans with pre-existing conditions. Voting by Latinos surged, alongside a flood of Democrats and crossover independents who recoiled from Trump and his party's fearmongering and the White House's anti-immigration policies and actions.

In House races, Democrats won overwhelmingly, gaining forty seats with the largest popular vote margin since the midterm election that followed Richard Nixon's resignation from office in 1974, a nearly 9 percent spread. More than a hundred women were elected to Congress—the most in history, and the majority of them Democrats. Both Native American women candidates won, as did both Muslim women candidates, placing the first Palestinian-American, Rashida Tlaib, and the first hijab-wearing representative, Ilhan Omar, in the House. In New York, a twenty-nine-year-old Puerto Rican woman from the Bronx, Alexandria Ocasio-Cortez, who'd toppled a Democrat once considered a candidate for speaker in the primary, became the youngest member of Congress.

Democrats swept Orange County, California, a former Republican stronghold that once produced Richard Nixon and Ronald Reagan. And even as Abrams lost her bid for governor, the excitement she created swept into office Lucy McBath, whose seventeen-year-old son, Jordan Davis, was murdered by a white motorist in Florida in 2012. McBath won the House seat once held by Trump's health secretary Tom Price, and before that by Newt Gingrich.

Election analyst Harry Enten called it not a blue wave, but rather, a "blue tsunami," noting on CNN.com, "If you go back all the way to the first election of the post–World War II era (1946), there have only been three elections in which Democrats net gained more seats than they did in 2018. Put another way, this was the fourth best performance for Democrats in the 37 general House elections since President Donald Trump was born."[10]

With Democrats in control of the House of Representatives, California congresswoman Nancy Pelosi retook the gavel she'd wielded, historically, in 2007, as speaker. This meant a woman would face down Donald Trump as second in line to the presidency and the most powerful constitutional officer outside the White House.

The election revealed stark racial, gender, and regional distinctions between America's two major political parties. In fundamental ways, the parties were governing two starkly different and disunited Americas.

Nearly a month after the election, in Mississippi, former Clinton-era agricultural secretary Mike Espy—who in 1987 became that state's first black congressman since Reconstruction—conceded the Senate race in late November to Cindy Hyde-Smith, the appointed U.S. senator whose campaign was briefly roiled by her "exaggerated expression of regard" for a supporter, about whom she said, "if he invited me to a public hanging, I'd be on the front row." It was a jarring statement coming from the state that historically lynched more black people than any other. Hyde-Smith also faced revelations about her affinity for the Confederacy and her and her daughter's attendance at so-called segregation academies,[11] which were designed to allow white parents to avoid integrated schools after the landmark 1954 *Brown v. Board of Education* decision. The two parties seemed to exist not just in different regions but in alternate universes.

Dave Wasserman, editor of the *Cook Political Report*, tweeted on the Sunday after the election that "the percentage of white men as a share of House Democrats is 'set to decline from 41 percent to 38 percent as a result of the 2018 election.' . . . Meanwhile, the percentage of white men as a share of House Republicans is on track to rise from 86 percent to 90 percent."[12] Congressional Republicans would close out the 2018 election continuing to govern the vast majority of rural America, but with little of the more economically robust urban areas under their control.

Wasserman also reported that House Democrats now represented populations that were even more concentrated in the nation's urban areas, the West, and the Northeast; Democrats represented districts comprising eight in ten Asian-Americans, seven in ten Latinos, 66 percent of African-Americans, six in ten college graduates, seven in ten Americans who had voted for Hillary Clinton, and just four in ten who had voted for Trump, plus only 45 percent of white Americans, and a fifth of the nation's land area.[13]

In the states, Democrats took seven governorships, winning in Pennsylvania, Wisconsin, and Michigan, three states that gave Trump his Electoral College victory in 2016. Democrats were victorious in a majority of state offices of attorney general, picking up four seats to end the election with twenty-five such offices to Republicans' twenty-three, along with two independents.[14] Those offices, particularly in states such as California and New York, would pose fresh threats to Trump's agenda, his businesses, and potentially his family, as the myriad lawsuits and investigations against his administration and businesses proceeded.

Democrats clawed back one-third of the state legislative seats they'd lost during President Obama's two terms, and they captured crucial secretary of state posts in Arizona, Colorado, and Michigan (while keeping that position in Wisconsin). This put them in a position to do what the Roberts court would not: protect and defend voters of color from the scourge of voter suppression in the 2020 presidential race. North Carolina, Wisconsin, and Michigan—where heavily gerrymandered state legislatures had moved to strip power from the incoming Democratic lawmakers, arguing that the mainly urban and heavily black and brown voters who elected them were somehow less representative of the needs and interests of their states—surrendered their governorships and state legislatures to Democrats.

And in Florida, even as Gillum lost the governor's race, a constitutional amendment passed by more than two-thirds of voters restored the right to vote to some 1.4 million Floridians who had served prison sentences, a major feat in a state that, like many in the United States, disproportionately incarcerates African-Americans and Latinos.[15]

There remained a heart of darkness in American life and politics, and Republicans were signaling that they did not intend to go into the political minority without an all-out fight. Still, in the weeks after the 2018 midterm election, with Trump's legal woes mounting and the prospects for divided government in Washington on the near horizon, Democrats were feeling the fleeting but genuine beginnings of hope.

In January, Donald Trump learned his first lesson in the power of the speakership, when Nancy Pelosi exercised her constitutional authority to delay his State of the Union address, so long as a government shutdown, triggered just before Christmas over Trump's demand that Congress appropriate money for the wall he had failed to induce Mexico to pay for, remained in effect. And the Democratic House vowed to reopen investigations into Trump's campaign and businesses that the previous, Republican-led House had slow-walked, in their determination to shield the president from whatever demons lurked in his past. Washington was going to be a very different place for Donald Trump, with only one legislative body—the Republican-controlled Senate—there to protect him.

But protect him they did.

In late January, the shutdown became the longest in U.S. history, radiating misery beyond the 800,000 furloughed and unpaid federal employees affected and threatening to tip the U.S. economy into recession. There were fears of a looming national security crisis as FBI, Transportation Safety Administration, and other federal law enforcement agencies remained understaffed and stressed air traffic controllers and flight attendants warned of reduced safety in the skies.

Yet Senate Majority Leader Mitch McConnell continued to shield the president. He refused to take up multiple House bills to reopen the government and vowed to only bring the president's preferred legislation to the floor, including American tax dollars to begin building his vanity wall. Ultimately, the shutdown ended with Trump giving in—and signing a bill no different from the one presented to him in December, with no money for a wall. Trump then declared a national emergency to try to take the funds by fiat, attempting to seize the power of the purse with the support of congressional Republicans in defiance of their own Article I constitutional powers.

That same month, the Senate Republican majority voted to drop sanctions against businesses owned by Oleg Deripaska, a key figure in the investigation into Russian interference in the election.[16] Even when a dozen Republicans crossed party lines in March 2019 to support a House resolution overturning Trump's national emergency, all but one Senate Republican up for reelection in 2020 refused to join them. Self-declared constitutional conservatives like Ted Cruz of Texas, Ben Sasse of Nebraska, and Thom Tillis of North Carolina, who had been impassioned opponents of the emergency decree, nonetheless voted with the president.

"We've learned through Trump that the ability to count on the system of checks and balances is much more fragile than anybody could have imagined," said Harvard University constitutional law professor Laurence Tribe. "Trump has exposed the danger that a Congress in which people are so obsessed with raising money and getting themselves reelected is not likely to be an effective check." Trump, Tribe said, exacerbated the weakness, "by showing the power of a demagogue to generate a lemming-like following."

Tribe contends that Trump has "shown that the letter of the law and the architecture of the constitution are considerably less powerful than what I would call the constitutional culture and the norms and expectations that we have over time."

Indeed, but for the midterm elections, and one wing of Congress changing hands, it seems impossible to imagine any guardrails being placed on the Trump presidency at all.

In January 2019, the Government Accountability Office's inspector general admitted, belatedly, that it had failed to fully consider the implications for the Constitution's Emoluments Clause when it allowed Trump to lease the old D.C. Post Office and remake it into his latest Trump Hotel. As every foreign dignitary who leased rooms there was a potential partner in bribery with the president of the United States, former prosecutor and Georgetown Law School professor Paul Butler saw the red lights flashing there, too.

"It's clear that it limits the ways that a president can profit while he's in office," Butler said. "The question is: A, who interprets it in terms of President Trump's own financial dealings, and B, who enforces that interpretation? [Trump] has managed to hijack the Supreme Court, now that he has five conservative justices. It's one of the most conservative courts in history. In fact, it has two justices, Clarence Thomas and Samuel Alito, who might actually be in the top three of the most conservative justices since the beginning of the Supreme Court. That's not counting the two men who the president has placed on the Court himself. We don't have a long enough track record to determine exactly how they'll rule on issues, but we have every reason to believe that they'll be in the same camp as the other two extremely conservative people."

Many wondered what, if anything, could be done to stop a president who counterintelligence investigators said was a potential threat to national security, acting on behalf of a foreign power. And what if Michael Cohen, who knew Trump better than nearly every member of Congress, wasn't employing hyperbole when he expressed doubt, during his public congressional testimony in February 2019, that Trump would leave office peacefully if he lost reelection? The Constitution, for all its supposed genius, did not seem to answer any of that.

"The idea has always been that if there is a president in office who's a despot, there is a constitutional remedy, which is impeachment," Butler said. "Now, I think that that remedy might be insufficient because we had a Congress—and we now have a Senate—that is unwilling to exercise its responsibilities to check the President. That means that he has essentially a blank check."

Likewise, what could be done about the racial division and antagonism laid bare by Trump's political success, and which he seemed determined to drive even more? A Pew study conducted before the midterms found that roughly three-quarters of those supporting Republican candidates viewed illegal immigration as a "very big problem," versus fewer than one in five voters who planned to vote for Democrats.[17] When Pew asked if "the way racial minorities are treated by the criminal justice system" was a "very big problem," seven in ten supporters of Democratic candidates agreed, versus just 10 percent who supported Republicans. That polarization extended to nearly every salient issue in American life, with Democratic and Republican voters differing on the importance of everything from gun violence (81 to 25 percent), to racism (63 to 19 percent), the gap between rich and poor (77 to 22 percent), climate change (72 to 11 percent), and sexism (50 to 12 percent) in diametric opposition.[18]

Six in ten Americans in the survey *opposed* building a southern border wall, according to a January 2019 Pew poll[19] that mirrored nearly every other major survey, but that figure flipped to 82 percent *in favor* of building a wall among Republicans and Republican-leaning independents.

And what to make of the ways in which Trump had inched his party closer to the messaging of white nationalists? An August 2018 study by University of Alabama demographer George Hawley, published by the University of Virginia's Institute for Family Studies, sought to quantify "white identity politics" in the larger population. The study, of 3,038 non-Hispanic white Americans, found that "about 28 percent expressed strong feelings of white identity; about 38 percent expressed strong feelings of white solidarity; and about 27 percent felt that whites suffer a meaningful amount of discrimination in American life. A much smaller minority, about 6 percent of respondents, expressed all three opinions."[20]

The percentage of white Americans exhibiting the full range of attitudes signaling support for white nationalist movements like the alt-right was small—much smaller than an ABC News/ *Washington Post* poll a year earlier that put the alt-right's support among white Americans at close to 10 percent of the white American population.[21] The "alt-right" remained a small, unpopular movement. But it fed on racial resentments and anxieties that were real, and more widespread than most Americans felt comfortable acknowledging.

America had always been a nation divided by race. Racism was built into the country's founding as a slave republic wrestled from the hands of indigenous people at the barrels of guns. But the prospect of interference by a foreign enemy in a national election had revealed the extent to which our racial polarization could become more than just a moral crisis. It could be exploited and weaponized into a threat to our national security. Our racial divides provided Russian intelligence with an opening through which to drive wedges into the electorate. And the combined effect of interracial suspicion, hyper-partisanship, and sexism, and one of the most cynical presidential campaigns in modern U.S. history, may have flipped a presidential election. Who, if anyone, had the moral authority to walk the 30 to 40 percent of Americans who were vulnerable to that kind of messaging back from the edge?

KURT BARDELLA BEGAN WORKING FOR THE REPUBLICAN PARTY straight out of high school in Southern California, starting with a summer internship that turned into a legislative job and later a move to Washington to work for congressmen including Brian Bilbray and then Darrell Issa, who in 2010 became chairman of the powerful House Committee on Oversight and Government Reform and the chief congressional antagonist to President Barack Obama.

"I was already working for the Republican Party without even knowing what it really was," says Bardella, who is Korean-American but was raised by adoptive parents who gave him his Italian-American surname. "I think much like many things, once you're in, that's your tribe, and you're kind of programmed to believe that this is your team and the other guys are the opposition, and the objective is to beat them."

Bardella's exit from his job as the Oversight committee's deputy communications director would be public: Issa dismissed him for sharing emails with a *New York Times* reporter who was writing a book about the political culture in Washington. So, he did what many a former D.C. staffer would do: he became a consultant, and in an only-in-Washington twist, signed Issa as his first client. His second client: Breitbart.com, then led by future Trump campaign and White House chief strategist Steve Bannon.

"At the time, Bannon pitched to me the idea of building a media platform that was much more credible than what [the site] had been during Andrew Breitbart's life," Bardella said. Bannon wanted an outlet "that was going to be taken seriously by policymakers and leaders within the Republican Party, but that told the story of the center right." At the time, the Tea Party had swept Republicans into the majority in Washington and "there was a lot of friction between the establishment and the Tea Party that had come in," Bardella says. Having grown up taunted for being different and inducted into a party where de-emphasizing your race was standard operating procedure,[22] there was a lot he was able to ignore.

That changed, Bardella says, when he realized that Bannon's goal was not to chronicle what was happening in the Republican Party, but rather to control it, and to promote one candidate in particular: Donald Trump. In interviews, he says Breitbart soon turned into "Trump Pravda," with Bannon failing to back one of his own reporters when she was allegedly shoved by Trump campaign manager Corey Lewandowski, then taking a "leave of absence" from the site to become CEO of Trump's campaign. In December 2017, Bardella abandoned his deal with Breitbart. He soon quit the Republican Party altogether, in disgust over Bannon and Trump's support for accused pedophile and Alabama U.S. Senate candidate Roy Moore. Bardella joined the Democratic Party, penning an op-ed for *USA Today*[23] to make his break as public as his exit from Capitol Hill had been.

Bardella believes Republicans are trapped. And he sees immigration as the vise. Having jettisoned the George W. Bush approach of "compassionate conservatism"—and switching to the anti-immigration warfare he witnessed firsthand at Breitbart—he says the party can't seem to find a way out.

"Marco Rubio is what they would say is a cautionary tale," Bardella said, "someone who was initially part of the 'gang of eight' immigration reform effort in the Senate" during the Bush years, who "got annihilated by the base for it, which was a real hindrance to his presidential ambitions. Every time that the right exerted themselves, it seemed that the posture of everybody else in the party was to hide and to just hope that the venom wasn't directed at them."

Bardella says the nativists' takeover of the Republican Party was accelerated when Tea Party outsider David Brat defeated House majority leader Eric Cantor in a primary in Virginia's 7th Congressional District in 2014. When Brat beat Cantor, "out of nowhere," Bardella said, "it was the clearest example of that friction between the base and the traditional Republican leadership. Cantor was very conservative, I think anyone could argue. And he was one of the top leaders in the party, and he lost to a right-wing lunatic, who campaigned exclusively on the immigration issue."

Two years later, Bardella said, "you had Trump go through the Republican primary and insult his way through it with this tough posture and his superficial 'build the wall' catchphrase, and he beat everyone from [then-Wisconsin governor] Scott Walker to Marco Rubio to Jeb Bush to, you name it. They had no answer for it. It's almost a hostage situation. They were taken hostage by their base, and they've always been too afraid to do anything about it other than to just go along with it."

Michael Steele, who led the Republican National Committee in the immediate aftermath of Barack Obama's election, traces his party's fragmented state farther back—to the bargain made by Ronald Reagan on his way to the presidency in 1980: "A lot of what Reagan was able to do was to create a relationship between conservatives (who existed in both parties) and Republicans," Steele said, noting that Reagan had been a Democrat and a union man, who himself reflected the kind of right-of-center voter who was struggling to find a place in a party that under Lyndon Johnson was increasingly concerned with black civil rights and anti-poverty programs, and that had also bungled the war. Reagan secured the nomination by bringing in another coalition that for decades had been uninterested in large-scale politics, making common cause with the newly minted "Moral Majority" of the evangelical Christian right.

Dartmouth professor Randall Balmer, and others, have documented that these newly empowered Christian conservatives, led by men like conservative activist Paul Weyrich and fundamentalist preacher Jerry Falwell, used abortion to activate evangelicals on something more palatable than their anger at losing federal tax exemptions for segregated schools.[24] With Reagan's ascent, an anti-abortion plank made it into the Republican Party platform for the first time, seven years after the Supreme Court decision in *Roe v. Wade*. "What Reagan recognized was something that Nixon did too in '68," Steele said, "which was that the disaffected Democrats who felt abandoned by their party around issues of civil rights in the 1960s now felt abandoned on issues like family values and abortion. He gave them a home."

What united each of these groups—whether social, religious, or economic conservatives—was a deep discomfort with demographic change.

"As the demographics change in this country, and the reality that white people are going to be the minority, probably by 2050 according to the Census, sinks in, there are those in the party who are desperate to hold on to as much of power as they can get, even though that pie is shrinking," Bardella said. "And really what happened to the California Republican Party is a great example of what that ultimately looks like because the California Republican Party used to be a very dominant presence. It was the organization that gave you Ronald Reagan and Pete Wilson, who was governor in the mid-'90s, and there was a Republican-controlled legislature. And then something called Proposition 187 happened."

The ballot measure, approved by California voters in 1994, denied undocumented immigrants access to public schools and healthcare.[25] The result of "Prop 187," signed into law by Republican governor Pete Wilson, was to doom Republicans' electoral prospects in the majority nonwhite state ever since, with the exception of the improbable election of action movie star Arnold Schwarzenegger as governor in 2003, following the recall of Democrat Gray Davis.

"You flash forward a decade and a half later," Bardella said, and "there are no Republicans in statewide office. There is a super majority of Democrats in the state legislature. They control a veto-proof majority. Two-thirds of the state legislators are Democrats. The Republican Party is an endangered species now in California because they got hijacked by their base and were too afraid to fight back. They were paralyzed by the fear of being 'primaried,' and they let the crazies take over and where did that lead them? Into a place of permanent political exile. And that's exactly what will happen nationally."

Indeed, when Bardella's former boss Darrell Issa retired ahead of the 2018 midterms, a Democrat took his seat. So how did the party that styled itself the party of Lincoln, the party that ended slavery and once commanded the lion's share of black voter loyalty, get here?

CHAPTER 3

The Trump Republican Party

"I did nothing worse than Lyndon Johnson. He was for segregation when he thought he had to be. I was for segregation, and I was wrong. The media has rehabilitated Johnson, why won't it rehabilitate me?"

—former Alabama governor George Wallace,
during a 1991 interview with the *Washington Post*

TOM NICHOLS WAS NINETEEN YEARS OLD IN 1980, THE YEAR Ronald Reagan was elected president, and he sees himself as part of a "generation of working-class, highly mobile young voters who saw the Republicans as optimistic and dynamic." Having grown up in Massachusetts, he calls himself "genetically programmed to be a Democrat"—living in a white ethnic factory town; "part Irish, part Greek." Yet he watched as his "post-'68 Democratic" parents left the party they felt had left them. After Nichols attended Boston University, adding degrees from Columbia University and Georgetown, he worked for Senator John Heinz, a moderate Republican from Pennsylvania, until Heinz's death in a plane crash in April 1991.

Nichols now teaches at the U.S. Naval War College and at Harvard University, and he is also a senior contributor to the conservative magazine *The Federalist*. With Donald Trump in the White House, he's not sure his old party exists anymore. Indeed, he quit and became an independent in 2018. He describes a number of friends from back home who "voted Reagan, Reagan, Bush, Clinton, Clinton, Bush, Bush, Obama, Obama, Trump." For him, the "connective tissue of those disparate votes" is " 'what's good for me? Who's going to give to me, who's going to do best by me as a small business owner?' All the rest of this stuff: foreign policy and all that other stuff, that all happens far away."

Nichols recalls a conversation twenty-six years ago with his childhood best friend who was voting for Bill Clinton. Nichols told him that "sooner or later you're going to end up with the choice of voting for his wife." The friend replied, "I don't care. [George H. W.] Bush is a rich guy. He doesn't care about people like me." In 2016, Nichols reminded his friend of this talk, and the friend said, "Yeah, but I couldn't vote for Hillary."

According to Nichols, his friend wanted to get back at everybody he thinks destroyed their hometown: "towns don't just die," his friend insisted. "Someone did that to them." Trump filled in that blank of "here's all the people you can blame." His supporters somehow didn't hold it against him that he was rich, the way they had against Bush or Mitt Romney. Trump convinced these voters that a self-declared billionaire real estate tycoon was on their side. They didn't even necessarily believe he could revive their town, but he would punish the people—the Mexicans or the Chinese—that they blamed for its decline.

Nichols bristles at the suggestion that the Republican Party's Alex P. Keaton spirit was always little more than a cover for old-fashioned racism. To him, the Republican rank and file has "internalized this notion that the Republicans are *not* the party of the rich." Rather, "the Republicans are the party of everybody who's not a Democrat." And Democrats represent the black and brown, the LGBT, the feminists, and in short, "everyone who's not a white conservative."

Nichols describes his parents as perfect examples of this. His mother worked in a Great Society antipoverty program but became a hard-core Republican when she came to believe that "everybody gets a break from the government except people like her and her husband."

Nearly fifty years later, Donald Trump stepped in to take advantage of that simmering resentment among white Americans. But not everyone bought the act.

Nichols recalls a family member who was impressed when Trump teased a presidential run in 2000 and even had some campaign paraphernalia made up. "I had a crazy uncle who showed up in a Trump hat," Nichols said. "And my father just tore the bark off him for being an idiot. Dad said, 'Donald Trump doesn't give a shit about you. Government has to be run by people who know what they're doing.'"

Nichols's family sometimes called his father Archie Bunker. He voted for Nixon and Reagan, though both he and Nichols's uncle passed away years before Trump attained the presidency. "But you could already see in 2000 the precursor" of the Trump era. "It wasn't really a Republican or Democratic sentiment," Nichols said. "It was the sentiment of a guy who worked with his hands his whole life, and all he wanted to do was just piss somebody off that [in his view] hadn't worked as hard as he had."

This notion, fueled by conservative media and an almost frantic rage against Barack Obama, led to the rise of the Tea Party movement, which eventually succeeded in swallowing the Republican Party whole, rendering the lower chamber all but ungovernable for consecutive Republican House speakers, Ohio congressman John Boehner, and Wisconsin's Paul Ryan, a Koch brothers acolyte and Ayn Rand true-believer who allowed countless floor votes to try to repeal the healthcare law that came to be known as Obamacare. The Tea Party's electoral successes in 2010 and 2012 placed men like Ted Cruz of Texas in the Senate, where in 2013 the future presidential candidate triggered a sixteen-day government shutdown after egging on the House Tea Party–inspired "Freedom caucus" to demand the defunding of the Affordable Care Act as a condition of funding the federal government.[1]

The Tea Party politicians who went to Washington were of the party's far right base—viewed as not typical politicians, but ordinary "Joe the plumbers," storming the barricades to finally set things right and succeed where they felt their traditional leaders had failed: stopping the creep of "Kenyan socialism" in the form of healthcare, ending the forced racial reckonings every time a police officer "did his job" and a black person was shot dead, curtailing libertine social reforms that elevated gay marriage, mosques, and "Sharia law" to the status of old-fashioned Christian values. And most of all, stopping illegal immigration. In short, the base was mad—not least at the Republican Party.

With its obscene signs attacking Obama as a witch doctor, a "lyin' African," and a black Hitler, its racist invective and period costumes evoking the Revolutionary War, and its professionally printed signs that said things like "bury Obamacare with [Senator Ted] Kennedy," the Tea Party was perhaps the ultimate expression of the power of a wealthy few to channel the GOP base's populist instincts and undifferentiated rage at the country's first black president toward the preferred policy outcomes of the rich—and even to stir demands by citizens for the repeal of their own healthcare.

In 2010, Florida's Republican and independent voters rallied to narrowly elect Rick Scott, a multi-millionaire former hospital executive whose firm reached a settlement in which they agreed to pay $1.7 billion in fines for Medicare, Medicaid, and military healthcare fraud. Embracing the Tea Party, Scott vowed to never allow Obamacare in the state, despite Florida having the second-largest pool of uninsured in the country.

Four years later in Kentucky, voters overwhelmingly chose to replace the outgoing Democratic governor with an investment manager aligned with the Tea Party movement: Matt Bevin, who ran on a vow to kill Obamacare in the state where the Medicaid expansion had extended healthcare to more than 400,000 Kentuckians. The Affordable Care Act program had been named "Kynect" by the previous governor, Steve Beshear, to make it acceptable to his constituents in a state that rejected Obama by 41.7 percent to 57.5 percent for John McCain in 2008, and by an even wider 37.8 percent to 60.5 percent for Mitt Romney in 2012.

The Tea Party movement ultimately failed to stop Obamacare, but their party's leaders didn't seem to acknowledge that because they were so flush with seemingly unlimited victory thanks to the base's Obama rage. And the 2010 census-year midterm rout, plus the Supreme Court's gutting of the Voting Rights Act and its rulings that unleashed unlimited campaign money to right-wing causes, freed Republican politicians to gerrymander, suppress, and spend their way to a future in which they believed they couldn't lose. But as former RNC chair Michael Steele stated in frequent appearances on MSNBC, the plutocrats who bankrolled the Tea Party had grabbed a tiger by the tail and soon found out how a tiger behaves.

BRUCE BARTLETT JOINED THE REPUBLICAN PARTY IN THE 1970S, as a student at Rutgers University. He would earn a master's degree at Georgetown, studying American diplomatic theory before working first for Texas congressman Ron Paul in 1976, and then for Congressman Jack Kemp. He saw the GOP as the "party of ideas" and felt the Democrats were just "proposing the same old policies they had proposed back during the New Deal." Bartlett now believes the modern Republican Party stands for little besides slashing taxes on the rich and gutting benefits for the poor. "Although there's lots of disparate interest groups, anti-abortion people, gun nuts, and various other groups," he observes, "the one issue that holds all of those people together and, particularly, the funders of the Republican Party, the ultra-wealthy, is tax cuts. I think that what people don't understand is that this isn't just about stimulating the economy. It's obvious that the tax cuts of the Bush and Trump eras had no economic effect whatsoever. Their agenda is to destroy government, to downsize it to such a point that we have virtual anarchy. I think that one of the problems with the Republicans is they've internalized a lot of the ideas of Ayn Rand. I think that they are de facto anarchists, even if they don't think so in their own minds."

After working for Paul and Kemp, Bartlett was a staffer to Senator Roger Jepsen, Republican of Iowa, and served as deputy staff director of the powerful Joint Economic Committee of Congress, and later as executive director when Jepsen became the committee chair. He was also a senior policy analyst in the Reagan White House, where he helped craft what he later called the "Republican tax myth" that powered the Reagan-era tax cuts. Bartlett's connections to the Heritage Foundation and other conservative think tanks made him a kind of father of supply-side economics.

Bartlett eventually renounced it all and wrote a bestselling book that accused George W. Bush of bankrupting America and betraying Reagan's legacy. In a 2017 *Washington Post* op-ed, entitled "I helped create the GOP tax myth. Trump is wrong: Tax cuts don't equal growth," Bartlett opposed both the Bush tax cuts and the Republican Congress's trillion-dollar tax cut, ultimately signed the following year, that went overwhelmingly to the wealthy and corporations.

Bartlett believes America is living through a new Gilded Age. "I don't think there's any question that history is repeating itself. But, keep in mind that the Gilded Age was followed by the Progressive Era," he said. "There does tend to be a pendulum that goes back and forth. But we'll need at least a generation to fix the mess that we've gotten ourselves into."

Bartlett believes that the modern Republican Party is, in fundamental ways, the creation of Newt Gingrich, who was elected to Congress from Georgia in 1978 and was House Speaker from 1995 to 1999. Bartlett points to Gingrich's strategy of running strong Republicans against conservative Democrats who would otherwise have been reelected since they fit the sensibility of their districts, as a way of taking control of the House and its committees. "It was extraordinarily successful and very important strategically," he said. "I think it happened so gradually, Democrats didn't realize what was happening until it was too late."

And as the Republicans became the party of the South, they picked up on the old-time Democrats' technique for winning elections, "which was you keep the blacks and the whites separated. Because if they vote together, they might vote for populists, and the populist threat was the only one Democrats were concerned about." Bartlett says, "the Republicans have adopted the same idea of using racism to keep poor whites from joining into an alliance with blacks. As long as they keep divided, you can keep control."

Bartlett is careful to say he doesn't believe all Republicans are racist. "But it is true that the party benefits from racism," and that "the existence of racism in society is per se beneficial to the Republican Party. I think it's also reasonable to say that although all Republicans are not racist, virtually all racists are Republicans today."

Republican concerns about law and order, illegal voting (haltingly rare), and welfare are code for racism, Bartlett says. "They're obsessed with cutting benefits for welfare," he observes. "They believe that all black people are on welfare, and that no white people are. Of course, that's complete nonsense. The vast bulk of people on welfare are in fact white. They have these ideas that are never fully articulated, because they use code to talk about them. They talk about lazy people on welfare. . . . Of course, they've also transferred their racism over to the Hispanic community as well. Again, people who are obsessed with illegal immigration, this is a code for racism, because the only immigration that they're concerned about are brown-skinned people from the South. You never hear anybody talk about needing a wall across the Canadian border."

Bartlett says that it is a matter of self-preservation for a party with little diversity to recognize that "within an election cycle or two, it may be impossible for them to win the White House again for a very long time, and they may lose control of Congress for a very long time as well. I think they're just shooting the last of their ammunition. They're trying to set into place for the long term as much of their policies as possible."

That strategy is most obvious in the courts. "That's why the [now associate Supreme Court justice Brett] Kavanaugh fight was so important," Bartlett says. "It's not just because he's a reliable conservative, not just that he's a movement conservative, but he's young. He'll be on the court for a very long time."

Bartlett believes that conservatives are looking for ways that the courts can both preserve those policies that are already in place and prevent the enactment of liberal democratic policies. "They have very much of an authoritarian mindset," he says. "I think in the conservative mind you can never trust democracy. You can never trust the people, because they're greedy. There are more poor people than rich people. They will vote benefits for themselves and pay for it by taxing the rich."

Donald Trump turned out to be the perfect vessel for implementing those plans. He spent the first two years of his presidency stacking the judiciary with young, far-right judges who would implement the policies favored by the wealthy for decades to come. He and his cabinet embarked on a frenzy of deregulation, unleashing polluters and corporations to dump at will into the country's rivers and lakes. And he signed record tax cuts including a temporary gutting of the estate tax that could balloon the maximum exemption for a wealthy couple to $22.4 million, a move that could benefit his own children.[2]

It's as if a new robber baron era has indeed begun, only with the armed everymen protecting the c-suites. Trump talked like a populist but presided over massive tax cuts for the superrich and a no-look government that unleashed an American oligarchy to do as it pleased.

Bartlett believes Newt Gingrich was thinking strategically when he significantly weakened Congress's ability to conduct investigations. "He wanted to neuter the one branch of government that had the power to [put a brake on] his executive fantasies, which have become true. I think Trump is so far beyond what Gingrich ever thought was possible. He must be the happiest person in Washington. Everything in his entire career was a buildup to the Trump Era, in which he can finally do all these things that Republicans have been dreaming about since the 1920s. Trump is doing them. I think Newt sleeps like a baby at night. I think he is simply a true believer and had a long-term plan. To his credit, he had a plan, and he implemented it."

HOLDING TOGETHER A PARTY LED BY PLUTOCRATS, YET POWered by a populist message, was never going to be easy. But the Tea Party movement proved that racial animus was a powerful binding agent. Racism and nativism have long been useful tools in the toolkit of American politics.

Trump's presidential advisers, including Roger Stone and Steve Bannon, intuited that after the simmering racial backlash Obama's two terms produced, anti-immigration sentiment was the strongest argument for a change of control in the White House. The base of the Republican Party was angry—angry at their own leaders for constantly losing to Obama, angry at the multiracial coalition that reelected him, and angry at a country that seemed to be drifting away from them.

None of Trump's sometimes jarring campaign promises bound him more closely to this increasingly nativist base than his pledge to "build the wall." It appealed to the modern heirs of those who pushed through the Johnson-Reed Immigration Act of 1924, which set strict national origin quotas to preserve the ethnic mix of the United States, discriminating against Italian and other southern European "lesser whites" and excluding Chinese and North African migrants.

Few old-line elected Republicans had any interest in erecting a 2,000-mile border wall, even if it could be done. As early as 2006, Iowa congressman Steve King, a nine-term Republican, had pushed the idea, even constructing a scale model on the House floor, and had been ignored. And the processes that would be required to even begin such a project, including filing eminent domain lawsuits against private landowners to take their land to build a wall on, were anathema to everything Republicans claimed to stand for.

In 2005, future Supreme Court justice Neil Gorsuch, whose nomination Trump touted constantly on the campaign trail as among his finest achievements, wrote a ringing email endorsement of Justice Clarence Thomas's withering dissent in a case called *Kelo vs. the City of New London*, in which the Court's majority decided that government could take private property from one owner and transfer it to another for economic development, broadening the interpretation of the Fifth Amendment's definition of public use in a way that set conservatives' hair on fire. At the time, Gorsuch was working for the George W. Bush Justice Department. Trump, who had used eminent domain for his building projects and casinos in ways that have been called abusive,[3, 4] thought the *Kelo* decision was "wonderful."[5]

Now Trump was leading a party that had become an inverted pyramid, with the angry base and the media entertainers on top, and the donors, conservative intellectuals, and traditional Republican politicians seemingly down below. It didn't matter that the base's (and the president's) belief that Central American migrants were a mass of diseased gang members bent on welfare dependency and mayhem was a twisted fantasy born on right-wing media and the dark corners of the Internet. Or that building a wall of concrete or steel (Trump's evolving plan) beyond the barriers that already existed along the southern border and had for more than a decade was completely unfeasible on a landscape that includes more than 1,200 miles of the Rio Grande River, which floods so often it would wash away any structure that the government might try to erect.[6] Or that a 1970 U.S.-Mexico treaty prohibits even trying to build in that massive floodplain.[7] Or that Trump's vow that Mexico would ever pay for such a project was an idea well beyond delusion.

None of it mattered. Trump, his media regents, and his most forceful defenders were determined to make it so.

It was a new world for Trump, the creature of New York who now led a party that was more rural, southern, and working class than he had ever been or tried to be. He had worked his whole adult life to join the Manhattan, Palm Beach, and Hollywood smart set. But now, he found himself allied with people like Pat Buchanan, whom he once despised.

Buchanan, the three-time presidential candidate who had been a staple of the broadcast and cable news commentariat until a book he wrote, which included chapter titles such as "The End of White America," was criticized, according to *Politico*, for being "homophobic, anti-Semitic and racist,"[8] derailed his career. Trump had considered challenging him for the Reform Party presidential nomination in 2000, attacking his then-rival as a "fan of Hitler" for his revisionist history of World War II.

Ironically, back then, it was Trump who said, during a speech at a museum of the Holocaust remembrance organization the Simon Wiesenthal Center, "We must recognize bigotry and prejudice and defeat it wherever it appears."[9]

A year 2000 pre-campaign book, *The America We Deserve*, ghostwritten for Trump by Dave Shiflett, assailed Buchanan's "history of defending Nazi war criminals" and his support for South African apartheid, accusing him of anti-Semitism in adding that "Buchanan's theory seems to be that Jews took over American foreign policy after the war and lied to us about everything, that Jewish global interests were paramount in American governmental thinking, and they even outweighed United States security interests." It was a passage that could have been written about David Duke, who endorsed Trump's candidacy during the Republican primaries, though Trump claimed not to know who he was;[10] or American neo-Nazi Andrew Anglin, the *Daily Stormer* editor who reacted to Trump's 2018 claim that majority-black countries are "shitholes" by claiming, "it indicates Trump is more or less on the same page as us with regards to race and immigration."[11]

The 2000 Trump book, which never became as popular as *The Art of the Deal,* went on to say that Buchanan "has been guilty of many egregious examples of intolerance. He has systematically bashed Blacks, Mexicans, and Gays. In 1983, saying that homosexuals had 'declared war on nature,' he said that AIDS is nature's awful retribution."[12]

Trump's distaste for Buchanan didn't last. By 2016, Trump had morphed into what political analyst Jeff Greenfield called "Pat Buchanan with better timing."[13] The shift toward bareknuckles nativism won Buchanan's support as the Republican establishment sought to jettison the Republican nominee when weeks before the election, outtakes from the NBC entertainment show *Access Hollywood* surfaced showing Trump in 2005 bragging about grabbing women's genitals as he joked with host

Billy Bush. Two years later, Buchanan heaped praise on Trump's stubborn refusal to abandon his demand that Congress fund his border wall. Trump eagerly shared the praise with his millions of Twitter followers.

"The Trump portrait of an unsustainable Border Crisis is dead on," Trump tweeted about himself, quoting a Buchanan article in the virulently nativist website Vdare.com. That was followed by a litany of frightening, yet false, statistics attempting to link undocumented immigration to grisly crime.[14]

On the night of January 13, 2019, two days before the one hundredth anniversary of Martin Luther King Jr.'s birth, the president tweeted another Buchanan quote: "America's Southern Border is eventually going to be militarized and defended or the United States, as we have known it, is going to cease to exist . . . And Americans will not go gentle into that good night." Trump then added a flourish of his own: "The great people of our Country demand proper Border Security NOW!"[15]

At the conservative *Washington Examiner*, which generally supported Trump's policies, editor Philip Klein lamented, "President Trump's decision to quote a Pat Buchanan alarmist op-ed peddling the sort of white grievance politics on which he built his political career is a signal that at this point, Trump is not interested in persuading anybody on the merits of his border wall."[16] The president hadn't just failed at persuasion—he made a remarkable statement of solidarity with Buchanan's well-trodden politics of white-male grievance and stark ethno-nationalism.

Trump's new and strange bedfellows weren't all from the South. And their enthusiasm for his "build the wall" pledge sometimes wreaked havoc on the GOP.

Congressman Steve King, in a January 10, 2019, interview with the *New York Times* about Trump's border wall and its racial implications, asked, rhetorically, "[w]hite nationalist, white supremacist, Western civilization. How did that language become offensive? Why did I sit in classes teaching me about the merits of our history and our civilization?" [17] The response was swift and brutal. Republicans joined Democrats in denouncing him. King's home state's junior senator, Joni Ernst, called his remarks "offensive and racist," linking her remarks to a *New York Times* op-ed by South Carolina senator Tim Scott, the lone black Republican in the 116th Congress, calling on his party to speak up when racism occurred within their ranks. And the senior senator from Iowa, Charles Grassley, who had endorsed King even after previous remarks prompted fellow Republicans to call King a white supremacist, condemned him, too.

King denied in a published statement and on the House floor that he was a white supremacist, saying he "reject[ed] those labels and the evil ideology that they define." [18] Yet he was stripped of his committee assignments, including what had been his chairmanship, when Republicans controlled the House, of the Judiciary Committee's subcommittee on civil rights.

Many asked, "Why now?" noting that Republicans had long been silent about King's rich history of nativist and racist statements and continued to be silent about Trump. Just months before, King had retweeted a post by white nationalist and YouTube host Lana Lokteff that depicted three blonde, white children and stated that "according to [Irish rock singer] Bono if your Swedish kids look like this, they are Nazis." King's retweet added, " 'Nazi' is injected into Leftist talking points because the worn out & exhausted 'racist' is over used & applied to everyone who lacks melanin & who fail to virtue signal at the requisite frequency & decibels." [19] And he ended with the factually inaccurate but well-worn right-wing flourish that Nazis, who were a far-right, purportedly Christian political movement of "National Socialists," were akin to the American left. Earlier that year, King tweeted his agreement with right-wing, xenophobic Dutch politician Geert Wilders, who said that, "our civilization cannot be restored with *somebody else's babies*."

During the 2016 campaign, King told MSNBC's Chris Hayes that no "subgroup" had contributed to civilization as much as Europeans had. In June 2016, he retweeted a post by British self-described "Nazi sympathizer" and Holocaust denier Mark Collett.[20] And that October, King traveled to Austria and met with members of the far-right Austrian "Freedom Party," which has historic ties to the Nazis. His trip was funded by a group that denies the Holocaust. Yet with all of this, his party had never done more than ritualistically condemn him; back home, he continued to win elections.

Few of the Republicans who raced to Twitter to condemn King noted his other comment to the *Times*, in which he dismissed the Democratic caucus's historic diversity in the House and Senate, by calling the opposing party "no country for white men." The election of minority candidates in the midterm elections caused the 116th Congress to have white-male representation at an historic low. But even so, the House was still made up of 60 percent white men and the Senate, 71 percent. Yet those figures stood in stark contrast to the white-male population of the United States as a whole, which as of 2019 was 38 percent.

"Republicans in Congress continue to be, for the most part, a party of white men," wrote Richie Zweigenhaft, a Guilford College (N.C.) psychology professor, in a statistical analysis of the 116th Congress for the academic site The Conversation. "About 41 percent of the Democrats but 88 percent of the Republicans in the House are white men. In the Senate, they make up about 63 percent of the Democrats but 82 percent of the Republicans."[21]

King was echoing Pat Buchanan's lament that the Democratic Party was engaged in a kind of conspiracy to drive white men out of power, an argument perfectly at home with the ethos of the white nationalist and "Western chauvinist" movements, and which reflected Buchanan's belief that America was engaged in a race- and religion-based culture war being fought through politics. King and his party recognized, as Kevin Phillips and

Lee Atwater had, that Democrats were increasingly beholden to black, brown, Asian, LGBT, and unmarried women voters— to the "new immigrants"—and that as such, they struggled to appeal to an increasingly resentful white working class.

Trump seemed to have signed on to those politics, or at least he was willing to use them to win. For a time, his business even sought to profit from them, as his adult children floated the notion, later discarded, of the Trump Organization building new, lower-cost hotel brands that would appeal to working-class Trump fans in southern states such as Mississippi.[22]

The modern Republican Party had taken a long march from the stoic bipartisanship of Dwight Eisenhower to the anti–civil rights "extremism in the defense of liberty" of Barry Goldwater, to the southern strategy of Richard Nixon and the "welfare queens" and cold war victory politics of Ronald Reagan, to George W. Bush's mix of "compassionate conservatism" and neoconservative adventurism, and finally to Trump.

As distasteful as Trump's tactics were, his party's leadership understood that its nativist elements were an important voting block they couldn't afford to turn away. The bogeymen had to be kept inside the house. So long as Trump continued signing legislation advancing the party and its donors' core interests—deep tax cuts for the rich and deregulation of industry—most seemed to find the Trumpian devil's bargain to be worthwhile. Some seemed downright enthusiastic.

The thing is, they'd been there before.

In the 1990s, Louisiana state legislator Steve Scalise told a political reporter that he was "David Duke without the baggage," touching off questions about his own racial attitudes that dogged him for more than twenty years as he rose through the ranks of Republican House leadership. The reporter he shared that self-description with, Stephanie Grace, later expressed her view that Scalise was doing what so many politicians, Democrats and Republicans, had done for years, when making pragmatic decisions about acquiring power.

For *The Advocate* in 2014, the year Scalise was vying for his role as the House minority whip, Grace wrote, "Scalise may have been naïve about how to express himself to a newcomer, but he was already a savvy politician who knew that, even though Duke had lost the governor's race a few years earlier, Duke voters were still around. And those Duke voters also were potential Scalise voters."

While Scalise was still a Louisiana state representative, it had been revealed during the lead-up to the election that in 2002, he spoke to the Duke-founded European-American Unity and Rights Organization (EURO).[23] Later Scalise's team claimed he had been unaware of the group's white supremacist ties, though considering Duke's prominence nationally and in the state, it's hard to imagine anyone in Louisiana politics being unaware of an organization founded by the 1991 Republican candidate for governor. "This is, in effect, a dirty little secret of Louisiana politics," Grace explained.

The truth, as Scalise suggested that day, was that the actual governmental philosophy that Duke espoused wasn't far off from what was becoming mainstream conservative thought, what with its suspicion of taxes, set-asides, and safety net programs such as welfare. The problem in his view was the messenger, not the message.

"The novelty of David Duke has worn off," Scalise told *Roll Call* in 1999. "The voters in this district are smart enough to realize that they need to get behind someone who not only believes in the issues they care about, but also can get elected. Duke has proven that he can't get elected, and that's the first and most important thing."[24]

While Scalise and other Republicans publicly and even forcefully rejected the racist views of these white nationalist elements, they shared a view on taxes and spending and welfare, as did many of their voters. There was a time when southern Democrats—even Jimmy Carter during his 1976 presidential run—could not afford to ignore the George Wallace voters, either. The rule of thumb was that white voters with "conservative views on race" had to be appeased with messages against multiculturalism and nonwhite immigration. But in the post–Civil Rights era the quiet parts—about explicit racial animus—were no longer to be said out loud.

This was made clear by men like South Carolina political strategist-turned-über-Republican operative Lee Atwater, who delivered the famously blunt explanation to political scientist Alexander Lamis: "you start out in 1954 by saying, 'Nigger, nigger, nigger.' By 1968 you can't say 'nigger'—that hurts you, backfires. So, you say stuff like . . . forced busing, states' rights, and all that stuff, and you're getting so abstract. Now, you're talking about cutting taxes, and all these things you're talking about are totally economic things and a byproduct of them is, blacks get hurt worse than whites." [25]

Before Atwater, Nixon strategist and "self-taught ethnologist" Kevin Phillips foresaw Republican dominance "premised on the alleged hostility of Irishmen, Italians and Poles, whose ethnic traits were conservative, toward Jews, Negroes and affluent Yankees, whom history had made liberal." [26]

Like Trump, Phillips grew up in New York City—in the multiracial borough of the Bronx. Rather than adhering him to the notion of an American "melting pot," Phillips would state in a May 1970 profile in the *New York Times* that his time in New York City convinced him that most people "still voted on the basis of ethnic or cultural enmities that could be graphed, predicted and exploited." [27] Phillips posited that "the old bitterness toward Protestant Yankee Republicans that had made Democrats out of Irish, Italian and Eastern European immigrants had now shifted, among their children and grandchildren, to resentment of the new immigrants—Negroes and Latinos—and against the national Democratic Party, whose Great Society programs increasingly seemed to reflect favoritism for the new minorities over the old."[28] At the time, Republican Party identification in the United States was at 29 percent, and Nixon was in the White House. By January 2019, it was 25 percent according to Gallup, having dropped two points from the month of Trump's election.

Phillips told his party they didn't need the black vote—and should actually encourage enforcement of the Civil Rights Act, since "the more Negroes who register as Democrats in the South, the sooner the Negrophobe whites will quit the Democrats and become Republicans."[29] Said Phillips: "That's where the votes are." (Decades later, conservative elections analyst Sean Trende would make the case that Mitt Romney's loss to Obama in 2012 was more related to white voters who went "missing" from the electorate than a surge in nonwhite voters who placed Republicans at an inherent demographic disadvantage. Turn out those largely rural white voters, Trende said, and Republicans could win at politics even in a browning America.)[30]

This brutal kind of logic was one the party would use again and again, sometimes successfully, but sometimes with disastrous results.

The 2018 midterm elections would see record Democratic turnout, driven by the demonstrated cruelties of Trump's first two years, including national anguish over the policy of taking migrant children—even infants—from their parents, and incarcerating them separately, sometimes hundreds of miles apart. The policy saw children kept in cages, to the horror of lawmakers and journalists alike. Sometimes parents were deported, leaving their children stranded in American shelters or foster homes. Nearly a year after the policy supposedly ended, shelter workers reported in whispers and off the record that they were still seeing separated children coming through their doors.

Adam Serwer, in a seminal piece in *The Atlantic*, declared that, much like the history of American lynching, in which upstanding, churchgoing members of the community gathered around the hanged bodies of black men who were deemed criminals in need of swift justice—"their cruelty made them feel good" [31]— Trump's base bonded around the ritualized pain inflicted on the brown, the foreign, and the poor. They enjoyed seeing them suffer, because it sent a message to the rest of the unwanted: "Stay away." And it reminded Trump's followers that at last, a president of the United States was working for *them*; he was putting them, the "real Americans," first.

On his "wall," Trump couldn't back down even if he'd wanted to. He was caught between an experienced House Speaker, Nancy Pelosi, who was determined to teach him the meaning of "no," and an entrenched right-wing media who were not about to let the president they helped put in place off the hook. Republicans were trapped, too. The Senate leader, Mitch McConnell, would not oppose Trump, but nor was he able to lead the president to a logical path. Those close to McConnell insisted that he would not go out on a limb unless Trump walked out onto it with him. He faced his own reelection in 2020, as did nearly two dozen of his members.

In autocratic regimes, an impotent legislature often rubber-stamps the erratic demands of a petulant leader. Without them, and a loyal military, he cannot rule. The Republican Party under Donald Trump, existing at the narrow end of the inverted pyramid, had become a kind of Politburo, acting only with his permission—and it was this relationship that made Trump's impetuous rule possible. Only the courts and a Democratic House stood in his way.

No one seemed more emblematic of the shift toward learned helplessness than South Carolina senator Lindsey Graham, the once-fierce Trump critic who during the 2016 primary called Trump "a race-baiting, xenophobic, religious bigot," but who now declared on his Twitter feed, "Declare emergency, build the wall now." The man who once stood with Senator John McCain to lambaste dictators and autocrats around the world now said of the opposition party in his own country, "I think Democrats hate Trump so much they want him to lose even though it would be good for the country to work with him on border security, and *if he doesn't break them now,* it's going to be a terrible 2019." [32]

That is what the Republican Party under Donald Trump had become. The GOP that emerged in the age of Trump was not just fully realized as the party of the angry, white man, raging against the onset of cultural, social, and racial change. They were a party of, by, and for Donald Trump. When they gathered around him in the White House, elected officials and businessmen alike submitted to lavish rituals of sycophantic praise and thanks to the president.

The vice president, Mike Pence, often did so in frankly humiliating fashion. It was the price of the ride. Mitch McConnell made it clear in the fall of 2018 that every degradation, every hit to the stature of the presidency of the United States and the institutions around it was worth it, because essentially all that mattered to him was transforming the judiciary for a generation. [33] That would be his legacy. Judges were what bound evangelical and archconservative supporters to Trump, whatever his manners and mores.

For rank-and-file politicians, including those who expressed disdain for Trump in private, the plain fact was that Trump's poll numbers were rock solid and not declining among Republican voters, no matter what he did or what was in the news. If they wanted to remain elected officials, they felt they had no choice but to go along. And so any criticism of him had to be quiet, like the many White House officials who become unnamed sources for tell-all books, or the unprecedented, scathing, anonymous September 5, 2018, op-ed published by the *New York Times*, written by someone who said they worked at the White House as part of an "internal resistance" that was working from within to "frustrate parts of [Trump's] agenda and his worst inclinations."[34]

The author's essay set off a fevered speculation in Washington and in the media about his or her identity. Could it be Trump senior adviser and staple cable television defender Kellyanne Conway, whose husband, George, scorched Trump almost daily on Twitter? Or perhaps Nick Ayers, described by one state-elected official who suspected him as the author, as "the Newt Gingrich of Georgia politics and the then-chief of staff to Vice President Pence?"[35] Whoever wrote the op-ed diagnosed "the root of the problem" in the White House as "the president's amorality. Anyone who works with him knows he is not moored to any discernible first principles that guide his decision making," the writer said, calling Trump's impulses, "generally anti-trade and anti-democratic"; the writer floated the notion—which would be repeated by ousted deputy FBI director Andrew McCabe in his 2019 tell-all book, and strenuously denied on the record by Justice Department leaders—that senior staff and cabinet members had considered invoking the Twenty-Fifth Amendment early in the administration to remove Trump as if he was incapacitated.[36]

"Although he was elected as a Republican, the president shows little affinity for ideals long espoused by conservatives: free minds, free markets and free people," the anonymous author wrote. "At best, he has invoked these ideals in scripted settings. At worst, he has attacked them outright." And yet, by the author's own admission, they were also fighting to preserve Trump's policies: tax cuts and deregulation that were anything but alien to conservative dogma.

For even some publicly declared "never Trump" Republicans (who over time drifted toward a conservative Democratic or a trial balloon independent run, as by Starbucks coffee mogul

Howard Schultz, who railed against "Socialism" and calls to hike billionaires' tax rates), for many Republicans, current and former, they loved many of Trump's policies and hated his manners.

The same week the op-ed ran, a bombshell book by veteran journalist Bob Woodward, entitled *Fear*, described a raving president being constantly undermined by his own staff, who went so far as to remove papers from his desk so he wouldn't sign orders they thought were dangerous to the country, and by his cabinet, who snapped to attention when Trump barked orders at them, even though they had no intention of carrying them out. This was no resistance—it was nothing short of an administrative coup.

Some Republican senators, such as John Cornyn of Texas, Bob Corker of Tennessee, and Jeff Flake of Arizona—all of them on their way to retirement—occasionally spoke out publicly about the president's temperament, but these men voted with him 96, 84, and 81 percent of the time, on everything from gutting the Affordable Care Act to approving his judges and affirming his policies neutralizing regulation of polluters. Nearly every elected Republican followed suit, with just a handful, such as Alaska senator Lisa Murkowski, occasionally breaking ranks.

In 2018, Mitt Romney, the former Massachusetts governor and presidential candidate, won a U.S. Senate seat from Utah, and he began 2019 with a New Year's Day *Washington Post* op-ed[37] denouncing Trump's character while expressing fulsome support for his policies, particularly the tax cuts that would surely benefit a man of Romney's immense wealth. Romney was sworn in to his Senate seat on January 3, 2019.

Even Senator McCain, who vivisected Trump over his humiliating performance in Helsinki, and whose heroic, stubborn vote on the Senate floor saved Obamacare from partial repeal, resisted Trump most strongly in the final months of his life, through statements and speeches that scorched the earth with Trump's lack of character and judgment. McCain did so most dramatically in death, by refusing to invite the president to his state funeral. And though even Lindsey Graham criticized Trump for excusing the murder of a U.S. resident journalist, Jamal Khashoggi, by a hit team tied to the crown prince of Saudi Arabia, there was little follow-up on the criticism, and it seemed to vanish into the vapor.

"What's different about the Republicans now under Trump," said Tom Nichols, "is that they are a party of negative aims rather than positive goals. It's just about tearing down instead of building. There is this resentment and I think a part of it has to do with the fact that the information age has created a chasm that's getting wider between the people who can live in the 21st century and people who just can't deal with it; who don't have the skills. They're kind of the buggy whip manufacturers of the modern era. They can't deal with diversity. And so what they want in that 'Freedom Caucus' is, 'as long as I make you miserable, that's my metric that I'm doing the right thing, because I don't really have my own goals and I can only judge my performance based on how angry you seem to be.'

"As for the rest of them, I think they're just scared," Nichols said. "The 'opportunity society' and the 'shining city on the hill' and rolling back communism'" are gone as Republican themes, replaced by the unfiltered, raw fear Trump thrives on. "I was walking across the campus at Cornell and I said, 'you know, these guys would burn the world down and live in the ashes if they thought it would make people on this campus uncomfortable for two hours.'"

Ironically, no one seemed to vocalize that truth better than Senator Graham, who said, in fiery opening remarks on the morning of the committee vote to confirm Kavanaugh to the high court, "I know I'm a single white male from South Carolina, and I'm told I should shut up, but I will not shut up, if that's okay."

Graham had voiced a Nicholsian truth: that his party was

increasingly the redoubt of white Christian men (and many of their wives), whose anger and desire to make those they deemed their adversaries uncomfortable was based on a real thing, fear of the consequences of demographic, social, and political decline.

With Trump pushing the pressure points of his party to the breaking point, and the demographic train barreling down the station toward a midcentury that will look quite different for white America, a question remained about what the party would be after it no longer had him as its standard-bearer. Would the GOP simply go back to what it was, sublimating the pockets of genuine anger and fear among the base, that Trumpism unearthed, so that the pyramid could right itself again? Or would the party's now-captive elite discover that the monster it unleashed over the decades from the Southern Strategy to the Tea Party to Donald Trump simply could not be forced back into its cage?

Two years into Trump's presidency, one Republican strategist who is white, worked for Trump's election, supports his tax and healthcare policies, and has vigorously defended the president's supporters for three years against the idea that they were motivated by racism has had a change of heart. "Donald Trump's election was about race. Just race," this strategist said in March 2019, calling the 2016 election a blend of resentment of Obama coupled with "a mix of racial attitude and a little hope and change."

"Rural white America wanted to get their kids out of their house," the strategist said. That was the "hope." Flag-waving white America "thought Obama had weakened us overseas" and replaced America's "swagger" with unbearable humility, unenforced "red lines," and contentment with "leading from behind." (Ironically, many on the left felt just the opposite: that Obama had failed to pull America back from its tendency toward intervention, military aggression, and, in particular, drone warfare.) Trump was more a vestige of the racial attitudes left over from the school desegregation and busing policies of the 1970s in the New York, Chicago, or Philadelphia suburbs than of the old-time racism of the Deep South, the strategist said. You could almost envision him posted up in a diner in his native Queens, carping about how Chinese imports and Japanese cars, affirmative action, "illegal immigrants," and political correctness were taking this country to hell. The fact that he reflected these core complaints of his base, combined with his celebrity, helped him quickly catch on. The strategist said that when interviewing Republican base voters about the healthcare law, for example, it takes just a few minutes before their anger at "Obamacare" becomes a diatribe about "that black SOB who ruined the country."

"I didn't want Obama to win, but I liked him," the strategist said, drawing a contrast with the venom that's out there. "I liked the fact that he smoked cigarettes out of the pack. I liked his family." That genial way of looking at a president of the other party seems like ancient history that will never repeat itself.

"Donald Trump may be the last president who can walk up on the line" of racism and divisiveness "and get away with it," he said. "The Republican Party can't stay this insane."

"I would like to think that there will be a reaction against Trumpism" when he's gone, Bruce Bartlett says. "And we can plough salt into the ground and destroy it completely. But, the problem with that is that you'd have to have some allies on the Republican side, and right at the moment, I don't see any. It is quite possible that the minute he's out of power, all of the sudden, all of these principled Republicans who [claim they were] in opposition to everything he's doing" will emerge. "There are a lot of Republicans I think out there who in their own minds have been the resistance, it's just they haven't publicized it. Partly, because they're liars, and, partly, because they're fearful of the consequences."

One prominent Republican fundraiser said that after Trump, "the plan right now is go back to the party of Reagan and Lincoln. That's the model that we're working on—to just pretend that Trump was never there. Of course, it's going to be difficult for a while to do that."

Indeed, things that have been seen can't be unseen. History can't be unwritten. And some in the party, including on its rightmost fringes, see Trump as a model, not a moment.

CHAPTER 4

A New American Civil War

"We're in a clear-cut cultural civil war."

—Newt Gingrich, during an interview with
Sean Hannity of Fox News, June 13, 2017

"THE RADICAL RIGHT ENTERED THE POLITICAL MAINSTREAM last year in a way that had seemed virtually unimaginable since George Wallace ran for president in 1968," reads the opening sentence of a February 2017 report by the Southern Poverty Law Center entitled, "The Year in Hate and Extremism." The annual report details the activities, growth, or decline of hate groups and hate-related attacks in the United States.

It was the second month of Donald Trump's presidency, and this was a sobering assessment of the effect his candidacy and election had had on the nation.

To further make that point, the report added that "a surge in right-wing populism, stemming from the long-unfolding effects of globalization and the movements of capital and labor that it spawned, brought a man many considered to be a racist, misogynist and xenophobe into the most powerful political office in the world . . . Trump's run for office electrified the radical right, which saw in him a champion of the idea that America is fundamentally a white man's country."[1]

The report included FBI statistics that indicate an increase in hate crime and hate incidents corresponding with Trump's election. SPLC's Heidi Beirich, who leads their Intelligence Project, which publishes data on hate and extremism as well as a blog called "Hatewatch," believes this rise in hate has been nearly twenty years in the making.

Beirich notes "a pattern of increase in hate groups going all the way back to 2000," when the Census Bureau first announced its statistical finding that white Americans would be a minority in the country by 2042. She says the significance now is "that the specific groups that have tied themselves to Trump . . . those particular organizations that have grabbed the Trump mantle, are the ones that are expanding." The SPLC quotes neo-Nazi "Stormfront" publisher Andrew Anglin, as crowing, "Our Glorious Leader has ascended to God Emperor. Make no mistake about it: we did this. If it were not for us, it wouldn't have been possible." It also uses quotes from "blood and soil" white nationalist Jared Taylor's boast that, " 'overwhelmingly, white Americans' had shown they were not 'obedient zombies' by choosing to vote 'for America as a distinct nation with a distinct people who deserve a government devoted to that people.' "[2]

Separately, an annual report of the Anti-Defamation League, "Murder and Extremism in the United States," found that "2018 was a particularly active year for right-wing extremist murders," and that "every single extremist killing—from Pittsburgh to Parkland—had a link to right-wing extremism." The annual report found that "the 50 deaths make 2018 the fourth-deadliest year on record for domestic extremist-related killings since 1970." The report found that the perpetrators of right-wing violence in the United States, often in the form of mass shootings, were most frequently tied to white supremacist, misogynistic "involuntary celibate or incel" and anti-feminist, so-called manosphere movements and anti-Semitic ideologies.

In October 2018, Cesar Altieri Sayoc of Fort Lauderdale, Florida, sent pipe bombs to a range of figures frequently targeted by Trump and his allies, including former president Barack Obama, former vice president Joe Biden, Hillary Clinton, former CIA director and current NBC News and MSNBC Senior National Security and Intelligence Analyst John Brennan, and Democratic senators Kamala Harris and Cory Booker, both of whom announced their presidential candidacies months later. Also targeted were frequent media presence and Trump critic California congresswoman Maxine Waters, and billionaire Democratic donors George Soros and Tom Steyer, along with actor Robert De Niro, who had been unsparing in his criticisms of Trump, a likely stinging rebuke of the former showman from a veteran of Hollywood.

Once again, the targets were frequent focuses of Trump's ire, and in February 2019 included Massachusetts senator Elizabeth Warren, whom Coast Guard lieutenant and self-proclaimed white nationalist Christopher Paul Hasson had listed in a manifesto discovered in his apartment along with a cache of weapons and steroids, calling her "Poca-Warren," a seeming permutation of Trump's epithet of choice for the Oklahoma-born Warren who drew controversy for her disputed claim of having Cherokee ancestry: "Pocahontas."

Trump publicly rejected any association with these radical right groups, and according to a longtime political associate, he was "furious" when Hillary Clinton in a June 2015 interview with Nevada political journalist Jon Ralston referred to "a recent entry into the Republican presidential campaign [who] said some very inflammatory things about Mexicans" and how such negative talk could "trigger people who are less than stable to do something like"[3] carry out the massacre of nine black churchgoers by a white supremacist in Charleston, South Carolina, that month. Trump complained publicly that Clinton had blamed him for the Mother Emanuel massacre, and according to the longtime associate, it prompted him to "take the gloves off."

When confronted with the potential impact of his Obama birtherism, his attacks on black professional athletes including LeBron James, his calling Salvadoran-American MS-13 gang members "animals," his attacking a Muslim Gold Star family for criticizing his policies, and insulting the African-American wife of a second fallen soldier, he typically pleaded ignorance or blamed others. And he vehemently denied that his embrace of the self-description as a "proud nationalist" meant that he is a "white nationalist," saying in October 2018, "I've never even heard that." [4]

When an Australian white nationalist massacred 50 people inside two mosques in Christchurch, New Zealand—live streaming the terrorist attack on Facebook—the killer named Trump in his lengthy manifesto as "a symbol of renewed white identity and common purpose." Yet Trump and his team rejected any notion that Trump served as an inspiration to white nationalists around the world. The president downplayed the global threat of white nationalism, calling it a "small group of people that have very serious problems." And his chief of staff, Mick Mulvaney, called any notion that Trump had stoked anti-Muslim sentiment "absurd," despite statements dating back to 2015 maligning Islam as a religion that "hates" the United States, Trump's Muslim travel ban, and his litany of statements calling for migrants to be driven out. The FBI in 2017 warned that white nationalist groups were responsible for more violence inside the U.S. than any other organized group. [5] And Donald Trump was serving as both a domestic and a global inspiration to those who like him viewed nonwhite migrants as an "invasion" of the West.

Trump may not have openly embraced them, but white

nationalist, neo-fascist, and neo-Nazi groups embraced him, Beirich says. They used their portrayal of Trump as their "God Emperor" to recruit young, white Americans, often on college campuses, with social media outreach, humorous Internet memes, "snark," and ridicule to appeal to young sensibilities, and affinity groups like the "Western chauvinist," sometimes violent Proud Boys. The SPLC says Trump—his image, likeness, and pronouncements—were the main drivers of increased hate group affinity.

These groups embraced his descriptions of Mexican migrants as "criminals," gang members, and "rapists" and his disparagement of the judge overseeing the (ultimately successful) fraud case against Trump University as unable to discharge his duties fairly because of his Mexican heritage. They cheered as he lashed out at black NFL players who kneeled during the National Anthem to protest police brutality. Even without direct reinforcement from the president, they believed that their affection for Trump was returned.

During the campaign, Trump and his namesake son retweeted Twitter posts by neo-Nazi and white supremacists who falsely claimed that 80 percent of murders of white Americans were committed by African-Americans.

Trump seeded his administration with immigration restrictionists and conservative hard-liners associated with the so-called alt-right, a thinly veiled rebrand of white nationalism. Chief among them was Steve Bannon, former head of Breitbart News, which he once bragged he'd made the "platform for the alt right." Bannon took up a place in the West Wing, armed with a whiteboard on which he scrawled what he meant to be the Trump administration's Bannon-ite "nationalist populist" agenda, initially meant to include a $1 trillion infrastructure plan to put Americans back to work with their hands (though that never became a formal proposal or legislation), draconian immigration restrictions including limiting family reunification (dubbed "chain migration" by the right), and curtailing special visas for foreign workers in the tech industries, as well as a virtual halt to multilateral trade deals including NAFTA in favor of bilateral deals (Trump ultimately settled for a partial NAFTA rewrite he called the USMCA).[6] Trump tried to seat Bannon on the National Security Council, though he would be fired just seven months into his tenure.

Months later, damning, on-the-record quotes from Bannon about Trump and his White House team surfaced in a tell-all book by journalist Michael Wolff. Even in exile, Bannon continued to pitch his framework for a new Western paradigm, linking a rebranded Republican Party to anti-immigrant, far right, Christian nationalist movements across Europe. But it was increasingly clear that Donald Trump was not just acting out Bannon's edicts. He was either a true believer or a far greater actor than he'd demonstrated on *The Apprentice*.

Another short-lived White House national security adviser was Sebastian Gorka, a Fox News regular who styled himself "Dr. Gorka" and claimed to be an expert on Muslim extremism and the Quran, though he didn't speak or read Arabic and had no direct subject matter mastery. Gorka became known mostly for wearing his father's pin from Vitézi Rend, a Hungarian organization tied to the Nazis, and for his over-the-top pronouncements about the impending end of Western civilization due to whatever liberal outrage was on his mind.

More durable was Stephen Miller, Trump's youngest adviser, in his early thirties, and who was widely believed to be the instigator of such ugly policies as the Muslim travel ban and the separation of migrant families at the southern border. Despite being of Jewish background, and the fact that part of his family fled anti-Jewish persecution in the Russian empire in the early 1900s and arrived in America as asylum seekers,[7, 8] Miller was associated with white nationalist Richard Spencer when both men were members of the Conservative Union at Duke University, where they made names for themselves among conservatives (and in Miller's case, on Fox News) in 2006, for their vigorous defense of a group of white fraternity members accused of sexually assaulting a black stripper who later changed her story.

Miller was a senior, writing angry screeds for the school newspaper, and according to a 2016 article in *Mother Jones*, "at DCU meetings, according to a past president for the group, [he] denounced multiculturalism and expressed concerns that immigrants from non-European countries were not assimilating."[9] Spencer was a PhD candidate who soon dropped out to pursue his new cause: a "white ethno-state" in America.

While at Duke, Spencer and Miller organized a debate between Peter Laufer, a journalist and author who had published a book advocating an open border between the United States and Mexico, and Peter Brimelow, publisher of the anti-immigrant, white ethno-nationalist website VDare. (Brimelow later turned up at a birthday party for President Trump's top economic adviser, former CNBC host Larry Kudlow, sparking fresh controversy over the administration's associations with extremists.) Spencer recalled the Duke debate in an October 2016 profile in *Mother Jones,* saying Miller helped him organize and fundraise for the event, though Miller later denied any association with Spencer, calling the entire story false and saying he rejects his views.[10]

Laufer distinctly remembers the two young men working in coordination. "They organized everything," Laufer says, "from the pickup at the airport, to the pre-debate dinner for the debaters and our wives, to the post-debate party that was nauseating to the point where my wife said, 'let's get out of here.'" They were the prime organizers. There is absolutely no question. Laufer says the two men "couldn't have been more cordial, nor their views more offensive."

In 2011, Spencer assumed leadership of a former nonprofit called the National Policy Institute following the death of its white nationalist founder (it lost its tax exemption in 2012). The NPI's stated mission, according to the Southern Poverty Law Center, is to "elevate the consciousness of whites, ensure our biological and cultural continuity, and protect our civil rights," and to "study the consequences of the ongoing influx that non-Western populations pose to our national identity."

Spencer, who earned his undergraduate degree at the University of Virginia in Charlottesville, wrote in 2014 for the NPI's publication that immigration is "a kind of proxy war—and maybe a last stand—for White Americans, who are undergoing a painful recognition that, unless dramatic action is taken, their grandchildren will live in a country that is alien and hostile." That same year, he coined the term *alt-right* as a rebranding of old-line, white nationalism, much as former grand wizard David Duke tried decades earlier to rebrand the Ku Klux Klan by trading in the white robes for a suit and tie. At a celebratory event in Washington following Trump's election as president, Spencer exclaimed, "Hail Trump, hail our people, hail victory!" to a chorus of cheers and Nazi salutes.

Miller may have denied being directly associated with Spencer, but he shared the alt-right founder's vehement opposition to the way mass immigration has evolved after the 1965 Immigration and Naturalization Act, which rescinded 1920s-era national-origin quotas and tipped the balance of migration away from Europe, where seven-eighths of immigrants to the U.S. came from in 1960, and toward other parts of the world, which produced nine in ten immigrants after the act became law.

Tom Gjelten, author of *A Nation of Nations: A Great American Immigration Story*, wrote in an article for *The Atlantic* that the shift was inadvertent, meant to mollify nativist opponents of the bill, who feared an influx of "Asians and Ethiopians," by shifting the emphasis from preferences for issuing visas to migrants "whose skills were 'especially advantageous' to the United States" to giving preference to "foreigners who were seeking to join their families in the United States." [11] The conservatives thought, erroneously, that family reunification would naturally favor "family oriented" Europeans.

In 2009, Miller became an aide to Alabama senator Jefferson "Jeff" Sessions, later Trump's first attorney general, whose desire to return to the immigration era of the first decades of the twentieth century was well known. As a senator, Sessions was fixated on preventing a comprehensive immigration reform bill that would legalize the status of millions of undocumented immigrants from becoming law. Miller was his ideological heir apparent, strategist, and sometime speechwriter. He hung on well into Trump's second year—outlasting a parade of senior staffers, cabinet appointees, and aides who left in scandal, resigned, or were forced out, including Sessions.

Miller emerged as the dark heart of the Trump administration, burrowed into the White House alongside Trump's preternaturally influential daughter and son-in-law who doubled as senior advisers. Miller wrote Trump's gloomy addresses, whispered into the president's ear, and occasionally emerged on CNN to shout demands that the resistance to the president immediately cease.

Trump was hardly the first rich man to take advantage of America's social upheavals. Members of the plutocratic class had long supported and even funded quasi-populist movements for their own material benefit. In 1934, the American Liberty League formed to oppose the New Deal, even as labor strikes crippled the country. The League, funded by the wealthy DuPont family and organized by a bipartisan cache of millionaire industrialists, former politicians, veterans of the anti-Prohibition movement, and even a handful of Hollywood figures such as legendary movie producer Hal Roach, quickly amassed more than three hundred chapters on college campuses. They launched "educational campaigns" inveighing against Social Security, the minimum wage, unemployment compensation, and federal labor laws, which they claimed were socialist outrages against liberty, promulgated by the class-traitor president, congenitally wealthy Franklin D. Roosevelt.

Generations later, Ronald Reagan, who after a childhood in poverty in Illinois made his money in Hollywood, all but defunded Lyndon Johnson's Great Society programs as president, crippled one of the nation's largest labor unions by firing striking air traffic controllers, and slashed taxes on the wealthy while becoming a hero of the white working class, whose anger was channeled into fears of welfare cheats and the Cold War. George W. Bush, the Brahman son of a namesake president and the candidate Americans were repeatedly reminded they'd most want to have a beer with, rode to the White House despite losing the popular vote, made good on his father's promise ("read my lips") not to raise taxes by slashing them even more for the wealthy, even as the country was in the midst of two wars fought largely by the sons and daughters of blue-collar workers.

Even Bill Clinton, the scrappy Arkansan who emerged from a troubled childhood to briefly lure some Reagan Democrats back into the fold with a booming economy and a generational reboot, ended the FDR-era Glass Steagall protections that kept banks from doubling as Wall Street casinos. Wealth inequality soared in the decades between the Reagan and Clinton years, even as household incomes continued to grow.[12]

And then came the Great Recession of 2007, which dropped the bottom out of the U.S. housing market, and the election of Barack Obama one year later.

The Tea Party movement, unleashed on live cable TV among financial traders outraged that the Obama administration might allow underwater homeowners to renegotiate their mortgages, found its billionaire backers in Charles and David Koch, the arch-libertarian heirs to an oil fortune. The Kochs' father, Frederick, was an acolyte of Nobel Prize–winning economist James McGill Buchanan and a founding member of the John Birch Society. Their modern-day Liberty League's goal was to stop the Obama plan from extending healthcare coverage to millions of Americans who couldn't afford it by raising taxes on Americans in the top one percent.[13] Even after the Affordable Care Act (Obamacare) was enacted, Republicans and their donors vowed to tear it out root and branch.

"This wealthy minority is very aggressive and very persistent," says Nancy MacLean, a Duke University–based historian and author, whose book *Democracy in Chains* traces the origins of McGill Buchanan's influence on the modern Republican Party. She considers his philosophy of property and wealth supremacy to be even more extreme than Ayn Rand's gospel of selfishness.

"They're willing to wait decades to get what they want," MacLean says of the modern-day DuPonts, including the Kochs, the Adelsons, Rupert Murdoch, the Mercers, anti-tax purists like Grover Norquist, and other purveyors of dark money in American politics. And "what they want is so radical that most Americans can't even believe it and think that they are safe from it because they think the majority would never vote for it."

In this "radical libertarian vision," MacLean says, government has only three legitimate functions: to provide for the national defense, ensure the rule of law, and guarantee social order. That means that all other functions of the federal government, all social welfare, safety net programs such as Social Security, Medicare, Medicaid, and food assistance, should be abolished, with each American privately meeting their own needs, such that "we should not be able to look to government at all." Of course, implied in this thinking is that the wealthy would pay dramatically less in taxes.

"Extreme is the new normal," says former Republican communications consultant Kurt Bardella, who traces the origins of the Tea Party's assumption of power not to the 2010 sweep, but to the surprise 2014 defeat of then-House majority leader Eric Cantor of Virginia by conservative economics professor David Brat in a primary. Brat's backing by the Tea Party and by right-wing media figures like Ann Coulter and Laura Ingraham was a watershed moment and his victory sent shock waves through the Republican establishment.

"It was the clearest example of the friction between the base and traditional Republican leadership," Bardella says. "Cantor was very conservative. He was one of the top leaders in the party. And he lost to a right-wing lunatic who campaigned exclusively on the immigration issue."

This was a sign of a shift that would ultimately alter the power relationship between the base of the party and its donor class, which for generations had been as content as southern Democrats had once been to nurture and benefit from working-class white voters' racialized views of federal welfare programs; desegregated, secular public schools; and the idea of universal healthcare. But as the Tea Party gained actual power, in Congress and in the states, and with a black family living in the White House as living reminders of the unstoppable tide of demographic change, the pyramid began to flip on its head.

Goaded by right-wing media stars who had nothing to lose and ratings to gain, the GOP base was growing bolder in its demands that the grievances they hashed out on talk radio, in their conservative evangelical churches, on conservative cable news, and in the comments sections of right-wing websites be given more than just lip service by their tax-cutting, deregulating party. Uppermost on their list of priorities were ending "illegal immigration" and beating back the "political correctness," multi-culturalism, and growing secularism that in the view of many on the right were "stealing" America.

Barack Obama's attempts to coax the country toward a deeper reckoning on matters of race and inequitable policing, as the Black Lives Matter movement swept the country in the wake of a series of police shootings of black men, women, and children—many captured on cell phone cameras—was a constant irritant to those disgruntled Americans. His plaintive calls for gun reform stoked seething anger and even paranoia, that this liberal president would begin confiscating guns and even rounding up their owners. But it was Obama's sweeping June 2012 executive order protecting from deportation some 700,000 young people brought to the country illegally as children by their migrant parents that seemed like a declaration of war.

These were the visible reminders of changing neighborhoods and changing times. Most were Latinx, who presumably would lean toward the diverse Democratic Party should they gain the right to vote. The suspicion among many on the right that advocates for liberalized immigration were scheming to create a future cache of Democratic voters didn't all go as far as Ann Coulter, who has placed herself on record as saying the problem is not just illegal immigration but all immigration.[14] But the vehemence and passion around the issue is real. And many on the right believed Obama had essentially legalized them by fiat. The right saw DACA as a form of executive tyranny, if not an act of civil war. When Obama was reelected with a historically large share of Hispanic votes, and Republicans responded by proposing to sign on to "comprehensive immigration reform" that could legalize the status of up to 11 million of the undocumented, the party seemed to have been tipped over the edge.

"Every time the right asserted themselves" on immigration, says Bardella, "it seemed that the posture of everybody else in the party was to hide and to just hope that the venom wasn't directed at them."

Having grabbed legislative power in 2010 and increased that power in 2014, Republican voters didn't understand why their party wasn't fighting harder. Why were they willing to abet the browning of America at the behest of their corporate donors? Why did they look the other way while their steel towns died and "Mexicans took their jobs"? Why was "Obummer"—the "Kenyan, Muslim socialist"—allowed to get back in office?

Donald Trump, who never studied a policy brief or political manual, seemed to intrinsically understand those questions, and he at least was willing to try to get some answers.

Whitney Dow has for years studied white Americans' views on their racial identity. His documentary series, *The Whiteness Project*, has taken him across the country, probing white Americans' views. Reflecting on his time in Cheyenne, Wyoming, conducting interviews, he notes that "Wyoming is one of the whitest, if not the whitest state in the union. And yet the media they consume—when you turn on your TV, you're seeing Verizon ads with interracial couples and gay couples, when you're looking at sitcoms, there's always representational people.

"When you turn on your local news, there's usually a racially diverse cast of people. There's this relentless drumbeat on this change, so it's almost like what they're seeing looks like the future, and it's so fundamentally different from what their actual experience is." The disconnect seemed to strengthen Fox News and other conservative media outlets that could provide a visual and ideological worldview that felt closer to what these Americans felt inside.

"They're afraid of the change," says Dow. "What's always confusing to me is their lived experience doesn't reflect it. When I was in Wyoming, a lot of people talked about immigration, though there aren't a lot of immigrants in the state. They talked about defending themselves and having Second Amendment rights and carrying guns, and it's a very, very safe state. When I was interviewing one police officer, he said, 'you know, 80, 90 percent of the times I'm shot at, it's a libertarian with an automatic weapon.'"

University of Virginia political science professor Gerald Alexander, in a May 12, 2018, column for the *New York Times*, chided liberals for abusing what he described as their "control of the commanding heights of American culture."[15] He argues, "liberals dominate the entertainment industry, many of the most influential news sources and America's universities. This means that people with progressive leanings are everywhere in the public eye—and are also on the college campuses attended by many people's children or grandkids. These platforms come with a lot of power to express values, confer credibility and celebrity, and start national conversations that others really can't ignore. But this makes liberals feel more powerful than they are. Or, more accurately, this kind of power is double-edged. Liberals often don't realize how provocative or inflammatory they can be. In exercising their power, they regularly not only persuade and attract but also annoy and repel."[16]

In July 2018, Brandon Morse, writing on the conservative site RedState, excoriated liberal complaints over a satirical video lampooning then-candidate Alexandria Ocasio-Cortez, who had become a fixation of the American right.

"The left has moved entire industries and brands into attack mode against the right using exactly that kind of humor,"[17] Morse complained, echoing Trump's own apoplectic reaction to NBC's *Saturday Night Live*'s satirical treatment of him. "Comedy Central utilizes 'The Daily Show' and other programs to mock Republicans without cease. HBO's 'This Week Tonight with John Oliver' is a bash-fest of venom against Republicans, and values they often espouse. Samantha Bee, Michelle Wolf,

Steven Colbert, and Jimmy Kimmel are comedians who weap-onize their comedy to mock, slander, and denigrate the right so it looks stupid, racist, and ridiculous. . . . The left has an entire armada of brands and programs specifically dedicated to turning the right into a group to be laughed at, yet whenever the right gets off a good shot the left has to feign that it goes too far. They'll denounce it as bad-natured, and even try to have it removed." [18]

These complaints extended to enraged responses to the multi-cultural recasting of *Star Wars* or proposals to cast a black Briton, Idris Elba, as James Bond, and even calls for boycotts. TV ads calling for men to eschew "toxic masculinity" produced ven-omous responses. The right seemed to feel constantly besieged, and in their view, without the cultural currency to respond, de-spite the fact that actual power—political, economic, corporate, and governmental, from Silicon Valley to the White House—remained almost entirely in white male and often conservative hands. Donald Trump, now holding immense political power but no cultural influence, seemed to heartily agree.

The right was seizing upon anything they could to create a blanket exoneration of Trumpism from charges of racism or hate, and to not just immunize themselves, but to warn the media away from any such insinuations, under penalty of legal action. A teenaged Catholic school student had already filed a $250 mil-lion lawsuit against the *Washington Post*—pointedly the amount Amazon chief Jeff Bezos had paid for the newspaper—alleging he was accused of racism against a Native American activist simply because he is white and was wearing a "Make America Great Again" hat. It was a new front in the media messaging war: demanding that Trumpism and the signature expression of it, the red MAGA hat, receive blanket immunity from charges of racism, or else.

For those on the right, Trump had become their general in a what former House speaker and Georgia political brawler Newt

Gingrich, who tried to take down President Bill Clinton via impeachment, in June 2017 called a "clear-cut cultural civil war."[19]

Even Trump's self-contradictions—a onetime celebrity born into wealth who exhibited the same racial and class resentments as the average Fox News viewer from Ohio or Mississippi or Florida—helped bind him to the Republican base. His 2016 victory locked elected Republicans into a vortex of submission and ostentatious loyalty and fear, lest Trump—the president brought to you by Rush Limbaugh, Ann Coulter, Laura Ingraham, and Fox News—turn the base against them.

Trump, perhaps simply by accident, turned out to be the perfect leader for the post–Tea Party, post-Obama Republican Party. He knew what the base wanted to hear. Yet he was perfectly willing to enact the priorities of the plutocrats, so long as everyone kept the praise coming.

It's hard to imagine another Republican president calling for trade wars with China and Europe, risking the health of the economy, and his party and donors standing quietly by. Trump channeled ethno-populist rage as naturally and charismatically as George Wallace had during the 1960s, while seating a billionaire cabinet as elite (and in some cases as corrupt) as a claque of Russian oligarchs. Trump used the power of the presidency to sell rank-and-file Republicans on a familiar GOP menu of tax cuts for the rich and deregulation of business, while thrilling the Christian right by handing them the power to drag the country back from modernity through the courts.

To the horror of many, including those who could no longer call themselves Republicans, Trump seemed to normalize corruption, cronyism, kleptocracy, and the public display of thuggery and open racism by white Americans who felt empowered to assert themselves as the arbiters of cultural legitimacy in his name. They would decide who was really an American, who belonged in public spaces, and who had any rights they were bound to respect. Donald Trump was indeed waging a new American civil war. And unlike the mere "politicians," he was fighting for real. America was learning what might have been had Governor Wallace won the White House in 1968 after all.

Unlike Wallace, though, Trump benefited from both the increased boldness of his party's base in demanding what seemed like impossible cultural reversals and from the country's—and the media's—regionalized interpretation of America's fraught racial history. In other words: being a New Yorker helped him pull it off.

"I think in some ways Trump is a creation of the big media and the New York media because I think [he] was given a pass that a white southerner never would have gotten," says Steven L. Reed, an African-American probate judge and the highest-ranking elections official in Montgomery, Alabama. "What I got throughout that campaign was, 'yes Trump says this, but we know Trump. He's been on the New York scene, on the national scene and on the world scene for decades. That's not what he really thinks.' If that had been a southern businessman or a southern elected official, I don't think there's any way [he] would have gotten the media path that he got in the Republican primary."

Indeed, the tendency of many Americans to view racism as both stuck in time—ending with the stroke of the pen that signed the Civil Rights Act of 1964 or with Obama's election—and confined mostly to the American South helped shield Trump early on. Members of the traditional media were as reluctant to make direct pronouncements about Trump's racism as they were to call him a liar. Yet Reed says Trump appears, to his southerner's eye, to be no different from Wallace or Bull Connor.

"I certainly think Trump is the bogeyman in the most classic sense," says Reed, comparing Trump to the politicians of the Jessie Helms era, "who ran race-based campaigns that spoke through not just dog whistles, but yells, on issues that appealed to a certain segment in this country that is very hesitant about the progress of people of color; African-Americans and Hispanic

Americans in particular." He says that "by the time the media realized that's who [Trump] truly was, it was too late. He had caught fire with the extreme right, and he had caught fire with those people who have a false angst about the cultural and racial changes in this country."

"MY MOM'S PARENTS WERE CONSERVATIVE REPUBLICANS; MY dad's were liberal Democrats," says writer and anti-racism activist Tim Wise. His parents raised him in Nashville, Tennessee, and sought to inculcate a specific value set in him by sending him to a preschool at predominantly black Tennessee State University. "I was one of only maybe three white kids in a class of twenty-five kids," Wise says. "Most of the women who ran the program were black."

That educational experience would shape Wise in later life, he says. "By socializing me in a nondominant, nonwhite space, once I got into elementary school and I was seeing the way the black kids, who I identified with; who were my friends; who were the kids I'd gone to TSU with—I could see them being treated differently. I could see them being punished more harshly for childhood behavior that I was doing and engaging in as well, or I could see them being tracked into the lower-track classes."

Wise, who went to Tulane University in New Orleans, now writes, teaches, and educates on race. The year Wise graduated, David Duke ran for the Louisiana senate seat, and the next year he ran for governor. Wise became first the youth coordinator, and then the associate director of an organization formed to defeat the former Klansman. He says it was eye-opening to watch Duke, "a politician who was so skilled at manipulating white racial anxiety and resentment, in that one state, around everything from crime, to taxation, to failing schools—effectively scapegoating people of color for those problems."

Wise notes "the effectiveness of racial scapegoating" and points out that "approximately 635,000 white Louisianans,

60 percent of the white population of Louisiana, voted for David Duke in the Senate race, and then 55 percent did that in the governor's race. For me, it was a very eye-opening thing on two levels. Number one, because I knew that 60 percent of my people were not Nazis, it intrigued me that six in ten of my people were willing to vote for someone who they knew full well was, because everybody in Louisiana knew that David Duke was a white supremacist. No one could claim innocence or ignorance; there were children in utero that knew the man was a Nazi, for God's sake. It was obvious. Everybody knew it.

"So, what white people were saying in effect was, 'Well, I know he's a Nazi, but I think I'm going to vote for him anyway.' When you're willing to do that—which is one of the reasons that Trump winning didn't shock me—I knew this was possible if you had the right package and the right rhetoric, and the right narrative, and in Trump's case of course, he didn't have the baggage that David Duke had. But even with the baggage David Duke had, six in ten white folks were like, 'Yeah, I think I'll do that.'"

Wise also took inventory after those campaigns and asked what he'd learned. After noting that six in ten white people who are not Nazis still voted for one, he asked, "Whose job is it to help save white people? It's clearly not black folks' job, and yet in that campaign, the only people that saved us were black people. It was black folks who went to the polls and stopped David Duke. Because, if it had been up to us, he would have been the United States senator from Louisiana, or he would have been the governor of Louisiana. So, at that moment, I'm like, 'wait a minute, it's not black folks' job to rush in and save us from our own bullshit. That's our job. So, we as white folks have to actually struggle with our people. If we really believe we're not all Nazis, we have to be willing to struggle with our people to bring them to a different level of consciousness and awareness.'"

Indeed, despite losing the governor's race by 61 to 39 percent,

Duke, running as a Republican, got 75,000 more votes than he did in his run for United States Senate a year earlier. A November 18, 1991, *Baltimore Sun* story declared that "the 680,000 Duke votes were also the most chilling measure yet of the discontent raging among working-class whites," and it quoted Duke: "Perhaps the messenger was rejected in this state of Louisiana, but the message wasn't. The people believe in what I believe. The polls all show that." [20]

Duke was threatening to support a Pat Buchanan run in the Louisiana Republican presidential primary the following February, against President George H. W. Bush's appeal for a second term. Perhaps protectively, Vice President Dan Quayle lauded Duke's "thorough" defeat, but during an ABC News interview was sure to add that "Mr. Duke's agenda of anti-big government, get-out-of-my-pocketbook, cut my taxes, put welfare people back to work [is] a very popular message." [21]

The *Sun* article also quoted Louisiana senator John Breaux, who at the time led the Democratic Leadership Council, which had a primary goal of reclaiming working-class white voters, as warning "that Duke-like candidates would emerge 'in every other state unless politicians and elected officials offer programs to respond to the concerns that he's raising.' " [22] Breaux said Duke had "raised some important questions," and went on to posit that "middle-class Americans," presumably white Americans, "think government doesn't serve their needs. They're concerned about government programs that spend more than we can afford, and they want somebody to address it." [23]

Wise sees a bridge between actual extremists and the ordinary white Louisianans who pulled the lever for the former Klan grand wizard. "Sometimes [Duke voters] would just say blatantly racist things," Wise noted. "But a lot of times they would couch it in, 'I'm tired of paying all these taxes for people that don't want to work.' And then they would say, 'but I'm not racist, I'm just talking about people who get government assistance, and I realize there are a lot of white folks that get that too.' But you knew that, that was the image in their mind . . . They would talk about, 'we need someone to stand up for us.' Sometimes they would just say straight up, white people. . . . It's all the same kind of grievance politics that Trump preys upon. It's the grievance politics that Lee Atwater acknowledged in 1981, that the Republicans and the conservatives had been manipulating all since the 1960s."

Wise points out that Duke is actually a national socialist (or Nazi), whose real focus is Jews. His position is that "blacks are the bullets that Jews used to destroy the white race." But Louisiana had only 14,000 Jews, and Duke's consultants told him that Louisiana residents wouldn't see that as a big enough problem and to shift to blacks. Duke quickly "learned how to do that."

Wise describes talking to these white folks and having them say they weren't in the least bit racist. But "if you talked to them for two minutes," he recalled, "it didn't take long before they either brought up some experience or they talked about crime, [or] the job they didn't get because of affirmative action, rather than the fact that the oil industry had collapsed, and that obviously had nothing to do with black people. Or, they would talk about their high taxes for welfare, even though at that time, the AFDC program in Louisiana was paying about $138 a month for a family of three. So clearly, that wasn't what was bankrupting anybody in Louisiana, but Duke was very skilled at manipulating it, and like a lot of other politicians, got people to believe it."

The history of merging racial appeals to voters' genuine fears is long. Brutal campaign tactics, from the Willie Horton ads against Michael Dukakis in 1988 to the crusade to disprove Barack Obama's American birthplace, were a toxic vein running through American politics that has shown no signs of slowing down. And many voters who are susceptible to these tactics are as certain of their distance from anything even close to racism as Trump has declared himself to be.

One woman in Cheyenne whom Whitney Dow interviewed for his "Whiteness Project" lived with her husband on a modest ranch where they raised chickens. Dow says he tried to discern why she was such a fervent Trump supporter. "I asked her— you're a thoughtful, nice, hardworking person," Dow says. "You make your living off the land here. It's tough here. What attracts you to this guy who lives in a golden penthouse on Fifth Avenue in New York City? She said, 'you know, he's had a lot of failures like I have.' I think everybody feels like they're on the outside, and Trump is an outsider as well." Indeed, says Dow, "I think some of the same things that powered Obama to the presidency are what powered Trump. It's this yearning for something fundamentally different that could change things.

"We, on the left, really believed that Obama could change things," says Dow. "I was stunned when he got up there and didn't tear into the system and remake it. I think that's the same motivation that people have with Trump. And in some ways, he is remaking it," in ways that many Americans view as tragic, ugly, and even dangerous.

THE CHARLOTTESVILLE RIOTS OF AUGUST 2017 WERE PERHAPS the first physical manifestation of the Trump-era cultural civil war. They began as a protest by hundreds of torch-bearing, mostly young, white men gathered on the campus of the University of Virginia to protest the planned removal of a statue of Confederate general Robert E. Lee.

The groups leading the march, under the banner "Unite the Right," drew from a grab bag of white supremacist leaders, including lead organizer and neo-Nazi Jason Kessler, a 2009 graduate of the university who briefly wrote for the *Daily Caller*, a Washington-based conservative news and opinion website cofounded by Tucker Carlson. Other organizers included Richard Spencer and a twenty-something Internet troll named Elliott Kline.²⁴ Duke was scheduled to speak.

Late in the evening on the night before the march, I was asked by Bishop William Barber, the former head of the North Carolina NAACP, who was leading a revival of Dr. King's Poor People's Campaign, to take a call from Rev. Traci Blackmon. Blackmon was the senior pastor at Christ the King United Church of Christ in Florissant, Missouri, and an executive minister in the United Church of Christ. She had been on the streets of Ferguson, Missouri, during the Black Lives Matter protests over the killing of a young black man, Michael Brown, by a police officer, so she knew what it felt like to be in the middle of a racial conflagration and had also been part of an Obama administration task force on racial and police justice.

When she called, she was trapped with other clergy inside a church on the University of Virginia grounds, where they had gathered to pray for peace during the march and counterprotest planned for the next day, a Saturday. Outside were the torches and the guttural chants of hundreds of young men who were converging on the gathering on foot. On the phone, as she recounted what happened, her voice was trembling.

"You will not replace us!" and "White lives matter!" they shouted, as the Reverend Blackmon and her fellow ministers and laypeople saw the lights flicker through the windows. The local police helped them hustle out of the church's rear doors to the safety of their cars. Blackmon said nerves she felt in the pit of her stomach were the same ones she had had as a young girl in the 1960s when the Klan marched through her Birmingham, Alabama, hometown.

The next day, Saturday, August 12, Reverend Blackmon was live on the air with me when an officer grabbed her, bodily, and pulled her out of frame as she screamed. Another crowd, a wave of "Unite the Right" marchers in helmets and body armor, was clashing with "antifascist" protesters and things were getting violent. Neo-Nazis with brass knuckles began beating pastors wearing their clerical collars. The scene that unfolded live on television was pure mayhem. Racist rioters punched, kicked, and even shot at antiracist protesters, scattering black and white counter-demonstrators into the street.

Two hours after law enforcement deemed the gathering an unlawful assembly and Virginia governor Terry McAuliffe declared a state of emergency, an avowed neo-Nazi named James Alex Fields drove his vehicle into a crowd of antiracist protesters, mowing down thirty-two-year-old Heather Heyer, killing her and injuring nineteen others. A Virginia jury eventually convicted Fields of ten charges including first-degree murder and sentenced him to life in prison plus 419 years. Some thirty-four people were injured in Charlottesville, in clashes in and near the park and during the car-plowing incident. In addition to Heyer, two state patrolmen pilots died when their helicopter crashed as they monitored the turmoil on the ground.

Across the country, an increasing intolerance for the emblems of the Confederacy culminating in the removal of the Confederate flag from the South Carolina statehouse in 2015—as well as calls to remove the names and likenesses of Confederate generals from college buildings, parks, schools, and municipal grounds—tripped a wire on the far right, leading them to defend the racist "heritage" of the antebellum South and the breakaway states that fought a civil war against the United States to protect their system of human slavery.

It was the photo negative of the Black Lives Matter movement, which had used street protest as a primal scream against the police killings of unarmed black men and women, and even children. The police had sometimes responded violently to those marches, as they did in Ferguson in 2014, or when their actions led to all-out riots in Baltimore a year later. But Charlottesville gave American history something new to contemplate: an American president taking up the mantle once reserved for revanchist southern politicians like George Wallace and Bull Connor.

At 12:19 p.m., nearly an hour before Heyer was mowed down, Trump or his aides sent out the standard tweets, calling for "national unity." But later that afternoon, Trump walked out to cameras at his Bedminster, New Jersey, golf club for a scheduled press conference on the signing of a Veterans Affairs bill, and what he said was unrestrained, clearly off script, and for many, unthinkable. "We condemn in the strongest possible terms this egregious display of hatred, bigotry, and violence, on many sides," Trump said, repeating "on many sides," a second time, seemingly for emphasis. "It's been going on for a long time in our country. Not Donald Trump, not Barack Obama. This has been going on for a long, long time."

Even Republicans seemed stunned, with Florida's Marco Rubio and Colorado freshman Cory Cardner firing off tweets calling the events in Charlottesville domestic terrorism by white supremacists. Condemnation of Trump's remarks rippled through the media, with Democrats expressing their revulsion at the president for drawing a false equivalency between neo-Nazis and their antagonists.

On Sunday, the White House issued a statement attempting to clean up Trump's remarks, saying the president "condemns all forms of violence, bigotry and hatred, and of course that includes white supremacists, KKK, neo-Nazi, and all extremist groups," and ending with another call for "national unity." But on Tuesday, Trump took questions again and defended his early statements. He falsely claimed that Heyer's mother had thanked him for his remarks. Reporters peppered him with questions about Steve Bannon, whose alt-right ties never seemed more relevant.

"Look, look, I like Mr. Bannon," an increasingly testy Trump said. "He is a friend of mine. Mr. Bannon came on very late. You know that. I went through seventeen senators, governors and I won all the primaries. Mr. Bannon came on very much later than that. And I like him. He is a good man. He is not a racist. I can tell you that. He is a good person. He actually gets a very unfair press in that regard. We'll see what happens with Mr. Bannon. He is a good person and I think the press treats him frankly very unfairly."

Trump also railed at Arizona senator John McCain, who had called on Trump to condemn the alt-right groups who rioted in Charlottesville. "Senator McCain?" Trump sneered. "You mean the one that voted against Obamacare? You mean Senator McCain who voted against us getting good health care?"

When a reporter pressed the president on the alt-right, Trump all but spat out, "When you say the alt-right. Define 'alt-right' to me. You define it. Go ahead. No, define it for me. Come on. Let's go. What about the alt-left that came charging at—Excuse me—What about the alt-left that came charging at the, as you say, the alt-right?"[25]

Trump was visibly angry. He interrupted reporters and challenged their premise that the white nationalist right was solely to blame for the deadly events that had occurred live, before the eyes of the world.[26]

"Do they have any semblance of guilt?" Trump demanded. "Let me ask you this: What about the fact that they came charging, that they came charging with clubs in their hands swinging clubs? Do they have any problem? I think they do. So, you know, as far as I'm concerned, that was a horrible, horrible day. . . . Wait a minute. I'm not finished. I'm not finished, fake news. That was a horrible day."

Trump wasn't finished. "I will tell you something, I watched those very closely, much more closely than you people watched it. And you had a group on one side that was bad and you had a group on the other side that was also very violent. And nobody wants to say that. But I'll say it right now. . . . You had a group on the other side that came charging in without a permit, and they were very, very violent."

A reporter asked if Trump believed the alt-left and the neo-Nazis are the same.

"All of those people—excuse me—I've condemned neo-Nazis," Trump said. "I've condemned many different groups. But not all of those people were neo-Nazis, believe me. Not all of those people were white supremacists by any stretch. Those people were also there because they wanted to protest the taking down of a statue, Robert E. Lee. So—excuse me—and you take a look at some of the groups, and you see and you would know it if you were honest reporters, which in many cases, you are not. But, many of those people were there to protest the taking down of the statue of Robert E. Lee. So this week, it is Robert E. Lee. I noticed that Stonewall Jackson is coming down. I wonder, is it George Washington next week? And is it Thomas Jefferson the week after? You know, you really do have to ask yourself, where does it stop?"

Reporters continued to press, and the president refused to concede, and the whole exchange seemed to reveal the insides of Trump's mind on a crucial aspect of American history. And he appeared to come down squarely on the side of the rebellious South.

When asked if he really believed there was "blame on both sides" in Charlottesville, he replied, "I think there is blame on both sides. And I have no doubt about it. And you don't have doubt about it either. And if you reported it accurately, you would say."

Trump was again reminded that the neo-Nazis had started the violence in Charlottesville, and that it had unfolded during their march.

"Excuse me," he interrupted again. "They didn't put themselves down as neo-Nazis. And you had some very bad people in that group. But you also had people that were very fine people on both sides. You had people in that group—excuse me, excuse me—I saw the same pictures as you did. You had people in that group that were there to protest the taking down of, to them, a very, very important statue and the renaming of a park from Robert E. Lee to another name."

Trump was digging in. "George Washington as a slave owner," he said. "Was George Washington a slave owner? So, will George Washington now lose his statue? Are we going to take down—excuse me—are we going to take down statues to George Washington? How about Thomas Jefferson? What do you think of Thomas Jefferson? You like him. Good. Are we going to take down the statue? 'Cause he was a major slave owner. Are we going to take down his statue? So you know what? It's fine. You are changing history, you're changing culture. You had people, and I'm not talking about the neo-Nazis and the white nationalists, because they should be condemned totally. You had many people in that group other than neo-Nazis and white nationalists. Okay? And the press has treated them absolutely unfairly. Now, in the other group also, you had some fine people, but you also had troublemakers, and you see them come with the black outfits and with the helmets and with the baseball bats. You had a lot of bad people in the other group too."

To distance themselves from a president whose toxicity was reaching maximum levels, members of Trump's manufacturing advisory council began stepping down. The first to go was Merck CEO Ken Frazier, the only African-American member, who said he was leaving "to take a stand against intolerance and extremism." Next came the CEOs of Under Armour and Intel, followed by the heads of the Alliance for American Manufacturing, the AFL-CIO, and the Campbell Soup Company.[27] Even the CEO of Walmart criticized Trump by saying he had missed an opportunity to bring the country together, though he didn't exit the council,[28] which soon disbanded.

Members of Trump's own cabinet were appalled. Some, according to books that exposed the administration's dysfunction, felt pressured by their families, friends, and consciences to resign. But none did. Not one.

The country's white nationalist groups, on the other hand, were elated.

David Duke tweeted: "Thank you President Trump for your honesty & courage to tell the truth about Charlottesville & condemn the leftist terrorists." A headline on Breitbart.com blared: "POTUS comes roaring back with press smack-down at Trump Tower." Richard Spencer also tweeted and called Trump's take on events "fair and down to earth," claiming that "#Charlottesville could have been peaceful, if police did its job [*sic*]."

Beirich believes that Trump's contention about good people being "on both sides" was "a very calculated Bannon-esque moment, because Trump knows he's appealing to these people, they know he's talking directly to them." But it's not just words, she said. "He has reposted white supremacist propaganda over and over again on that Twitter feed. He posted this idea that black people are rampaging through the streets killing white people, the same idea—'black on white crime'—that motivated Dylann Roof. He posted that South African white farmers are under assault. That's a lie. That's a white supremacist lie," she said.

"He's had hate group leaders in the White House, meeting with White House staff, and he's hired people from hate groups to run key positions in DHS, immigration, and so on," Beirich says. "The links are not distant. They're pretty clear."

In August 2018, Ian M. Smith, a Trump-appointed immigration and refugee policy analyst at the Department of Homeland Security, resigned after being confronted about his ties to white nationalist groups, including emails from 2015 in which he responded to a dinner invitation from a host who vowed the gathering would be *judenfrei*, a German word Nazis used during the Holocaust to describe areas that had been "cleansed" of Jews.

There were other troubling signs. For the Trump administration's first Holocaust Remembrance Day in February 2017, they omitted any mention of Jews in their pronouncements and instead chose the Russian formulation of honoring "the victims, survivors, and heroes of the Holocaust," drawing condemnation from groups like the Anti-Defamation League. When asked to explain, the White House's Hope Hicks provided CNN with a link to an online story about the other groups the Nazis killed, suggesting the explanation was that other people were killed, too.[29] The White House corrected the omission in 2018—yet that October, Trump drew outrage for his jokes about a "bad hair day" at a political rally following the slaughter of eleven people at Pittsburgh's Tree of Life Synagogue.

And Stephen Miller, publicly denounced[30] by his own uncle as an immigration hypocrite for his radical immigration views, was subjected to the ultimate insult by an unnamed adviser to the White House; as the images of caged children separated from their weeping moms struggling to reunite with toddlers who no longer seemed to know them spread across the airwaves, the adviser told *Vanity Fair* reporter Gabriel Sherman, "Stephen actually enjoys seeing those pictures at the border. He's a twisted guy, the way he was raised and picked on. . . . He's Waffen-SS."[31]

Meanwhile, Miller's boss, Donald Trump, with his own history of housing discrimination and racist provocations, was now being blamed for emboldening violence, anti-Semitism, and racism. With each violent incident, at a mosque or a synagogue, or on the streets of cities around the country, people shifted their gaze to the White House, and the man who stubbornly refused to take a vocal stand against white supremacy. Trump's refusals begged the question why, as did his party's reticence to condemn him for not doing so.

In March 2019, Trump's "acting" chief of staff, Mick Mulvaney, declared, unprompted, on Fox News that Trump was "not a white supremacist." The question he had been asked, by the network's Chris Wallace, was why the president wouldn't give a national address condemning white nationalist violence in the wake of a deadly, white supremacist terrorist attack on two mosques in New Zealand. That question—of why Trump could not bring himself to issue an outright condemnation of white nationalism, when he spent so much time attacking everything from late night comedy to Democratic politicians—went unanswered.

Outright racial populists and white Christian nationalists are not only a minority of the country but also of the white population. But they make up enough of the electorate to matter to Republicans, as they once did to Democrats. And having failed, from George Wallace to Pat Buchanan, in electing one of their own to the White House, they finally succeeded with Trump, whose celebrity (and help from a foreign power) helped him claim the highest office in the land.

Those who view themselves as being at war with an increasingly alien, multicultural, multilingual, secular, and feminist society saw Trump as their ideal warrior—including against the "political correctness" they believed had all but silenced them in the public square, at the workplace water cooler, and on social media. Even when Trump was accused more than twenty times of sexual harassment or misconduct[32] and pilloried for bragging about being free, as a celebrity, to "grab [women]" by their genitalia, he refused to back down or bow to modern feminist norms. He defied anyone whose sensitivities sought to strip football and baseball teams of their Native American monikers and mascots, even mocking Senator Elizabeth Warren with the "Pocahontas" slur in the presence of Navajo Code Talkers being honored at the White House as he made them stand beneath a portrait of Andrew Jackson.

He stood up for the traditional veneration of the National Anthem, savaging black NFL players as "sons of bitches" for kneeling in protest against police brutality during its rendition. And he spoke the inner truths felt by many grandsons and granddaughters of European immigrants, who believed that the Central American migrants, refugees, and asylum seekers sprinkling or pouring into their communities were the enemy. These pronouncements may have made him an anathema to most Americans, even an embarrassment, but they placed Trump in the pantheon of American perspectives that are both unavoidable and real.

"Anybody who really thinks that Donald Trump is unprecedented or not normal, isn't paying attention to four hundred years" of history, says Tim Wise. "The oldest play in the American playbook, going back to the colonies, is the play of rich white men telling 'not rich' white people that their enemies are black and brown." Wise says that playbook led to the once-scorned indentured European servant suddenly being inducted into the American family of "whiteness."

When these indentured servants reached the colonies, Wise says, rich Virginia landowners worried they would "figure out they have more in common with African enslaved folks," so the colonists created laws and customs that did away with indentured servitude and "put the poor white people on the slave patrol," and made them believe they had authority. "You convince them that, if they just work really hard, one day maybe they can own a slave, and maybe they can own property," creating the notion of "every man a king." Wise says this quickly morphed to "'if these people get free, they're going to take your job.' It worked, and during the Civil War hundreds of thousands of poor white folks in the South went and fought for other people's property interests."

This notion of binding working-class white Americans to their wealthy racial peers stretched into the early twentieth century, when factory owners and coal mine operators feared that racial integration would make the labor movement bigger and stronger, and that black, white, and brown working-class Americans would come together to demand higher wages and better benefits, and to pay for it they would raise taxes on the wealthy. Racism was a convenient wedge between white and nonwhite workers that served the interests of the rich, from the robber barons to those who bankrolled the Tea Party.

W.E.B. Dubois called this "the wages of whiteness," by which late nineteenth- and early-twentieth-century wealthy industrialists didn't compensate white laborers in wages but nevertheless provided them with intangible benefits tied to their skin color.

"They were given public deference and titles of courtesy because they were white," DuBois wrote in *Black Reconstruction in America,* published in 1935. "They were admitted freely with all classes of white people to public functions, public parks, and the best schools. The police were drawn from their ranks, and the courts, dependent on their votes, treated them with such leniency as to encourage lawlessness. Their vote selected public officials, and while this had small effect upon the economic situation, it had great effect upon their personal treatment and the deference shown them. White schoolhouses were the best in the community, and conspicuously placed, and they cost anywhere from twice to ten times as much per capita as the colored schools. The newspapers specialized on news that flattered the poor whites and almost utterly ignored the Negro except in crime and ridicule." [33]

As a result, DuBois wrote of white and black workers that "there probably are not today in the world two groups . . . with practically identical interests who hate and fear each other so deeply and persistently and who are kept so far apart that neither sees anything of common interest." [34]

Wise calls this "fear of the other" a "deeply encoded human tribal trait that we haven't evolved through yet, and that we haven't confronted adequately yet," that also plays to the notions of meritocracy and rugged individualism that are fundamental components of the American myth. "It's what allows that rich person to look at that poor white person and say, 'no really, if you just work hard, one day it'll be within your reach,'" he says.

The election of Barack Obama created what Wise calls "a perfect storm of white anxiety." Obama "confronted white people with an image of the leader of the country that's obviously very different than that which we're used to, not only visually, but even his name, his story, his narrative." This also came at a time when white people were facing being confronted "with a level of economic insecurity that we were not used to for three generations" and during a "quarter-century shift in popular culture that saw black and brown faces proliferating across popular culture, from music, to television to sports.

"You could be in a cornfield in Nebraska," says Wise, and suddenly, "white, black, and brown peoples' soundtracks of their lives, the music they have on their iPod, the stuff they listen to, the television shows they watch, the movies they watch, are a mélange of cultures. You've got country music artists who are making records with hip-hop artists. So, there's been a pretty significant shift, in terms of pop culture icons in the course of that twenty-five, thirty years. So now, if you're already insecure as a white person who's maybe middle aged, and you've got the black guy running the show, and you've got the economy melting down, and the posters on your kids' walls are from all over the world. Some of the signs in your community are in Spanish now. And you're starting to realize that maybe the notion of what an American is, is no longer specific to you. You're having to share space, you're having to share a concept, with people that you didn't have to share it with before."

Wise agrees with Heidi Beirich that the creeping knowledge of the coming shift into the minority is further stoking white cultural anxiety.

"As we continue to talk about, and people become aware of, because they're either living it or hearing about it, the fact that by

2043, half the country will be people of color, there is a degree of perceived displacement," he says. And even though it's not displacement that has altered the economic and political advantages white Americans continue to enjoy, Wise says the prospect "strikes some of them as [akin to] genocide."

For those gripped by that distress, the Tea Party's calls of "we want our country back" or Trump's declarations to "Make America great again" offer powerful nostalgia.

But what can be done about it?

Wise proposes "brutal honesty" about the causes of white anxiety, combined with a message that affirms the capacity for change. "Economic anxiety is a very real phenomenon in a global economy where the top one-tenth of one percent has so much of the wealth," he says. But "the research tells us that white economic anxiety is filtered through the lens of racial anxiety and cultural anxiety," so it's wrong to think that "if you just take care of economic anxiety, racial prejudice will diminish."

Wise says the reverse is true. "White people are feeling economically anxious, because they fundamentally believe that immigrants are going to take their job, which is a racialized stress. Or they believe their kid is not going to get into the right college, because some black kid is going to take their spot. So, I think we have to be brutally honest about that, and acknowledge the way that race drives these divisions. . . . The mistake that the left has made, broadly speaking, from the Democratic Party to actual leftists, is that we tend to start with the economy, and think that if we dance around race, and talk about everything but race, we can appeal to people's 'real interests,' and they'll do the right thing."

Wise believes that racism must be confronted head-on. He says that if Hillary Clinton had not called Trump's supporters "deplorables" and instead had said, "Donald Trump thinks his voters are so racist that they will fall for this phony scapegoating of black people and Mexican immigrants, but I know the people in this country are too smart to fall for that," she might have found a way into a conversation with white voters who were not yet deeply entrenched against her.

He suggests Democrats adopt a message to voters lured away from the party by Trump that goes something like this: " 'This guy thinks you're racist. I'm not saying you're racist, these people think you're racist. For four hundred years, these rich folks who don't care about you have believed that they could just push these buttons, and you would do this dance for them. I'm suggesting to you, that even if we all have some racial biases, we're better than that. We can be better than that. Let's show them that we're better than that.' "

Wise has found in his decades researching bias, including for his book *White Like Me: Reflections on Race from a Privileged Son*, that when most people are confronted with their subconscious biases, and are "encouraged to respond to the better angels of their nature, they will do it. It's when you don't let them believe that they have better angels; if you make it seem like, 'you're just a horrible, irredeemable human being,' they will show you just how horrible and irredeemable they are.

"The research tells us . . . that most white folks don't want to think of themselves as racist, and don't want to be racist," Wise says. It's a matter of convincing them that there's another way to allay their fears.

Whitney Dow sees the key to overcoming racism among the willing as finding a "righteous narrative" to replace the "wholesome, all-white" America of their nostalgic vision. He says people naturally recoil from the notion that the America they "want back" was fundamentally corrupt, in that it excluded and even injured nonwhite people. "I benefited from generations of white people building a country that's for someone like me," he says. "How do I navigate that?" But since the myth so many grew up on is just that—a myth—Americans must find a way to write a new and more complex story that speaks to both the villainy and the redemption that comprise the United States.

Dow and Wise agree on something else: that solving racial divisions in this country and drawing out the better angels of our nature cannot be the job of nonwhite Americans alone. White America and the institutions that wield political and economic power have to engage. The challenge today is doing so against the determined opposition of the person with the ultimate bully pulpit: the president of the United States.

CHAPTER 5

The Man Who Sold the World

"Being president doesn't change who you are—it reveals who you are."

—Michelle Obama

"AMERICA IS AN IDEA." THIS PHRASE IS BANDIED ABOUT SO often that it's hard to attribute it to any one person. Behind its meaning is an assertion of "American exceptionalism"—of the young nation's ability to persuade the world to move toward democratic ideals, based not just on the strength of our armed forces but on the moral force of our founding creed: that all men are created equal.

The idea that America is a unique democratic experiment that the rest of the world should view "as a city upon a hill" dates back to seventeenth-century Puritan John Winthrop, the first governor of the Massachusetts Bay Colony. Winthrop included the phrase as part of a 1630 speech entitled, "A Model of Christian Charity." He wanted the European settlements in New England to be watched and modeled by the world.

This preferred myth—that America is what Thomas Paine

called an "asylum for mankind"—frequently overshadows the bitter ironies embedded in our founding ideals, causing our true and complete history to be consigned to the margin of this Great American story. Winthrop trafficked in human cargo, meticulously noting in his famous journals the trade in Native American slaves [1]—for example, the "little Squa" [2] (*sic*) requested of slavers by respectable settlers who planned to work them near the areas where Logan Airport stands today, or to ship them off to the Caribbean to be traded for "cotton, tobacco and Negroes." [3] Winthrop was the first to write laws codifying the enslavement and breeding of African men, women, and children.

A sanitized version of our history becomes a chorus of the American songbook and is used to build good citizens while leaving out the more problematic verses. (How many of us know the third stanza of "The Star-Spangled Banner"—designated in 1931 as our National Anthem—which condemns runaway slaves who sought their freedom by fighting for the British in the War of 1812?) A belief in the nation's gilded origin story has helped immigrants transcend their unique cultural origins and immerse themselves in "Americanness."

On their way to being good and patriotic citizens, schoolchildren learn a postcard version of the American story, often with little mention of the continent's indigenous people, who were cut down by the colonizers' twin weapons: guns and germs (diseases like smallpox and measles devastated native populations as much as violence and war).

The native tribes who survived genocide were shunted off to reservations, many forced to march hundreds of miles to be resettled in unfamiliar lands. Those truths are too often ignored, buried, or even mocked, while the nation's first people have been reduced to mascots for our favorite sports teams, or totems to spruce up a TV or movie script or a European family tree.

We know little about the Chinese laborers who built the nation's railroads only to be barred as unwanted migrants in the early twentieth century, the Japanese Americans interned as enemy aliens during World War II, or the conquered people of Mexico or Puerto Rico who were conscripted into the country by force and annexation, and whose descendants are now treated as invaders. Yet each group holds on as strongly to American ideals as the European descendants who lay claim to über-Americanness.

African-Americans acutely know the contradictions of the American myth, having inherited the American story from the millions of black souls dragged as slaves through a Hell on Earth, bought, sold, and bred like cattle in the "land of the free" and then subjected to more than a century of discrimination, lynching, and police brutality. When black abolitionists like Frederick Douglass, anti-segregationists like Homer Plessy, and human rights advocates like Ida B. Wells argued for freedom and equality, they did so on the basis of the constitution that was written to exclude their humanity. African descendants fought in each of America's wars, including its war of independence. Every age of American invention was contributed to by black hands. Black Americans emerged from bondage and Civil War and fully bought in to the idea of American democracy, demanding the vote and running for office almost as soon as the Civil War was won.

The first black United States senators came from Mississippi during Reconstruction. First, Hiram Revels, a free man and second-generation minister, was among 30 black state lawmakers elected out of 140 before being named by the state senate to fill one of the U.S. Senate seats vacated by onetime Democratic governor Albert Gallatin Brown and self-styled Confederate "president" Jefferson Davis upon secession. He was followed in 1874 by Blanche K. Bruce, a former slave.[4] Upon Revels's accession to the Senate, Republican Massachusetts senator Charles Sumner exclaimed: "All men are created equal, says the great Declaration. And now a great act attests this verity. Today we make the Declaration a reality."[5]

The quest to truly make real the ideals of those founding documents fueled the antilynching movement and the civil rights movement and the quest for women's suffrage, and eventually helped elect a black president and a Congress as diverse as America. Even with its deep flaws and contradictions, "the American idea" has power.

The United States has long viewed itself as a land of superheroes, of brave men pioneering the western frontier, captains of industry and inventors of the future, from the electric lightbulb to the mass-produced motorized car, to the miracle of airplane flight and rockets to the moon. Mandrake the Magician, the first documented costumed crime fighter, debuted as President Franklin D. Roosevelt was beginning to steer us out of the Great Depression.[6] Four years later, in 1938, Superman was introduced as an alien from another planet who had been raised as an idealized American.

The Marvel and D.C. Comics superheroes invented in the 1940s and '50s still dominate the box office today. These uniquely American versions of ancient myths from much older cultures have been our way of saying we are a special kind of people. During the last century's two world wars, America sent its sons to Europe to save those ages-old civilizations from tyranny, furthering the idea that this continent-spanning nation, just two and a half centuries old, is a country set apart.

America's decisive role in defeating Nazism and the Axis powers, as well as our first-to-the-finish-line development (and deadly use) of nuclear weapons, placed in this country's hands the effective stewardship of the Western global order. While Europe was in tatters, we were the counterweight to Joseph Stalin's U.S.S.R., and the Cold War divided the world into spheres of American and Soviet influence. The comic book hero-villain narrative of the twentieth century became "mighty capitalism versus dastardly communism." American presidents wielded the powerful notion of a free and democratic United States to justify military interventions—some wise, some not, and some scandalous, including the toppling of uncooperative governments from the Middle East to Latin America.

The idea that something unique about America had allowed us to resist fascism also gave weight to our attempts to spread democracy around the world. This message of American exceptionalism was used effectively by presidents from John F. Kennedy, when he faced down the Cuban Missile Crisis, to Ronald Reagan, when he declared, "Mr. Gorbachev, tear down this wall." Bill Clinton called on these themes in joining NATO's intercession in the Balkans and calling for peace in Northern Ireland. George H. W. Bush arguably misused it to intervene militarily to expel Iraq from oil-rich Kuwait, as did his son in invading Iraq after the September 11, 2001, terror attacks, which his administration misled the American people into believing had occurred with the help of Saddam Hussein. Barack Obama called on the notion of America's unique progression toward heroism and grace when he went to Cairo in 2009 and proposed a new relationship between the Muslim world and the West, hoping to draw down the suspicions, exacerbated by the Iraq War, that America's true gospel was the theft of Middle East oil.

For better or worse, the American myth has been a principal tool used by American presidents. We have used it to present ourselves to the world.

And then along came Donald J. Trump.

Trump never seemed to believe the words in the American songbook. From the time he entered the public consciousness during the 1980s, he has declared himself superior to every American president, including Reagan, the Grand Old Party's secular saint.[7] In Trump's own mythmaking, he is bigger than the America idea. In his mind, the United States has long been a running disaster, a "joke" run by men who let our country be laughed at and treated like suckers by foreign, *alien* countries like Japan and China.

In Trump's telling, America is the constantly bullied and be-littled Steve Rogers, the pipsqueak World War II soldier who agrees to be given an experimental strength serum, and Trump alone is the resulting Captain America. Given the chance, *he* could better negotiate nuclear disarmament with the then Soviet Union—just as he could outdo the legendary Merv Griffin at developing casinos in Atlantic City (he couldn't), or build a better pro football league than the NFL (he bought the fledg-ling USFL's New Jersey Generals franchise in 1983 but his idea of suing the NFL for antitrust backfired, and helped drive the league to ruin).[8]

Trump has long benefited from a particular kind of shame-lessness. He "worked" the New York tabloids, sometimes pre-tending to be his own publicist by calling reporters with the pseudonym "John Barron." He hung a framed *Time* cover in his golf clubs with his face on the cover, his name in bold letters and the subhead: "The Apprentice is a television smash!" The *Washington Post*'s David Fahrenthold reported in 2017 that the magazine cover is fake.[9] It's also not entirely clear if Trump truly is a billionaire as he claims, or if he has simply gamed the docu-mentation of his wealth and income over the years so he could say he is one.

Trump was an aggressive licensor, and as his fame grew, he slapped his surname on neckties, water, and even a short-lived board game (the catchphrase on the Parker Brothers/Hasbro cover was, "I'm back and you're fired!"). He took over the East-ern Airlines Shuttle, but the Trump Shuttle was a failure. And he strung Trump-themed golf clubs and hotels around the world. Trump believed he could make a better deal than anyone for absolutely anything. All it took was his "superior genes" and business know-now.

The Trump myth was never true. He was never the up-by-his-bootstraps business success he claimed, having inherited the equivalent of $413 million from his father,[10] Fred Trump, then the most prolific real estate developer in Queens, New York, largely through a series of tax dodges and schemes.

The elder Trump was a hard man who was arrested at a Klan riot in Queens in 1927[11] and who, with Donald and their family business, originally started by Fred Trump with his mother (his father, German immigrant Friedrich, died when Fred Trump was twelve years old), was cited by the Nixon administration's Housing Department for their refusal to rent to black tenants.

Tony Schwartz was writing for *New York* magazine about Donald Trump's redevelopment project at 100 Central Park South in the early 1980s when they first met. Trump wanted to empty the building of the tenants who were paying modest rents under New York's rent control laws, making way for him to redevelop the valuable property into luxury condominiums.

According to Schwartz, Trump hired Urban Relocation, Inc., which was notorious for harassing and forcing tenants to relocate.[12] Their tactics, he says, included "breaking the elevators and not making repairs," refusing to address heat, sewage, or other ills, and "making life so miserable for the tenants that they had no choice but to leave."

This was Schwartz's introduction to Trump, and he says the irony is "that he failed miserably at it. The tenants didn't leave. There were enough educated, well-off tenants that they fought him for years and years, and it cost him a fortune." Schwartz came away with the impression that Trump was "a hustler." He says, "I thought he was just a guy without a lot of conscience, maybe none, and interested in making money however he could, and not particularly bright, but slick and good at managing the media." To Schwartz's surprise, Trump loved the resulting article, which he thought made him look like a tough guy. He especially loved that it landed him on the cover.

In May 1984, Trump got another cover—of *GQ*, featuring a faux-hagiographic piece written by Graydon Carter, one of his future antagonists. The article's subhead told the story:

"New York's brash new landlord can afford to sit pretty. He has powerful friends, a beautiful wife, a football team, and some of the choicest turf in Manhattan. It's wild, it's crazy. Isn't it?"[13] Carter began his piece with Roy Cohn, the notoriously ruthless lawyer and political fixer, with whom Trump had "what passes as a friendship." At the time, Trump was trying to break out of his father's Queens-based empire and crack the glittering high-end social circles and high-rises of Manhattan. The *GQ* article helped set up the grand myth of Trump—part real estate tycoon, part celebrity.

"Meet Donald Trump. Age 38," Carter wrote. "Eyebrows by Henry Luce. The sandy hair—longish on the sides in a Chamber of Commerce sort of way and brushed flat over the ears—by George Steinbrenner. The six-foot-two-inch frame is trim but well-nourished. The hands small and neatly groomed. The suit is blue and stylish—maybe a little too flared in the leg for someone who lives east of the Hudson. About the only thing that gives away this striver from an outer borough are his cuff links: huge mollusks of gold and stone the size of half-dollars."[14]

In 1986, Carter cofounded *Spy* with novelist and radio host Kurt Andersen. Two years later, for the first of a dozen times, *Spy* skewered Trump as a "short-fingered vulgarian" in a mock advertisement[15] for Trump's 1987 memoir, *The Art of the Deal*, touching off a grudge that has stretched into Trump's presidency. (Trump has sent Carter photos of himself over the years with the hands circled, defensively attempting to demonstrate the normal size of his hands.)[16] Carter went on to become the long-running editor of *Vanity Fair*, stepping down from the magazine soon after Trump became president. But his ability to tick off Trump with a written piece or an interview remained undiminished.

Despite Schwartz's dim initial impression of the rising real estate baron, he "coauthored" *The Art of the Deal* with Trump, to what he calls his eternal regret. Decades later Schwartz told *The New Yorker*'s Jane Mayer that the idea for the book came from legendary publisher S. I. Newhouse, whose company owned Random House and Condé Nast, whose portfolio includes *The New Yorker* and *GQ*. Newhouse noted how well the Trump *GQ* covers had sold and thought a Trump autobiography would sell, too. According to Mayer, "At one point, Howard Kaminsky, who ran Random House then, wrapped a thick Russian novel in a dummy cover that featured a photograph of Trump looking like a conquering hero; at the top was Trump's name, in large gold block lettering. Kaminsky recalls that Trump was pleased by the mockup, but had one suggestion: 'Please make my name much bigger.' " [17]

After securing a half-million-dollar advance, Trump signed a contract with Random House and, to Schwartz's surprise, asked him to write the book with him, agreeing with no negotiation to Schwartz's demand for half of the $500,000 advance and half the royalties.

With the title suggested by Schwartz, the book was part biography and part "how to succeed in business." The book included a skein of carefully woven falsehoods. "There were three chapters about [Trump's Atlantic City] casinos" in *The Art of the Deal*, says Schwartz. "All three later went bankrupt."

Over the years, he had failed or refused to pay scores of contractors who worked on his buildings, and when they demanded payment, he sometimes sued them as a way of running them off. He was accused of overworking and often refusing to pay the largely Polish and often undocumented workers, who did the dangerous work of stripping the wiring out of the old Bonwit Teller department store building on Manhattan's Fifth Avenue where the first Trump Tower would be built.[18]

Even the Trump surname, so ubiquitous around the world, was a fiction, anglicized from "Drumpf" to "Trump" either by his grandfather, Friedrich, or his father, Fred.[19] According to Gwenda Blair, in *The Trumps: Three Generations that Built an Empire*, and a Trump cousin, John Walter,[20] Fred Trump for years tried to pass off the family as Swedish, to avoid anti-German public sentiment during World War II and to make the family real estate business more palatable to prospective Jewish tenants. Schwartz says Trump told him that his grandfather came to America from Sweden as a child, a falsehood that made it into *The Art of the Deal.*

Trump was building his personal legend on a lie, but it didn't matter.

The Art of the Deal became a massive success when it was published in November 1987, spending forty-eight weeks on the *New York Times* bestseller list and making Trump a household name. This led the brash real estate mogul to more magazine covers, late-night talk show interviews, and movie cameos. Suddenly, everyone wanted to know what he thought about everything, from business to showbiz to politics.

Donald Trump had by then taken over his family's real estate empire, which was valued in the hundreds of millions of dollars. But behind the scenes, he had begun losing money,[21] taking serial loans from his father to try to save his foundering projects. By the early 1990s, he was deeply in debt—$900 million in the red, by some estimates[22]—and when he failed to pay back the loans he'd taken out in the United States, he became wholly reliant on foreign banks.

Trump had purchased the old Marjorie Merriweather Post estate, Mar-a-Lago, in Palm Beach, Florida, in 1995 and was almost immediately reviled by the residents there. Due to his enormous debt, he was forced to refashion the estate as a money-making private golf club, which he cynically marketed as open to Jewish members, unlike the other two main private clubs on the island that were restricted; it was the perfect payback to his snooty, WASP-y neighbors.

The man who decades later would be denounced as a casual racist who courted and excused neo-Nazis enjoyed welcoming black celebrities including rap music stars, pop stars, pro athletes, and others deemed "undesirable" in the stuffy, nearly all-white enclave. His name was dropped in countless hip-hop songs as a synonym for ostentatious wealth.

Trump cultivated an image as an irresistible ladies' man, in part by pitched items—as "John Barron"—to the New York gossip tabloids or getting salacious stories planted, or negative stories killed by friendly publications like *The National Enquirer*, whose publisher, David Pecker, is a longtime ally. For years, he did raunchy interviews with radio shock jock Howard Stern, talking openly about his alleged conquests.

Trump lied about having a chance to date everyone from actress Salma Hayek to Princess Diana, as he careened from marriage to marriage, to Czech model Ivana Zelníčková, American actress Marla Maples, and finally Slovenian model Melania Knauss. And as would later be alleged by Trump's own lawyer and fixer Michael Cohen,[23] marriage and children didn't stop him from pursuing dalliances with *Playboy* models and porn stars whom Cohen would be convicted of paying off to buy their silence ahead of the 2016 compaign-according to Cohen, at Trump's direction.[24]

Trump eagerly cultivated his celebrity image, becoming what the late reporter Wayne Barrett called a "star struck groupie, attaching himself to Don Johnson, Michael Jackson, and just about anyone else who would allow him to climb into photographs with them."[25] Barrett, in his 1991 biography, *Trump, The Greatest Show on Earth: The Deals, the Downfall, The Reinvention*, wrote that Trump once tried to persuade *Playboy* to do a "Girls of Trump" spread, featuring his prettiest, most buxom employees, in various states of undress.

Eventually, his eager celebrity courtship worked.

Michael Jackson and Lisa Marie Presley honeymooned at Mar-a-Lago in 1994, according to Jackson biographer J. Randy Taraborrelli. And Sean "P. Diddy" Combs and Jennifer Lopez, who were a couple at the time, spent an Easter holiday there.[26]

Trump made sure the famous people who visited were photographed with "The Donald," or that the news of their presence leaked to the tabloid press. Everything was part of the show.

By the time he married his third wife, Melania, in 2005, Trump's serial business and financial failures were forgotten. He had been fast-tracked to the celebrity A-list by the runaway success of *The Apprentice*—a reality show launched by *Survivor* producer Mark Burnett a year earlier on NBC to a record viewership. As journalist Patrick Radden Keefe wrote in a lengthy January 2019 profile of Burnett for *The New Yorker*,[27] Burnett conceived of *The Apprentice* as a kind of "*Survivor*, in the city"—with would-be entrepreneur contestants battling it out in the concrete jungle rather than the real thing, for a chance to work for and learn from a genuine business tycoon.

Trump, whom Burnett had met years before at the ice rink in New York City's Central Park—Trump had taken the renovations off the city's hands in 1986 and convinced contractors to work for free while he got all the publicity and ongoing fees to manage it—had just enough medium-level fame and more than enough ego and narcissism to pull off the *Apprentice* role. He even got his adult children involved in the show.

"'*The Apprentice*' portrayed Trump not as a skeevy hustler who huddles with local mobsters but as a plutocrat with impeccable business instincts and unparalleled wealth—a titan who always seemed to be climbing out of helicopters or into limousines,"[28] Radden Keefe wrote. Trump had only recently emerged from a series of bankruptcies. Producers found his Manhattan offices run-down, with signs of a "crumbling empire" everywhere, and Trump could barely perform the scripted material, most of the time going off the cuff. He was at his most charismatic when berating contestants who didn't perform well, and when delivering the show's signature line: "You're fired!" It became his catchphrase, his version of Schwarzenegger's "I'll be back." A takeoff on the line, declaring "Melania, your hired"[29] (*sic*), even flew over Palm Beach strung behind an airplane on the day of their wedding—signed by someone initialed "J.D." As one former editor put it in the *New Yorker* article, "it was like making the court jester the king." [30]

None of that mattered. The show was a hit. And Trump had achieved full membership in the celebrity club that he had always craved. His and Melania's wedding at the Episcopal church of Bethesda-by-the-Sea in Palm Beach featured a veritable red-carpet parade of celebrity arrivals: Arnold Schwarzenegger, model Heidi Klum, media stars Barbara Walters and Katie Couric, Billy Joel, Simon Cowell of *American Idol* fame, Kathie Lee Gifford, and Russell Simmons, and vintage stars including Tony Bennett and Paul Anka.

Even some members of the Manhattan elite whose favor Trump had coveted for decades were there, including *Vogue* editor Anna Wintour, alongside more Trumpian cartoonish characters like boxing promoter Don King.[31] Among the Trump "political friends" in attendance: former New York mayor Rudy Giuliani, then–U.S. attorney Chris Christie, and Bill and Hillary Clinton.[32]

Most of Trump's "celebrity friends" would disappear once he launched his presidential bid with open appeals to racism and nativism. Few stars would talk publicly about ever having known him.

Former *Celebrity Apprentice* stars, with a few exceptions, remained silent. Trump's most vocal celebrity supporters, like Kid Rock and Ted Nugent, had long since fallen to the fringes of fame. Some of those to whom Trump had once sought proximity became objects of his disparagement, both as a candidate and as president. He engaged in epic public feuds with A-list stars like Robert De Niro, attacked award-winning actress Meryl Streep and the stars of *Saturday Night Live* (a show whose cast had been forced to host him during the campaign) for parodying and mocking him, and said of Klum in a 2015 interview with *New York Times* columnist Maureen Dowd, "sadly, she's no longer a 10." [33]

In October 2015, I interviewed[34] rapper Luther Campbell for *The Daily Beast*. Campbell popularized raunchy rap music in the 1980s and '90s as the frontman for the group 2 Live Crew, before taking a free speech–related case all the way to the Supreme Court. At the time of our interview, he had become a respected political columnist in Miami. Campbell was among the rap stars whom the real estate mogul cultivated in those early years.

As hard as it is to believe, Trump was a hip-hop totem for decades. His name and references to Trump Tower were routinely dropped in rap songs, and Campbell and other music stars, from Sean "P. Diddy" Combs and pop singer Jennifer Lopez to rap mogul Russell Simmons, were among the celebrities who flocked to Mar-a-Lago during the 1990s. Trump even recorded cameos for Staten Island, New York–based Wu Tang Clan's lead rapper Method Man and for Fugees (as in *refugees*) "Ghetto Superstar" rapper "Pras,"[35] though Trump later admitted he had never heard of him.[36] It was pure marketing. According to former campaign aide Sam Nunberg, Trump "loved the hip-hop success culture. He didn't listen to the music."

Campbell told me he never thought that Trump's racist rhetoric about immigrants would hurt him with the black men who were inclined to vote for him, and not just because of his place in rap music's cultural firmament. "Whether they want to come out and say they do or not, when [Trump] talks about 'I'm gonna put a big old wall up [on the border with] Mexico,' he's tapping into a lot of people who won't say it on the surface, but [for the] man in the barbershop, it's, 'Man, I can't get a job because the Mexicans got the jobs,' "[37] Campbell said.

With Trump in the White House, and his aggressive racist rhetoric in full flower, hip-hop's love affair with all things Trump was decisively over. Veteran rap stars who "knew Trump when" were attacking him. And the president's lone remaining hip-hop "friend," Kanye West, after repeatedly donning a "Make America Great Again (MAGA)" hat and imploding in a bizarre October 2018 appearance in the White House, announced he was no longer willing to be "used for an agenda" he didn't believe in, and stopped talking politics.[38]

Responding to the notion of how "crazy" it was that Trump had gone "from a random, iconic celebrity to the despised leader of the free world," and "from a cameo in *Home Alone 2* to defending Neo-Nazis," African-American culture writer Michael Arceneaux wrote in a March 2018 *Essence* column that "what's crazier to me is we kept touting [Trump] as some sign of wealth and success despite evidence that one, he didn't give a damn about us, and two, he wasn't really that successful when you pull back the veneer of it all." Arceneaux added that, "in many ways, hip hop—much like 'The Apprentice'—helped perpetuate that folklore that Donald Trump was some masterful businessman whose image and fortune were to be marveled."[39]

The artifice that Donald Trump created around himself proved to be more fragile than he thought. It was easily pulled down once he ran for president. His attacks on Mexicans as "rapists and killers" led NBC to cut ties with him by dropping the Miss USA and Miss Universe pageants in June 2015 (Trump stepped down from his role in *The Apprentice* franchise in order to run). Macy's followed days later, ending its clothing deal with him. His daughter Ivanka Trump faced a consumer backlash as a campaign called "Grab Your Wallet" urged consumers to boycott retailers that carried her eponymous clothing and shoe lines, and several retailers, including Nordstrom and Neiman Marcus, complied.[40]

Trump's presidential bid prompted deeper scrutiny of his business empire. Reporters excavating his background revealed that far from owning hundreds of properties, most of the buildings with his name on them were owned by other developers. He simply leased his name to them like a celebrity brand of cologne. Far from being a hugely successful construction firm, the Trump Organization was in a fundamental way a small but highly effective licensing factory with just one product: Donald Trump.

Trump's attitude toward women has long veered from the Byzantine to the bizarre. His 2004 book, *How to Get Rich*, included the pearl of wisdom that "It's certainly not groundbreaking news that the early victories by the women on 'The Apprentice' were, to a very large extent, dependent on their sex appeal,"[41] and he told a contestant on the 2013 edition of the spinoff series *Celebrity Apprentice: All Stars*, former *Playboy* model and onetime *Baywatch* costar Brande Roderick, that "It must be a pretty picture, you dropping to your knees."[42]

Trump had purchased the Miss Universe multipageant franchise in 1996, including Miss Universe, Miss USA, and Miss Teen USA, reportedly complaining that the previous owners placed too much emphasis on brains over beauty.[43] He generated a few headlines with his insults against the first winner during his tenure, referring to Alicia Machado's postpageant weight gain (he called her "Miss Piggy" and "an eating machine").[44] But America let it slide. Trump continued to attack Ms. Machado when he became a presidential candidate, and she dared to speak out against him. He allegedly barged in on Miss Teen USA contestants, some as young as fifteen years old, while they were naked.[45] He had even bragged about doing so on Howard Stern's show.[46]

And then there is Trump's strange and inexplicable public fixation with the beauty and body of his eldest daughter, Ivanka. He reportedly compared his paramours Stormy Daniels and *Playboy* model Karen McDougal[47] to Ivanka as a form of flattery. An early draft of a post-election *Washington Post* column[48] by Richard Cohen included an anecdote in which Trump reportedly queried someone the columnist knew, regarding the then-thirteen-year-old Ivanka: "Is it wrong to be more sexually attracted to your own daughter than your wife?"[49] (The anecdote was deleted from the final column.)

After the *Access Hollywood* video surfaced,[50] nearly two dozen women, including at least one former *Apprentice* contestant, came forward to accuse Trump of making unwanted sexual advances over the years.[51] That former contestant, Summer Zervos, would sue Trump for defamation for denying her claim, setting the stage for the president to be deposed while in office, just as Bill Clinton had been in the Paula Jones lawsuit during his term as president.

Black former *Apprentice* contestants—including Kwame Jackson, Tara Dowdell, and the first African-American to win the show, Randal Pinkett—who Trump said should share his prize with a white female runner-up—came forward during the campaign to denounce Trump's racism and divisiveness. Even his staunchest African-American defender at the time, former *Apprentice* contestant Omarosa Manigault-Newman, who became a celebrity in her own right and then took a job in the White House, wrote a tell-all book (after she was fired by Trump's then-chief of staff) and said a tape of Trump calling Kwame Jackson "the n-word" exists. (Two years into his presidency, no such tape had surfaced, and Burnett steadfastly refused to release any behind-the-scenes footage of the show.)

Running for president, in the way he chose to, was undoing decades of Trump brand-building, and the undoing was happening quickly. One black former celebrity friend who says he still has a hard time viewing Trump as personally racist (while acknowledging the ample public evidence) believes Trump made the mistake early on of "hitching his wagon" to birtherism and Steve Bannon's white nationalist populism, and it took him on a ride he may not have intended, but that he can't extricate himself from now.

"I think he latched on and said, OK, let me ride this out. This is where my power is going to come from," the onetime friend said. "Business-wise I don't understand it. When it's over, in four years or eight, and people see you as this racist, what are you gonna do, start a chain of Motel 6's?"

Most celebrities are in one way or another inventions, changing their names, altering their bodies, or sometimes shaving down their ages to make them more marketable to a fickle public. During the "golden age" of Hollywood, Archibald Leach became Cary Grant, Frances Gumm became Judy Garland, and Norma Jean Baker transformed into Marilyn Monroe. Even today, Whoopi Goldberg is really Caryn Johnson, comedic actress Tina Fey is actually named Elizabeth, and comedian Jon Stewart leaves off his true surname: Leibowitz. It's a simple fact of show business that what you see on screen or on social media is mostly an illusion. Even John Wayne, who built the archetype of the "western" and stood for a particular brand of twentieth-century (white) American manhood, had his real name, Marion Morrison, changed to the iconic moniker by a movie producer.

Some myths are more than name-deep. Wayne, who also starred in more than a dozen war-hero epics, including *Sands of Iwo Jima* in 1949, never saw a day of real combat, having avoided service in World War II. For a time, he claimed a football injury kept him from the front lines, when other, much more famous actors at the time, such as Jimmy Stewart and Clark Gable, enlisted and served. A sympathetic 1995 biography, *John Wayne: American,* made it clear that Wayne sought deferments to avoid interrupting his burgeoning movie career.[52]

When a 1971 *Playboy* interview resurfaced in 2019 in which Wayne was quoted as disdaining movies with same-sex themes and favoring white supremacy "until the blacks are educated to a point of responsibility," with no qualms about white settlers having taken America from the indigenous who were "selfishly trying to keep it for themselves,"[53] it touched off angry and partisan debates over the ongoing value of fundamentally American mythologies, and whether re-litigating the arcane social views of a man who was born in 1907 and died in 1979 is entirely fair. We Americans have gotten used to having our youthful faith dashed, as the famous drink or drug themselves to death and even "America's dad," Bill Cosby, goes to prison after the revelation of his decades of sexual predation.

Invitations to disillusionment have frequently visited the White House. Civil War hero Ulysses S. Grant actually testified, as the sitting president, on behalf of his personal secretary in a rollicking scandal over whiskey distillers skimming liquor tax revenues and bribing IRS officials that saw more than 230 indictments and 110 men convicted by the nation's first special prosecutor in 1876.[54] Presidents Andrew Johnson and Bill Clinton were impeached, and Watergate, which "stole the innocence" of a generation of Americans who believed in the fundamental honor of our politics, forced Richard Nixon to resign, less than one year after his vice president, Spiro Agnew, resigned to avoid going to prison for tax evasion.[55] Ronald Reagan, heralded by many Americans as the hero of the Cold War, in July 1987 had to give a televised address taking responsibility for his administration selling weapons to Iran and funneling the cash to a Central American militia.[56]

Americans have become almost inured to presidential scandal in the post-Watergate age. And while the person of the president has been a more closely guarded commodity, no fewer than four early presidents, including George Washington, Thomas Jefferson, and even William Henry Harrison, were accused either contemporaneously or decades later of fathering children with women they enslaved, and two others scandalized for having children out of wedlock.[57] The public didn't learn of the extramarital affairs of FDR or JFK until they were long dead, thanks to a twentieth-century tradition of probity by the press in such illicit personal matters, an unwritten rule that didn't survive the later sex scandals of presidential candidates such as Gary Hart and Bill Clinton.

Voters in the United States have long embraced the idea of turning fame—gleaned from military heroism or even absurdist celebrity—into power. Abraham Lincoln's seven public debates in the U.S. Senate campaign of 1858 with Stephen A. Douglas made him famous enough for the leaders of the nascent Republican Party to nominate him for president two years later. The war exploits of politically unfortunate but humane General Grant; venal, populist Andrew Jackson; swashbuckling Teddy Roosevelt; John F. Kennedy, whose quick thinking aboard his sunken PT boat was anthologized in *Reader's Digest* magazine and a hit Hollywood film; and the World War II heroism of General Dwight Eisenhower propelled them to the White House.

Modern voters sent familiar TV faces—Gopher from *The Love Boat*, Cooter from *The Dukes of Hazzard* (representatives Fred Grandy and Ben Jones, respectively), and late variety show star Sonny Bono to Congress. Clint Eastwood was for a time the mayor of Carmel, California, and "The Terminator," Arnold Schwarzenegger, and WWE wrestler Jesse "the Body" Ventura became governors. And *Saturday Night Live* sketch comic Al Franken was a United States senator. Reagan was the ultimate celebrity-to-politics transference: from B-movie actor to California governor to president.

There have been many stars who've tried and failed, from would-be president Fred Thompson of *Law & Order* fame, to a grown-up Shirley Temple (Black), who made a bid to become the lone woman in California's thirty-eight-member congressional delegation in 1967 but lost her race to a candidate who opposed Nixon on the Vietnam War.[58]

The myths Trump had for decades created about himself, and the celebrity he so eagerly cultivated, helped make him president. Americans believed what they saw on TV. Unless you lived in New York City when he was damning the Central Park Five in the '80s or were a black tenant denied an apartment in one of his buildings in the '70s, or a contractor or creditor left unpaid, you likely had no idea who he really was. Even some who did know looked past it, faced with the chance to put an "outsider" in the White House.

Alongside the negative motivations he cynically pitched—hurting immigrants, humiliating Mexicans, and pummeling

China—for many Americans there were affirmative motivations for voting for him, too. For millions of Americans, a President Donald Trump meant jobs and opportunity and a gaudy, joyous spectacle of gold-plated success.

But if the entire architecture of the Trump myth was a house of lies, nothing was more false than the notion that he was a crusader for American greatness. Trump built his buildings with Chinese steel and mob concrete, according to journalist David Cay Johnston, who had covered Trump for decades. He used foreign, undocumented labor in his golf clubs right up to the time he was in the White House, according to exposés in the *New York Times*,[59] NBC News,[60] and the *Washington Post*.[61] He was, in every conceivable way, artificial: a product that was packaged, marketed, and sold to America, including by himself.

Trump seemed to exhibit the greatest personal affinity, not for the hymnal of America, but for the pure love of money and fame, and the siren song of another nation: Russia.

CHAPTER SIX

American Strongman

"Despotic power is always accompanied by corruption of morality."

—Lord Acton

DONALD TRUMP'S ATTRACTION TO STRONGMEN AND AUTOCRATS was never hidden. He told his biographers, including Tony Schwartz, that being strong, tough, and a "killer" were the qualities his father taught him to admire. His onetime *Apprentice* castmate Omarosa Manigault-Newman, also his 2016 campaign's African-American outreach director, told PBS's *Frontline* in a documentary that aired during the primaries that after President Obama ridiculed him during his set at the 2011 White House correspondents' dinner, Trump vowed to get the ultimate revenge by running for president. "Every critic, every detractor, will have to bow down to President Trump," Omarosa recalled him seething. "It's everyone who's ever doubted Donald, who ever disagreed, whoever challenged him. It is the ultimate revenge to become the most powerful man in the universe."

Trump seemed determined to make good on those threats now that he actually was president. And he seemed to have a particular country in mind as a role model for the America he envisioned with himself as the leader: Russia.

Donald Trump's attraction to Russia has been on display since at least 1987, when he and his first wife, Ivana, traveled to Moscow to inquire about a potential real estate deal, a trip widely believed to have been arranged by Soviet intelligence services. The Soviets were reportedly alarmed by Ronald Reagan's hawkishness and were looking to develop contacts with Americans they might turn toward their point of view.[1] Experts suggest the Soviet Union's interest in Trump and his family likely stretches back much further. Luke Harding, in a November 2017 article for *Politico Magazine*, wrote that the KGB may have opened a file on Trump as early as 1977, when he married the Czech-born Ivana.

Harding also wrote that Ivana, as a citizen of a communist country, would have been "of interest both to the Czech intelligence service, the StB, and to the FBI and CIA."[2] Craig Unger, in his book *House of Trump, House of Putin: The Unfolding Story of Donald Trump and the Russian Mafia*, points out that Trump and Ivana attracted Czech security services' attention even in America, where the StB likely monitored her father when he traveled to the United States for the Trumps' 1977 wedding, and wiretapped her phone calls with him as early as 1979. Unger reports that Ivana even began using code names to obscure the conversations.[3] Unger writes that "the StB thought there was a chance that the U.S. intelligence agencies could use Ivana," too. He quotes a Prague-based historian on totalitarian regimes in adding that these intelligence services "wanted to use [Mrs.] Trump to gather information on U.S. high society."[4]

In 1986, as Trump claimed he was pushing for a posting by the Reagan administration and touting his unique ability to achieve nuclear disarmament and end the Cold War, he sought out Bernard Lown, a Boston cardiologist who had invented the defibrillator and shared the Nobel Peace Prize (on behalf of the

International Physicians for the Prevention of Nuclear War) with Yevgeniy Chazov, who was Mikhail Gorbachev's personal physician. Trump invited Lown to Trump Tower, where, according to Unger, he asked Lown to tell him about Gorbachev and bragged to the doctor, "If I know about Gorbachev, I can ask my good friend Ronnie to make me a plenipotentiary ambassador for the United States with Gorbachev."[5] "Ronnie" was President Ronald Reagan, whom Trump didn't actually know.

A year later, Trump gave the Russian ambassador to the United Nations and his daughter a tour of Trump Tower, later boasting to Tony Schwartz that he was "talking about building a large luxury hotel across the street from the Kremlin, in partnership with the Soviet government." When Trump and Ivana arrived in Moscow a year later to try to close the deal, the couple reportedly stayed in the Lenin Suite at Moscow's National Hotel, near Red Square, and they were treated like visiting celebrities.[6] But the tower never materialized.

Trump's eagerness to be embraced by the Russians unfolded in a public embarrassment two years later when he welcomed a Mikhail Gorbachev impersonator to Trump Tower after falling for a prank while the real Russian leader was in New York.[7]

Trump would be dogged by his real estate pursuits and the shady financial schemes surrounding them—a central tenet of his longtime lawyer Michael Cohen's public testimony before Congress and of ongoing investigations in New York and Virginia. But the myths and fundamental lies Trump had sold the world about himself were what had gotten him into that suite near Red Square and had presaged his ability, decades later, to explode nearly every American myth, along with his own.

As president, Trump adopted a style that was more reflective of the Russian president, Vladimir Putin, and other strongman figures and autocrats around the world than of traditional American leaders. His calls for violence by his supporters were not unlike the Philippine leader Rodrigo Duterte, who boasted of killing drug dealers in his country himself and threatened to "slap" the United Nations raconteur if she tried to probe his prosecution of his country's drug war. He mirrored the klepto- cratic thuggery of his friend, the crown prince of Saudi Arabia, Mohammed bin Salman. He went from threatening "fire and fury" against North Korea to saying he "fell in love" with that country's brutal congenital dictator, Kim Jong Un. And Trump's harsh, anti-immigrant rhetoric and policies were not unlike those of Hungary's nativist, some charged, neo-fascist prime minister, Viktor Orbán, or Poland's far right nationalist president, Andrezej Duda, or Italy's Lega party and its leader, Matteo Salvini, whose confrontational approach was threatening to upend the Euro- pean Union.

Nonwhite immigration—particularly by Muslim refugees from war-torn Syria and from North Africa—was fueling a metas- tasizing right-wing nationalism across Europe that in some coun- tries bordered on a return to fascism. Anti-immigrant zeal (and Russian interference) fueled the "Brexit" vote for Britain to leave the European Union. Hatred of Muslims fueled a deadly terror- ist attack in New Zealand in which a white nationalist gunman shot up two mosques, killing 50 men, women, and children in March 2019—an attack the killer live-streamed on Facebook. And rather than stand against the tide of right-wing nationalism roiling countries from Germany to France to Sweden, the Ameri- can president, Donald Trump, was joining in.

The first policy enacted by the incoming Trump administra- tion was an executive order barring travel to the United States from seven majority-Muslim countries, including Iraq, where the 2003 U.S. invasion had helped create tens of thousands of refu- gees. The travel ban, which threw airports around the country into chaos,[8] wound up in the Supreme Court. The courts at first rejected what Trump had during the campaign called a "total and complete shutdown of Muslims entering the United States until our country's representatives can figure out what the hell is going on." The Supreme Court upheld a later version of the ban when the administration added two non-Muslim countries to the list, with Chief Justice John Roberts calling the new version "facially neutral toward religion." [9]

Trump and his administration flaunted their goal of slashing both unlawful and *legal* migration to the United States, with the president openly declaring his preference for immigrants "from Norway." The administration all but shut down the processing of asylum claims and canceled temporary protected status for refugees from Latin American, Caribbean, and African countries. On Twitter, in February 2019, Trump referred darkly to a Gallup poll that said: "Open borders will potentially attract 42 million Latin Americans," and he commented, "This would be a disaster for the U.S. We need the wall now!" America, suddenly, was no longer a beacon for the world's huddled masses to come and "breathe free." The president of the United States was slamming the doors shut.

In 2018, the Trump administration forcibly separated thousands of Central American migrant children from their parents at the southern border, detaining them and denying them even the chance to ask for asylum. In some cases, the administration shipped the parents back to their countries without their kids, declaring that it would be too difficult to track all of the stolen children or reunite them all with their moms and dads.

Reporters and United States senators traveled to the military-style camps set up by the administration in Texas, and witnessed some of the children locked in cages. As it emerged that the administration had separated perhaps hundreds, perhaps thousands more children than they first admitted, the howls of outrage were global while members of the Republican Party were largely silent.

I was among a group of reporters permitted to tour one encampment in Tornillo, Texas, in the summer of 2018, and we watched as hundreds of Central American boys lined up to eat or to make brief phone calls in what looked like a military prison camp. We toured tents filled with sparse bunk beds and canvas walls lined with artwork depicting gloomy religious scenes.

When the smaller boys looked at us—this group of strangers there to gawk at them and scribble in our notebooks—it was with a mixture of confusion and dread. Some of the older boys smiled at us as they ringed a soccer field made from sod that looked like it had been rolled out that day. We weren't allowed to talk to the children, beyond asking "¿Cómo estás hijo?" and "¿Cómo está la comida?"—"How are you," and "How is the food?" Anything more, and we would be ejected.

When we reached the tent where the smaller group of unaccompanied girls lived, all but one refused to come out, and one reporter was admonished for attempting, in Spanish, to ask what country the teen girl was from. These children were not the ones separated from their parents, but rather those who had traveled from their faraway homes alone. The idea that they were not prisoners was belied by the wide, hot desert surrounding them, the palpable sadness of the place, and the military men with guns guarding the gates. Even the man running the facility called the policy of separating children from parents at the border "stupid" and said he looked forward to going back to erecting his tent cities for natural disasters, not children.

Trump twisted the presidency into a performance of autocracy. He openly attacked the press, calling media who reported critically about him and his administration "the enemy of the people." He looked the other way when violence was done to journalists, whether in a mass shooting at a Maryland newspaper or at the behest of the Saudi crown prince. And he took both comfort and counsel from the right-wing media outlets and figures who had helped him ascend to power.

Besides the ritualized public praise and effusive loyalty he required from his cabinet, his vice president, and his party, Trump personally attacked those whose actions displeased him. This included not just politicians and members of his own administration, but also private companies who failed to comply with his tweeted demands, sometimes causing the stock market to lurch and plunge. Some corporate leaders responded by giving him undue credit for policies or decisions taken even before he entered office. Fear of Trump's Twitter attacks kept his party strictly in line. And Republicans bent over backward to stay in his good graces, turning themselves into little more than Trump subordinates and sycophants, willingly giving up their power by voting to weaken congressional authority over the White House.

During and after the campaign, he repeatedly threatened to jail his presidential rival Hillary Clinton—a move out of the playbook of the world's worst dictatorships. At his frequent political rallies, the crowds chanted "Build the wall!" and "Lock her up!"—usually directed at Clinton, but sometimes targeting other women who drew Trump's ire. He publicly threatened potential witnesses against him, including Michael Cohen and Cohen's father-in-law.

Even as his presidency and business empire stood on the brink of unraveling under pressure from multiple prosecutors and investigative committees in the Democratic House, which were poised to subpoena his chief financial officer, his personal secretary, his seediest former business partners, and his tax returns, Trump remained in full ownership of the GOP. He gave a rambling, two-hour address at the annual Conservative Political Action Conference in Maryland in February 2019, holding forth in a mock rally reminiscent of a modern-day Fidel Castro.

Washington Post political reporter and NBC News/MSNBC contributor Robert Costa wrote of Trump's iron grip: "Acquiescence to Trump is now the defining trait of the Republican Party more than two years into his presidency—overwhelming and at times erasing principles that conservatives viewed as the foundation of the party for more than a half century." [10]

Trump did take up conservative causes, vowing to issue an executive order "requiring colleges and universities to support free speech if they want federal research grants."[11] The right has long accused colleges and universities of squelching conservative speech and thought, and churning out an army of "social justice warriors" programmed to oppose traditional values. The desire to bring academia to heel is an authoritarian staple. Trump's announcement came as Prime Minister Orbán—an ally of both Trump and far right Israeli prime minister Benjamin Netanyahu—kicked Central European University out of Hungary. The university, founded by Hungarian-American philanthropist George Soros—a frequent target of the right both in and out of the United States—had been vilified by Orbán as he consolidated power and clamped down on dissent.

Violent incidents on U.S. college campuses increased in the years since the 2016 election, as right-wing figures, including members of the white nationalist alt-right, faced pitched opposition to planned university speeches, and some events were canceled amid fear of violence. Sensitivity by university leadership to this hate speech enraged those on the right who had long battled the notion of "political correctness" as little more than a way of oppressing conservative views. Christian fundamentalists frequently complained that their First Amendment rights were being curtailed on campuses where public prayer, or prayers led by faculty, were prohibited. Trump was now taking up the baton.

Trump's affinity for mob violence by his supporters was put on garish display during his campaign rallies, when he whiffed that those gathered in his name should "knock the hell out of" protesters. He encouraged the country to "toughen up" during a March 2016 campaign rally in St. Louis, Missouri, lamenting that it took too long to remove a group of hecklers, saying "part of the reason it takes so long is nobody wants to hurt each other anymore." Thirty people were arrested outside the venue amid violence and mayhem that included anti-Muslim slurs hurled at protesters.

In rhetoric reminiscent of George Wallace's references to violently evicting protesters from his 1968 campaign rallies, Trump made appeals to violence a "dark comedy" feature of his campaign appearances. He offered to pay the legal fees for a supporter who physically assaulted a protester at one of his rallies and told supporters at a North Carolina rally in March 2016 that protests didn't happen in the "good old days" because "they used to treat them very, very rough."[12] While stoking his supporters' fear that Hillary Clinton would do away with their gun rights if she were to be elected president and got to appoint judges, Trump said "Second Amendment people" could take matters into their own hands.[13]

As president, Trump kept up the violent rhetoric. Surrounded by uniformed police onstage as he spoke in Long Island in August 2017, Trump veered from raging about gang violence and "thugs being thrown into the back of a Paddy wagon" to suggesting that cops not be careful to protect suspects' heads from hitting the roof of patrol cars.

In March 2019, Trump entered the darkest territory of all, saying during an Oval office interview that while the left "plays tough," he had a way to play tougher. "I actually think that the people on the right are tougher," he said. "But they don't play it tougher. O.K.? I can tell you I have the support of the police, the support of the military, the support of the Bikers for Trump. I have the tough people, but they don't play it tough—until they go to a certain point, and then it would be very bad, very bad."[14] Trump's rhetoric stoked fears of how far he was willing to go to protect himself from the reach of the criminal justice system, the special prosecutor, or even the voters in 2020. Whispers of whether Trump would even willingly leave office if he were to lose reelection were turning into alarm.

Perhaps Trump's most lethal defiance of the norms of the American presidency was his seemingly open invitations to kleptocracy.

Trump continued conducting personal business while in office: operating golf clubs in Florida, New York, New Jersey, California, and Scotland, with new contracts for golf courses in Dubai. Upon becoming president, he doubled the fees at his Mar-a-Lago private club to $200,000 and signed a lease with the Government Accountability Office for a new Trump hotel based in the old D.C. Post Office, putting him in business with the federal government.

"We've never had a president who has come into office, who's basically got conflicts of interest all over the world," said Nick Akerman, who as a young lawyer was part of the team that investigated Watergate under special counsel Archibald Cox. He says Trump's operation of the D.C. hotel, where Republican politicos and foreign leaders and diplomats lined up to pay to stay, was particularly problematic. "We have never before Trump had a president who is basically using the office to make money, and to conduct his business while at the same time being president of the United States. That has just never happened before. We've never had the kind of a conflict of interest where the emoluments clause has even been at issue." Yet, Trump's hotels and golf courses are "basically being funded by foreigners," Akerman says, whose goal in spending money at Trump properties is "to influence the president."

And then there were Trump's attacks on his own country's national security apparatus.

James Comey, the former FBI director, told Congress that before Trump fired him, the president asked for a pledge of personal loyalty, something Comey, as a federal law enforcement officer, could not do. Trump constantly derided and publicly humiliated his first attorney general, Jeff Sessions, who as a senator had been an early supporter and an adviser to his campaign, but who recused himself from the investigation, as required by law and propriety, and who refused to end the investigations against Trump. The president ultimately hounded Sessions out of office.

Trump questioned his own administration's intelligence services and elections system, publicly attacking and berating FBI officials including fired deputy director Andrew McCabe, the man who ordered the counterintelligence inquiry into whether the sitting president was operating as an agent of Russia, against American interests.[15]

McCabe disclosed in a 2019 autobiography that Trump ridiculed his wife, who had run for state office in Virginia as a Democrat, for losing the election, and asked McCabe whom he'd voted for. And McCabe, a lifelong Republican, said that when briefed by his national security team about North Korea's nuclear capabilities, Trump refuted them, saying he believed Vladimir Putin, who had told him something different.

Trump hired his daughter and son-in-law as senior White House advisers and gave them top-secret security clearances despite their extensive overseas business ties—a flagrant display of cronyism. Trump invested immense authority in them, including announcing in 2019 that Ivanka Trump would help choose the next president of the World Bank, even while her company holds hundreds of foreign patents, including some acquired in China after his election.[16]

According to the *New York Times*,[17] Trump ordered Kushner's clearance to be granted over the objections of his own national security apparatus, including the CIA, and his then-chief of staff and the White House counsel.

Trump's adult children continued to operate the Trump business. His sons, accompanied by their U.S. Secret Service details, were known to jet around the globe seeking fresh contracts,[18] while they, Donald Trump Jr. in particular, and Eric Trump's wife, Lara, were actively involved in Republican Party politics.

Steven Mnuchin, Trump's Treasury secretary—who had served as his campaign's national finance director—arranged to lift the sanctions on a Russian oligarch implicated in the Kremlin's attack on the 2016 election, opening the way for hundreds of millions of dollars to flow to a man associated with Trump's indicted former campaign chairman, Paul Manafort (the man who also chose his vice president, Mike Pence). Democratic lawmakers soon questioned Mnuchin's own financial ties to a major investor in the aluminum business owned by that Russian oligarch.[19, 20]

In innumerable ways, Trump's presidency was a test of whether the constitutional framework erected more than 240 years ago could withstand the kind of populist tidal waves that have overrun governments from Europe to Asia, Africa, and South and Central America. Bruce Bartlett, the onetime Reagan-Bush Republican staffer, said, "I'm very fearful of having very serious confrontations, constitutional-level confrontations between Congress and the White House with Trump having Fox News in his pocket, talk radio in his pocket, and an extremely unified party behind him."

Trump used his infrequent trips to Europe and his attendance at global forums with other heads of state to berate and humiliate America's allies. He slammed Britain for failing to enact the Brexit withdrawal from the European Union swiftly enough—a referendum with Trump's brand of anti-immigrant xenophobia as well as Russian interference in their election.

He assailed multilateral trade deals and withdrew the United States from the Trans Pacific Partnership negotiated by his predecessor, while launching a global trade war. He pulled the United States out of other historic Obama-negotiated pacts on combating climate change and attempting to steer Iran away from producing nuclear weapons. Trump's only reason seemed to be that they were Obama initiatives.

Trump consistently flaunted his admiration for Putin, shocking even some Republican allies with his performance at a July 2018 joint press conference in Helsinki, Finland, during which he echoed Putin's denial of interfering in the 2016 election that made Trump president. He stood by this, even though his administration's intelligence services had concluded that Russia had done so, including hacking into the emails of the Democratic National Committee and distributing the content through WikiLeaks.

The Trump administration alarmed Democrats by slow-walking the implementation of Russia sanctions passed by Congress in the wake of Russian meddling in the U.S. election and the poisoning of a former Russian spy and his daughter on British soil. He called for Russia to be readmitted to the Group of 7, even though they had not ceased their occupation of Crimea—the act that triggered their suspension. A bombshell *New York Times*[21] story in January 2019 revealed that the president had openly discussed withdrawing the U.S. from NATO, sending shudders through the Pentagon and Department of State.

Trump heaped similar praise on the authoritarian rulers of Saudi Arabia, Turkey, the Philippines, China, and Egypt, seeming to induct the United States into what former naval intelligence officer Malcolm Nance called an "axis of autocracies," while spurning America's traditional role as the leader of the Western alliance.

The alarm in Europe over the conduct of the American president culminated in a November 2018 call by French president Emmanuel Macron for the creation of a nine-country European Union military force, independent of NATO, that could defend the Western nations against not just Russia and China but also the United States.[22]

Even Trump's attempts at seeking world peace showed his tendency toward autocratic behavior, and his soft spot for dictators. He held two unprecedented face-to-face summits with North Korea's Kim Jong Un, in Singapore and in Vietnam, declaring after the first that he had ended the nuclear threat from North Korea (they never agreed to give up their nuclear weapons), and ending the second summit early, having achieved nothing. For Kim, the meetings fulfilled his—and his late father's—long-held dream of standing equal with an American president on the world stage. At the second failed U.S.–North Korea summit, journalists were excluded from key proceedings by the administration, reportedly for daring to "shout questions."

At a press conference following the meeting, Trump again genuflected before Kim, saying he "took him at his word" when the dictator denied his regime's involvement in the torture of a long-detained American student, Otto Warmbier, who was returned to his family in the United States in a coma, and later died.[23] Trump seemed more concerned about North Korea's potential as a site for future real estate development than with its disrespect for human life, Korean or American. He praised North Korea's "great beaches," telling the assembled reporters, "you see that whenever they're exploding their cannons into the ocean. I said, 'Boy, look at that view. Wouldn't that make a great condo?' You could have the best hotels in the world right there."[24]

The Gallup organization's annual survey of global power and leadership reported on the first year of the Trump presidency by saying, "the median global approval rating of the job performance of U.S. leadership across 134 countries stands at a new low of 30 percent. This is down nearly 20 points from the 48 percent approval rating in the last year of President Barack Obama's administration, and four points lower than the previous low of 34 percent in the last year of President George W. Bush's administration.

"More important is the shift this has created in the global balance of soft power and what that means for U.S. influence abroad. With its stable approval rating of 41 percent, Germany has replaced the U.S. as the top-rated global power in the world. The U.S. is now on nearly even footing with China (31 percent) and barely more popular than Russia (27 percent)—two countries that Trump sees as rivals seeking to 'challenge American influence, values and wealth.' "[25]

The damage to the United States's reputation was most acute in Latin America and Canada, and among our closest allies, in Europe, where approval of U.S. leadership declined in 21 out of 28 members of the European Union. American leadership saw its highest approval in Israel and the Philippines, and its lowest approval in Pakistan and the Palestinian territories. Even Russians had a net negative view, with just 8 percent approving and 58 percent having a negative view.[26] China was a major beneficiary of America's decline—along with Germany, newly christened as the world's most admired country. The ironies couldn't be starker for the United States, the nation that saved Europe during World War II from a very different German Republic.

At the end of 2018, when Gallup asked the nearly 47,000 respondents in 45 countries to name the best and worst global leaders, two things stood out for researchers: the across-the-board downward trend for nearly all of the world's heads of state and Donald Trump's unrivaled spot at the bottom, behind the Saudi king, Turkey's autocratic Recep Tayyip Erdogan, Russia's Vladimir Putin, Israel's hawkish prime minister, Benjamin Netanyahu, and Hassan Rouhani, the president of Iran.[27] Meanwhile, China's newly minted president for life, Xi Jinping; India's Narendra Modi; the embattled British prime minister, Theresa May; and France's Emmanuel Macron lined up behind the German chancellor, Angela Merkel, who two years into Trump's term was in many respects the new leader of the free world.[28]

A poll is just a poll, of course, but the United States will someday have to face the damage Trump has done to the country's "soft power," a term coined by Harvard political scientist Joseph S. Nye Jr. that refers to the ability "to get others to do what they otherwise would not."[29] Not since George W. Bush's unnecessary war in Iraq dropped America's global standing has America been so reviled—creating fewer opportunities for the United States to cajole, persuade, and to promote democracy and to counter the military or economic aggression of countries such as Russia, North Korea, Turkey, Venezuela, and China.

FIVE DAYS BEFORE CHRISTMAS IN 2018, TRUMP'S SECRETARY OF defense, General James Mattis—whose nickname "Mad Dog" Trump delighted in using even though the general reportedly loathed it—became the first member of the volatile administration to resign on principle. In his resignation letter, Mattis displayed his disagreement with Trump over the fraying of our country's long-held alliances: "We must do everything possible to advance an international order that is most conducive to our security, prosperity and values and we are strengthened in this effort by solidarity of our alliances." Then in a clear rebuke to the commander in chief, Mattis wrote, "Because you have the right to have a Secretary of Defense whose views are better aligned with yours on these and other subjects, I believe it is right for me to step down from my position." [30]

Mattis had been one of the few cabinet officers to command universal respect and whose reputation remained unsullied by his association with Trump. His departure was triggered by Trump's abrupt announcement of a U.S. military departure from Syria, where he said the ISIS terrorist group had been unilaterally "defeated." This came two months after retired admiral William H. McRaven, who led the mission to kill terrorist leader Osama bin Laden, stepped down from a key Defense Department board days after he criticized Trump for revoking the security clearance of former CIA director John Brennan, who had become a consistent Trump critic.

"Few Americans have done more to protect this country" than Brennan, McRaven wrote in a *Washington Post* op-ed. "He is a man of unparalleled integrity, whose honesty and character have never been in question, except by those who don't know him. Therefore, I would consider it an honor if you would revoke my security clearance as well, so I can add my name to the list of men and women who have spoken up against your presidency." [31]

Donald Trump was increasingly isolated, surrounded by "acting" staff, with a dwindling cadre of advisers increasingly beholden to Jared Kushner or to Trump himself. And he was becoming bolder in appearing to do the Kremlin's bidding. The *Washington Post* revealed in January 2019 that Trump had met with Vladimir Putin several times since becoming president, never with a note-taker present, and he had consistently concealed the transcripts of those meetings and kept them even from his own cabinet.[32]

The Kremlin said he consulted with them before his second meeting with Kim Jong Un. And despite a White House announcement that a Trump-Putin meeting during a November 2018 Group of 20 summit in Buenos Aires, Argentina, had been called off in protest over renewed Russian aggression in Ukraine,[33] it was revealed in January 2019 that the two had met after all, with no U.S. staff present. The meeting was not revealed by the White House, but by a Russian government official.[34]

Vladimir Putin, a former KGB agent who ran counterintelligence duties in the spy agency's Eastern European bureau, had one dream, experts said, of restoring the glory of the shattered Soviet Union by collapsing the world order crafted during the "American century." Putin wanted to replace the post–World War II global order with a twenty-first-century free-for-all, made up of a string of autocracies led by populist strongmen running superficially democratic countries where immigration—particularly by the Muslims fleeing the Middle East chaos and violence created by the terrorist organization ISIS—was all but forbidden.

In Putin's ideal world, violence, on the streets and by governments, would not be scrutinized by any world body. Multilateral trade would be replaced by bilateral deals with the potential to financially benefit the country's leaders and their cronies. Putin was in his eighteenth year of power in a country that experts such as Malcolm Nance, Craig Unger, and authoritarian states scholar Sarah Kendzior likened to little more than a governmental version of the Mafia. In this new configuration of autocratic kleptocracies, Trump could assume the role of America's strongman. And it could make him and his family incredibly rich.

Edward "Ned" Price, who resigned as a CIA intelligence officer in February 2017, rather than remain in the agency under Trump, expressed his belief in a *Washington Post* op-ed that

Trump's leadership of the country is in service of something other than the national interest. "In kowtowing to people from Vladimir Putin to Rodrigo Duterte [of the Philippines] to Abdel Fattah el-Sisi of Egypt to Mohammed bin Salman of Saudi Arabia, he is preserving his well-being and his earning power once he leaves the Oval Office," said Price.

"The things he has said, and the tactics that he and his sons have used, even the relatively mundane developments like his Mar-a-Lago Club raising their membership fees after he was elected . . . [paint] a picture of a man who wants to preserve his earning power in places where he has earned tremendous revenue and income in the past, and that he sees as lucrative markets going forward. Russia, Turkey, the Philippines, Saudi Arabia, Egypt, China."

Price echoes the alarms of other members of the intelligence community, who became increasingly bold in their negative assessments of everything from the president's attention span to his willingness to believe his own briefers.

"Helsinki put on a stark display for everyone what we had come to see of Trump before that," Price says. "He regularly dismisses the work of the U.S. intelligence community and embraces the word of Vladimir Putin. What most bothers my former colleagues and myself is the uncertainty of what's behind this. Is it financial interest? Is it naiveté? Is it something much more sinister that I think a lot of us never thought would even be possible in terms of the occupant of the Oval Office? I think it's that continuing uncertainty that really vexes a lot of people in the national security realm."

Price sees Trump fitting perfectly into the new and unstable world he and Putin have helped create, where Britain is weakened by Brexit, countries like Poland and Italy teeter on the brink of succumbing to a second wave of fascism, and Germany and France are battling their own right-wing populist movements while struggling to hold together what's left of the global order. A new Mexican president and a young Canadian prime minister were navigating a new reality in which the quest for American global leadership might not begin in Washington, D.C., even as countries such as Brazil and Venezuela were destabilized by right- and left-wing populist presidents. Meanwhile, Trump was indeed being welcomed by many of the world's leading autocrats as a new member of the club.

Price believes the autocrats see Trump as "one of us," and "what drove them crazy about not only the Obama administration but previous administrations is that these presidents took their American values with them, even when we had interests that in some cases were countervailing."

NAVEED JAMALI'S PARENTS WERE IMMIGRANTS—HIS FATHER from Pakistan and his mother from France. They started a small defense-contracting firm in New York City in the late 1980s that sold textbooks to federal military academies like West Point and the U.S. Naval Academy at Annapolis. Just before the fall of the Berlin Wall and the collapse of the Soviet Union, a man walked into the Jamali family's business, saying he had a list of books he wanted to order.

"He showed my dad a card that said, 'Colonel Alec Tomakin, attaché, Soviet Mission to the United Nations,'" Jamali said. "And my dad was like 'This is great. I usually have to call thirty people before I get a contract, and this guy just is walking into my office and saying he wants to do business with us, and it's the United Nations.' Fifteen minutes later, the guy leaves a list of books, walks out, and my dad gets back to work. And then there's a knock at the door, and two more guys come in. This time, it's two FBI agents, and they say, 'The guy that walked in here was a Soviet intelligence officer. What did he want?'"

That brief interaction began what would become a twenty-year relationship between his parents, the Soviets, the Russians, and the FBI. "As a young boy, I grew up watching this stuff, and it became a joke at the family dinner table," he says. "We'd talk about the Soviets, and the Russians and the FBI—the way they're just watching each other. And when the Soviet Union collapsed away, the same people, a year later came back, and instead of being the Soviets and the KGB, they were now the GRU, with the same mission, the same assets they're targeting, and the same requests" as before.

Nothing much changed once the Soviets became the Russians, according to Jamali, other than the shrinking of the massive country when its former satellites became independent. In 2005, when he was in his early twenties, he applied to be a naval intelligence officer and was turned down. But the September 11, 2001, terror attacks were still fresh in his mind, and he was determined to serve his country.

"There's this thing about being first-generation," he says, "and what it means to be an American. It's who you are," he says. "This is my home. There are not many places where the son of a philosopher from Pakistan and a French, Jewish woman can have a kid who can thrive. I felt the real desire to do something, and I didn't get in."

Next he got the "harebrained idea that perhaps if I helped the FBI, they would write me a letter of recommendation. So I sat down with FBI agents and said, 'I know the Russians. An intelligence officer came to my parents' office years ago. I'm going back to New York, and I'd like to help you, and do you think if I help you, you'll get me a letter of recommendation?' I often joke that they probably walked out and were high-fiving each other, because usually people are asking for help getting out, not getting in."

Soon Jamali was working undercover for the FBI and was set up to be "recruited" by a Russian intelligence officer, positioning him to act as a double agent. "I had no idea what I was getting into," he said. He ultimately shared the same Russian case officer as the notorious Russian double agent Anna Chapman.

Jamali believes the real danger of Donald Trump's whirling dervish presidency is that it distracts Americans from the Russian intelligence operation that undermined the 2016 election and keeps us from taking actions to prevent it from happening again.

"We, as Americans, don't understand how much the Russian [leaders] dislike the United States," he says. "The collapse of the Soviet Union was such a black mark [for them], in terms of Russian nationalism. They see it as like something that fundamentally was an attack on who they are, and they hate the United States for that." He believes the current leaders of Russia "haven't changed their viewpoint of the United States since the Cold War. They still see us as their main adversary. They knew Hillary Clinton was going to run [for president], and they decided that the best way to hurt the United States was to make the conduct of our free and open elections and our democracy come into question, and [in the process] to hurt Hillary Clinton. Remember, Trump was saying, 'if I lose, I'm gonna contest the election. I'm not going to bow out peacefully.'"

Jamali thinks that Trump may well have been fed that messaging from the Kremlin, whose talking points and beliefs about everything from election interference to the Soviet invasion of Afghanistan to whether the United States should join in defending the tiny former Soviet satellite country and newly minted NATO ally Montenegro he seemed to echo.

As various investigations seemed to close in on Trump's presidency and his business, some wondered if Trump's increasingly erratic leadership and constant courting of global economic and political instability were an indication of how far he might go if truly cornered. According to journalist Garrett M. Graff, author of *Raven Rock: The Story of the U.S. Government's Secret Plan to Save Itself—While the Rest of Us Die,*[35] some of Richard Nixon's aides worried he might use a nuclear strike to save his presidency. Would military leaders prevent Trump from going too far?

Ned Price points out that "there are very, very few, scant checks when it comes to the Commander in Chief's ability to launch something like a nuclear war." What saves us, Price says, "and what could well save us as a republic is the fact written into the Military Code of Justice, that a military officer is not obliged to follow any orders that may be illegal. The problem, however, is that it requires these individuals"—from the chairman of the Joint Chiefs of Staff to the head of the U.S. strategic command and nuclear weapons command—"all of whom have had storied military careers, to put on hats that they have rarely if ever worn before, and that's the hat of a constitutional lawyer. We shouldn't have to require our top military officials to be experts in constitutional law in addition to all of what they need to know in order to lead our armed forces."

Some Democratic members of Congress seemed to agree, and by 2019 there were rumblings in the Democratic-led House about bills that would restrict a president's ability to deploy lethal force, reasserting Congress's unique constitutional ability to declare war.

Jamali is still plagued by the underlying reasons Russia was able to infiltrate our elections systems to help make Trump president, and these were the very fissures Trump was so expert at exploiting.

"Obviously, what Russia exposed is the divisiveness in this country," says Jamali. "And the divisiveness existed long before Trump, long before the Russians, and it reached a boiling point when we elected the first black president." He believes we should make a priority out of drawing down that rancor, as surely as conducting a real and thoroughgoing investigation of what the Russians did in 2016 and how they did it.

"Two things have to happen," says Jamali. "The first is we, as a country, have to have honest discussions about some of these topics. Because the reality is that racism, bigotry, intolerance, sexism, all these things are still incredibly prevalent in our society. It's not about economic anxiety. There are just people who hate other people because of who they are, and we're glossing over that. As a country, we need to have a discussion about this.

"The second thing is that someone in the Senate, or someone in the House, hopefully both, come up with a bipartisan hearing to talk about why [the interference] was such a failure" of American intelligence. Why were the Russians "able to cause such carnage to our democracy, and how were they able to do so undetected? Were they detected but we failed to act? Was it both? So those are the two things, and really until we do those two things, then we're building whatever comes next on a lie."

Finally, we must ask what the future of the American presidency, and American global leadership, will be after Trump. Will the next president of the United States, upon inheriting a country whose global leadership had been squandered so badly, be able to set it back on its once-storied course?

ZAINAB SALBI IS A GLOBAL ACTIVIST FOR WOMEN WHOSE FAMILY fled Iraq after breaking with Saddam Hussein. She believes Trump displays an aspect "in America that has always existed and has always been seen, but mostly from abroad." Salbi says this is an "aggressive part of America, the one that's not consistent with its values; that bully part of America." Salbi sees discrepancies between the American assertion that "'we are here to stand for freedom and democracy,' and how these values get significantly compromised when America invades countries like Iraq or Afghanistan or deals with oppressive regimes."

Salbi says this has long frustrated the world about America, but Trump has shattered any pretext, "making it loud and clear" through public corruption, electoral disenfranchisement, and mistreatment of minority populations, and even autocracy and authoritarianism, that "yes, this is also us."

Trump has ripped off the veil of America's exceptionalism that one African diplomat said caused Obama to "lecture African governments" rather than listen to them, frustrating leaders who saw him as a "son of Africa" who could have tried patience instead. That diplomat predicted that the rampant voter disenfranchisement in the United States combined with the Russian

influence in America makes it unlikely that any African government would let U.S. officials into their country to observe elections or to try to promote democracy on the continent.

Many worry about how much Trump's new American reality
has destroyed the American Myth. "[America] is a country that
does stand for values that are beautiful and unique in the world,"
Salbi said. "As an immigrant here, I honestly am deeply grateful
and touched by how America welcomed me. I have an accent. I'm
different. And yet, people don't care. They say, 'We just want your
values. We want your opinion.' That is uniquely beautiful about
America: the acceptance of the other, the embracing of them, the
freedom to speak and to act. That is so beautiful about America."

Trump, with his attacks on nonwhite immigrants and
by slamming shut the golden doors of welcome and mercy to
asylum seekers and those fleeing troubled lands, has shattered
that story, too.

"We look at America and . . . even though it has always been
a country full of hypocrisy, you could hold it up as an example
of a country striving to be better," says author and activist Sisonke
Msimang, who grew up in exile when her father, a member of
Nelson Mandela's militant wing of the ANC, fled South Africa
in the 1980s. "That was the American narrative. So when Obama
comes along, part of why we admire him is because we see him as
our son and our father and our brother in Africa, but also because
we see him as part of a tradition that demonstrates that no matter
what America embodies, it is a place that is constantly striving
towards a more perfect union. And then you have Trump. And
he reverses that narrative and reminds us of every piece of cynicism that we have ever had about what America is. All those
contradictions? He confirms them. He takes away the sense of
wonder [and] admiration that we had about America.

"Now," she says, "all bets are off."

CHAPTER 7

What America Can Learn
from South Africa

"In my country we go to prison first and then become president."

—Nelson Mandela

IN DECEMBER 2018, MY HUSBAND AND I TRAVELED TO SOUTH
Africa. The trip—my first to the African continent—was a gift
to myself for my birthday. The previous two years had been emo-
tionally and physically draining, as my country became almost
alien, with Donald Trump and his political party warping every
conceivable norm in their pursuit of a particularly thuggish
brand of power. Frankly, I didn't want to spend my birthday in
his America. So, in September, I bought two tickets to Johannesburg and reached out to friends of my father, to let them know
we were coming. A month later, I was invited to participate in a
small way in the Global Citizen Festival's South Africa edition,
which would be broadcast on MSNBC.

My father was Congolese, but he spent much of his adult life
living and working in South Africa, even during apartheid. He

worked in the mining industry by day and slept in Botswana, where Africans had more freedom, before returning to the Congo later in his life to run an environmental NGO on his ancestral land. This was his penance, I suppose, for what his profession did to plunder the earth. His best mate growing up is now an official in South Africa, and this trip was a chance to meet this extended family, get to know a faraway place, and maybe see a lion and an elephant in person (we saw elephants, leopards, and more, but sadly, no lions).

It turned out to be the trip of a lifetime. I'll never forget the breathless feeling of walking out onto that stage in FNB Stadium in Johannesburg alongside Rev. Al Sharpton, who is utterly re-vered in South Africa as a man who fought for black freedom in New York at the same time that black South Africans were fight-ing for Nelson Mandela's freedom as well as their own during the last throes of the apartheid regime.

Everywhere I went in South Africa, from Constitution Hill in Johannesburg, where Mahatma Gandhi and Nelson Mandela were among the dissidents jailed in the deep underground prison; to breathtaking, hilly Cape Town, which looks like a version of Beverly Hills; to Langa and Soweto townships, where the pov-erty is as biting as any I've seen in the world but where art, entre-preneurship, and hope also flourish, I was greeted with "welcome home." It felt good, and it felt like a known quantity, for better and for worse.

When the three of us who were traveling together—two black Americans (myself and my producer, who had come down to work on "Global Citizen" with Rev. Al Sharpton and me) and my husband, the Queens-raised black Brit—received ugly stares from white patrons in a Cape Town boardwalk restaurant and knowing glances from the black waiters, we immediately under-stood what that was. This was America, down under.

South Africa is like the United States in so many ways. The physical beauty of the land, from the vistas of the Cape of Good

Hope to the neat, manicured estate homes peeking up from behind high, concrete walls (nearly every home is behind high walls), belies a racial history as ugly and violent as our own. South Africa's white minority wielded the same power, with the same naked brutality, as America's white majority, and for roughly the same number of centuries. They, too, struggled to extricate themselves from the moral rot of slavery and segregation. The main differences are in the numbers: South Africa is America "upside down," with its black population in the vast majority (plus a small but robust Southeast Asian community). And yet their apartheid (Dutch for "apartness"), supported for decades by the U.S. government, outlasted our version by a generation.

Nearly a quarter century into statutory equality, South Africans are dealing with many of the same struggles to become "postracial" as Americans are. In so doing, they have innovated in ways we haven't been able to, confronted truths Americans have often been reluctant to face, and made some progress. Their government has struggled with corruption on a level we are only now becoming starkly conversant with, and with questions of racial equity we have long understood. Today in South Africa, they are confronting questions about who has a right to own the land, how to expand access to education and economic opportunity to those locked out for centuries by law, and what it means to be a citizen in a nation built for white people when you are not white.

South Africa, like America, is a study in contrasts. Even Robben Island, the remote outpost where Mandela was imprisoned for eighteen of his twenty-seven years in captivity, possesses a strange beauty. Prisoners there, when they were allowed to leave their dank cells, could see the cloud-swept expanse of Table Mountain, surrounded by a pristine bay. Today, some of those former prisoners guide long lines of tourists through their former cells, and past the 7-by-9-foot box, with just a modest desk and chair, where Mandela spent his years imprisoned and where he secretly wrote *A Long Walk to Freedom*, which he managed to have smuggled out.

Visitors to the island pass a pastoral church, a reminder of man's capacity to pursue God while acting like the devil, as well as the bleak prison yards and the bland quarries where Mandela and the other prisoners were forced to break up limestone for hours a day and to carry their own waste in pails, emptying them just once every twenty-four hours.

When Dutch colonists arrived at the Cape of Good Hope in the mid-seventeenth century, some fifty years after the Jamestown colonists reached "the new world," they, too, deemed themselves on a mission from God. Like the men who conquered the Americas, the Boers sought to "civilize" the indigenous black Khoikhoi and other tribes they encountered, first by dispossessing them, and then by enslaving them.

The settlers, later overtaken by the British Empire, imported more slaves, from India and Malaysia, and they soon set up an intricate system of racial hierarchy that was not unlike America's "Jim Crow." Apartheid was designed to privilege the Dutch and English settlers who seized the land from the Zulu, Xhosa, and other tribes. Instituted in 1948, the same year President Harry Truman issued an executive order to desegregate the U.S. armed forces, apartheid occupied the minds of civil rights leaders from around the globe for generations.

Mohandas K. Gandhi arrived in South Africa in 1893 as a twenty-four-year-old lawyer for a local Indian trader involved in a dispute, and he left for India twenty-one years later as "Mahatma," having spent those years fighting for equal rights. Gandhi's nonviolent protests inspired Dr. Martin Luther King Jr., who called South Africa home to "the world's worst racism." While American students were facing dogs and fire hoses and fleeing firebombed buses in places such as Birmingham, Alabama, in the early 1960s, the children of impoverished townships like Soweto were dodging bullets and tear gas while fighting laws that required them to speak a foreign language, Afrikaans, and carry a pass stating their racial identity and determining where they could live, work, and walk. As in most of America before the mid-1960s, racial intermixing and marriage were strictly forbidden, both by custom and by law.

In March 1960, after nearly seventy black protesters who had gathered at the Sharpeville township police station to peacefully protest the pass laws were massacred by police officers, Dr. King called it "a tragic and shameful expression of man's inhumanity to man"[1] and warned that the bloody incident "should also serve as a warning signal to the United States where peaceful demonstrations are also being conducted by student groups," adding that, "as long as segregation continues to exist; as long as gestapo-like tactics are used by officials of southern communities; and as long as [there are] governors and United States senators [who] arrogantly defy the law of the land, the United States is faced with a potential reign of terror more barbaric than anything we see in South Africa."[2]

The Sharpeville massacre came just one month after four college students launched sit-ins at a "whites only" lunch counter in Greensboro, North Carolina, and three years after President Dwight Eisenhower federalized the Arkansas National Guard in order to ensure desegregation of Central High School in Little Rock, Arkansas. That same year, 1957, Eisenhower signed the first of what would be a series of Civil Rights Acts, which southern senators—with the notable exception of Lyndon Baines Johnson, the tough, Texan Senate majority leader—vowed to meet with "massive resistance."

King's warnings about the bloody consequences of meeting nonviolent protest with violent repression would not be heeded. America had four bloody years ahead, until the signing of the Civil Rights Act of 1964, including murder, threats of murder, the firebombing of churches and buses carrying freedom riders by segregationist terrorists in the southern states, and assassinations of black leaders, some with the complicity of local law enforcement, while J. Edgar Hoover's FBI surveilled and even threatened national black leaders. American apartheid was persistent, violent, and enduring.

South African apartheid would hang on, too, until Mandela's liberation from prison on February 11, 1990 (which, incidentally, would have been my mother's sixty-first birthday had she lived). When Mandela made his triumphant first visit to the United States that June, I was in New York and spent the day watching the ticker-tape parade, squinting at the small dot of him as he greeted the massive crowd during a speech from City Hall.

Having grown up with his story in our home and in our church, even in my youthful soundtrack—the "free Nelson Mandela" and divestment movements were an integral part of pop culture and music—and even as a young woman, not yet out of college, I felt like Mandela was waving a magic wand over America. Like he was changing us. My God, I wish he had.

When Mandela took the oath of office as South Africa's president in 1994, his country faced a question that has roiled America, too: How can it reconcile the dishonorable aspects of its past and go forward to a multiracial future?

Fear of change and a fear of the loss of power, status, and dominance have been as real in South Africa as in the United States, particularly as Mandela retired from office and then from this world, leaving his party and government in the hands of uneven and arguably corrupt leaders, Thabo Mbeki and Jacob Zuma (though there's considerably more hope in the current president, Cyril Ramaphosa). And just as in the United States and Europe, far-right and white nationalist elements are taking advantage.

Between 1986 and 2000, more than 304,000 white South Africans emigrated to Europe, Australia, and North America, and another quarter million did between 2000 and 2011. (For perspective, South Africa's population as of 2019 was nearly 58 million people, of whom approximately 5.3 million are white.)[3] Some of these émigrés formed the nexus of organizations that claimed that a "white genocide" was in effect and that their former country was "going to the dogs." White nationalists worldwide went into a spasm when South Africa's governing party sought to reverse the Natives Land Act of 1913, which had allowed the white government to strip land from indigenous Africans by force.

In Britain, Katie Hopkins, an anti-immigrant, anti-Muslim columnist (who, incidentally, appeared in 2007 as a contestant on Britain's version of *The Apprentice* with U.K. billionaire Alan Sugar in the Trump role), spread the notion that white South Africans were being "slaughtered" and their property seized.

Afrikaner identity movements have latched on to the anxieties of white South Africans who are unsure of their place in the new, black-run country, and have sought to amplify those fears. In their dark lore, the minority white population—who are just over 9 percent of the population though they own approximately 72 percent of privately held agricultural land as well as the bulk of the nation's mineral and economic wealth—are oppressed and under threat of cultural and even physical extinction. (Black South Africans, who comprise approximately 80 percent of the South African population, own about 4 percent of the country's farmland.)[4] Seeking international support from other far-right and white nationalist groups, these Afrikaner alarmists issue dark warnings that when white Americans become the minority in the United States and are subjected to governance by formerly oppressed nonwhites, they will suffer the same fate.

In the days after Barack Obama's reelection in 2012, Dan Roodt, founder of the Pro-Afrikaans Action Group, wrote in the white supremacist magazine *American Renaissance*, "What lessons can white Americans draw from our tragic demise, as they ponder the outcome of a Presidential election in which the evidence of a demographic turn for the worse is clear for all to see?"[5]

Roodt saw a Republican Party locked in a "demographic death spiral as youth, single women, blacks, Hispanics, and Asians overwhelmingly vote Democrat."

Roodt warned that the Democratic Party "could become an American version of [the] African National Congress, as immigration and high nonwhite birth rates ensure a steady stream of Democratic voters eager for change." And he echoed American white supremacist Jared Taylor in calling for the Republican Party to become the explicit champion of white interests.

In an August 2018 tweet, Donald Trump invoked South Africa, seemingly out of the blue, saying he had asked Secretary of State Mike Pompeo "to closely study the South Africa land and farm seizures and expropriations and the large scale killing of farmers," adding, "South African Government is now seizing land from white farmers." The tweet echoed a sentiment voiced not long before by Fox News host Tucker Carlson, and caused white supremacists, including David Duke and Richard Spencer, to cheer.[6]

The South African government tweeted a rebuke of the American president, saying that the country "totally rejects this narrow perception which only seeks to divide our nation and reminds us of our colonial past."

Five days after Trump's tweet, Katie Hopkins continued the theme on Twitter, claiming without evidence that a "violent, ethnic cleansing of white farmers by armed, black gangs" was taking place, adding that "the world doesn't care. Or at least the mainstream media doesn't care." Hopkins had previously called the Syrians fleeing ISIS carnage and seeking asylum in Britain "cockroaches"[7] in a column in *The Sun* (later deleted), but now she was calling for refugee status in the United Kingdom for white farmers. She even traveled to South Africa to document the supposed rash of murders of white farmers, but she found little to back up her claims.

"There are some people in the American, British and Australian right who are trying to make a lot of political capital out of spurious stories intended to stir up white anxiety," said Andries du Toit, a researcher at the University of the Western Cape who specializes in the politics of poverty and inequality in South Africa. He also recognizes "very deep parallels between white racism in South Africa and in the U.S.," and believes Trump has traded on white anxiety, using South Africa's travails as a pretext.

"I'm not really even sure the right word for it is 'anxiety,'" du Toit says of South Africa's version of those fears. "Anxiety portrays a vulnerable person who is feeling that they are being attacked. I think 'resentment' is probably a better word for what's going on."

So, can America learn anything from South Africa's attempts to reconcile its past? From Johannesburg to Pretoria, South Africans—black and white—are almost preternaturally friendly but also incredibly frank about what their country was such a short time ago.

The Apartheid Museum in Cape Town is brutally honest. Nearly everyone, from car drivers to tour operators, acknowledged the ongoing disparity in wealth and opportunity based on race, and they said their country has a long way to go. On the bus ride to Robben Island, the young, lanky tour guide, a black South African in his twenties, with neatly coiled dreads, joked dryly with the mixed-race passengers after asking where everyone was from: "We have a complicated relationship with the Dutch and the English." The few of us on the bus who were black understood that this wasn't meant as mere humor. Such frankness about race, from black and white South Africans, felt refreshing and surprisingly healthy.

A group of black and white schoolchildren in identical uniforms bounced past our Marriott "African Pride" hotel, a hopeful sign. Everywhere we went, we were told that black South African children suffer from inferior schooling, poorer health and housing, and harder lives than white children. Some black middle-class South Africans have moved into the gated homes in Johannesburg. Before Mandela died, and after his divorce from his second wife, Winnie, who kept his legacy alive throughout his incarceration, and kept the freedom movement going in sometimes-controversial fashion, he lived in a charming, large estate, where his third wife still resides. Even after South Africa launched a groundbreaking commission to publicly reckon with its past, the country is still not whole.

Du Toit, who is white, said it's important to understand that South African society is "absolutely founded on white supremacy," and that under the official racial oppression in South Africa, "everybody who was white was part of it and was therefore in some way complicit and benefiting from the institutions of white supremacy, whether you were personally a racist or not." He believes many white South Africans were not racists and wanted blacks to be treated well and paid fairly, and they attempted to interact with their fellow South Africans with kindness. "But," he said, "even those people—all of us—were in some way systematic beneficiaries of white supremacy.

"Of course," he said, "a very significant portion of white society actively participated in actual discrimination, in belittling and reducing the dignity of black people, and were themselves part of the politics of resentment and hatred and rage against black people. That was just par for the course for South Africa during the time of apartheid." And then, he says, "in 1994, we changed from a society based on racial discrimination and white supremacy and the daily enactment of racism, to a society in which racism is the constitutive political sin."

Du Toit said that white South Africans have reacted to changes in their country similarly to the way Americans have— by banishing the notion of racism to the darkest corners of society, even while the real thing lingers on.

"To be identified as a racist [in today's South Africa] is to be defined as not being part of the political discourse at all," he said.

"You'd be very hard-pressed to find any white person who had lived in South Africa at the time who will ever admit to having supported apartheid at all. That whole history of complicity with racism and white supremacy has simply been erased from the collective memory."

But du Toit says that racism goes hand in hand with its denial. He recalls an incident[8] in 2001 when a group of four white policemen set their dogs on a group of detained black immigrants and videotaped it, "for their own amusement."

"When this came out, it caused a paroxysm of outrage in the country," he says. "But many people said, 'Why are you assuming these guys are racist? They may have other reasons for doing this.' Well if letting dogs loose on defenseless black prisoners isn't racism, what is? And yet it was possible in South African discourse at the time to say, 'No, no, this is not racist.' So that sort of politics of denial is very much part of the context of the time."

Du Toit says Katie Hopkins speaking out on behalf of white farmers was unwelcome in the new South Africa. He said that even white South Africans said, "We don't want anything to do with that." And the reaction to Donald Trump taking up the cause of the Afrikaner minority was, according to du Toit, " 'butt out. We don't need you to come in here. You're just going to make things worse.' "

Much as it happened in America after the 1954 *Brown v. Board of Education* ruling, after apartheid fell, many white South African parents pulled their children from the public school system, which had erected separate institutions for white, black, "colored," and Indian or "Malay" students. The school culture of South Africa and America evolved in much the same way.

Author and activist Sisonke Msimang recalls a young woman at a rare high-quality mixed-race public school in South Africa who was told she could not come to school with her hair in an Afro—a story with echoes in the United States. Starting in 2015, black South African students began demanding the removal of statues on college campuses and public parks of Cecil John Rhodes, the brutal founder of the former Rhodesia—now Zimbabwe. (In photos taken of Dylann Roof, before he slaughtered nine churchgoers inside Mother Emanuel Church in Charleston, South Carolina, in June 2015, he had a Rhodesian flag affixed to his jacket, alongside the apartheid-era South African flag.)

Cries by black South African students of "Rhodes Must Fall" echo the calls on American college campuses for the removal of statues and plaques commemorating slave owners such as John Calhoun and Robert E. Lee. And those fights, which black South Africans, through their superior numbers and acquisition of political power, were often able to win, sometimes exacerbated white grievances.

In May 2018, members of AfriForum embarked on a tour of the United States. This ironically named group, formed in 2006 to oppose land reforms and counter the historical narrative of what they call the "so-called injustice" of apartheid, claimed to have more than 200,000 Afrikaner members and called itself a "civil rights organization." Washington, D.C., was the first stop on a tour to spread their message of impending doom and to make their case that white farmers were the true victims of South African racism.

In D.C., the group's CEO, Kallie Kriel, and deputy CEO, Ernst Roets, met with high-profile U.S. officials, including staffers at USAID and in the office of Texas senator Ted Cruz, plus a member of Congress the men would not name. Kriel and Roets said that while they were in the Capitol, they happened upon John Bolton, Trump's hawkish new national security adviser, and took a photo with him, which they posted to their social media accounts. They also had meetings at the CATO Institute and the Heritage Foundation, both of which had opposed divestment and trade sanctions against the apartheid regime during the 1980s. The AfriForum representatives distributed copies of Roets's book, and they appeared on Tucker Carlson's Fox News show, where they recounted alleged tales of violence against white farmers. Their message found receptive audiences in far-right U.S. figures including Mike Cernovich, Ann Coulter, and conspiracy theorist Alex Jones.

Msimang said that "AfriForum is a fringe group that has worked very hard to become less fringe." She wrote a widely read article that rebuked Trump for his "white farmers" tweet. "I remember a few years ago starting to worry that the message that they are preaching is so seductive to white people around the world because of the sense that South Africa is the last outpost of whiteness in Africa. I remember thinking to myself, this is actually a dangerous message, not because it's crazy . . . 'cause it is crazy, right? . . . but because of the ways in which global whiteness works."

Msimang was born in Swaziland and grew up in Zambia, Kenya, and Canada, after her father's flight from South Africa, where he was a member of Nelson Mandela's Umkhonto we Sizwe, the armed wing of the ANC, which her great-uncle helped to found. Her father's journey took him as far away as Russia, where she says she had many "Russian aunties" who married the freedom fighters exiled from the apartheid regime. The family returned to South Africa after Mandela was freed in 1990, when Msimang was a teenager, though she continued to globe-trot, attending Macalester College in Saint Paul, Minnesota, and ultimately settling in Australia.

She recalls a college professor in Cape Town, Njabulo Ndebele, who writes about the power and reach of "international whiteness," and says Ndebele "talks about how white South Africans have always had a special status as citizens who belong to the world because they're white," whereas "black South Africans have worked hard just to become citizens of South Africa. That's what the struggle against apartheid was. White South Africans were always part of something bigger, which is the white world. So when we see in America an increasingly overt embrace of racism—including very crude racism, AfriForum is able to appeal to that sense of 'international whiteness' that white South Africans have always enjoyed."

Msimang sees in South Africa "an increasing sense of desperation among white people as they lose relevance, as the population shrinks, and as black people's sense of self-assuredness, confidence, and education" come into play. "So white people aren't special anymore," she says. "And I think this is part of why you see this mentality of AfriForum feeling like they are very much under siege and therefore calling on that card of whiteness and using it to go to Canada, to go to the UK, and to go to America" to appeal for support. "The fact that they are able to have very senior-level meetings with U.S. diplomats is deeply problematic but also unsurprising if you think about this frame of international whiteness as a 'thing.'"

Msimang says even after apartheid, white South Africans operated on a fear of black violence, just as the United States had after the civil rights movement. But unlike the Kingian movement in America or the Ghandian defiance against British rule of India, Mandela's struggle began as a declaration of war. He was the son of a Xhosa tribal chief, and the Umkhonto we Sizwe were determined to ignite a revolution.

"Throughout the 1980s, you had a very tumultuous and violent people's revolution," she says. "Nelson Mandela is in prison. His party, the ANC, decides that the idea of a revolutionary war, of having a guerrilla war is not going to work because the South African army is big, it's mighty. South Africa is the U.S. of Africa in a sense, so they're very well equipped and very well resourced. And so our attempts as black people to fight them with guns was not working. We were a guerrilla army. It wasn't working.

"So," she adds, "in the 1980s a strategy is embarked on which says we will make this country ungovernable. We are demographically more than white people, so making the country ungovernable means burning tires at every street corner; it means making the townships where black people lived hard to manage and tiring them out. It meant cutting electricity connections and reconfiguring them so that we were getting free electricity, because we were saying it's an immoral government, so they have no right for us to pay them for electricity or water connections. So the 1980s is incredibly violent. There's chaos. This brings the apartheid government to its knees.

"What it also does is create this specter of black violence," she continues, which translated into a fear of black governance. After Mandela's release, however, the ANC did the unexpected. "They decide to completely pull back, renounce violence, and say, 'now we're at the peacemaking table,'" Msimang says. "In part, they do that because of a fear of the international financial markets and that the world was watching and was concerned about white South Africans and their safety. So black South Africans, represented by the ANC, embark on this negotiation process where it is foremost in our minds that we have to protect white people. We have to make them feel comfortable. This is how the Mandela narrative of reconciliation and unity emerges: that if we're going to move forward, it has to be on the basis of peace.

"One of the first acts of the new parliament once Mandela took charge was to pass the Truth and Reconciliation Act, which established a commission to look backwards at apartheid," Msimang says. It would examine "the crimes that were committed against black people, the murders that happened under the rubric of apartheid, and the places where black victims' bodies had been buried, so that black people could forgive white people, and we could move forward cleanly into the future."

But Msimang sees caution flags for Americans who believe that our future lies in a Truth and Reconciliation process of our own, to reckon with the ghosts of slavery, lynching, and Jim Crow.

"People will argue about this, but my view is that one of the crucial mistakes" of the Truth and Reconciliation process in

South Africa, she says, "was that although it's very concerned with individual crimes, it didn't accept that the overall crime of apartheid was that if you were black, you could not live in a particular area. You could not be educated." It didn't, she says, address the mass discrimination against black people, which was much like slavery in America.

She says the deficits were material. As with "the refusal of America to give reparations to black people," she says, "we never had the ability to make the calculation of the cost, in order for us to move forward. What it meant for you as a black person to have to live sixty kilometers from the center of the economy. What it meant for you to be placed on the least desirable land in the country. What it meant for you to have to flash a pass every time you had to move from one area to the other. This is how much black people economically have been disadvantaged. That discussion, that narrative, and that check never came.

"So white South Africans are forgiven," she says. "Nothing happens to their economic status, and many of them refuse to acknowledge fully the horror of apartheid and their complicity in it. Black people are being fed this narrative that we have to forgive, that this is part of the grace of the oppressed. And then slowly this new generation of 'born frees,' these kids who were born twenty-five years ago when South Africa became free and who have grown up in a post-apartheid country, but whose lives economically have been pretty crappy and who continue to ex-perience racism and continue to live in segregated communities while white people continue to live in really nice places and to operate with impunity and to be racist towards us. This genera-tion is like, 'we are not having it anymore.'"

That new sense of confidence, even militancy, which includes "refusing to use white people's language, debating about what it means to be black, becoming assertive and putting white people on notice, has terrified white people," Msimang says. "AfriForum is in part a consequence of this new, defiant, and very confident young black South African."

Du Toit agrees with the reasons the Truth and Reconciliation process largely failed.

"I think the TRC was a very important part of the transition," he says, "but one of its strengths *and* limitations was that it was very much framed in an explicitly religious, Christian discourse, in which notions of forgiveness were absolutely central to it." He says this was due in large part to the prominent role played by South African archbishop Desmond Tutu, who carries a tremendous moral authority as a Nobel Peace Prize winner (in 1984) and South Africa's best-known religious leader.

That Christian vision of amazing grace "short-circuited the moral reckoning that was necessary," says du Toit. "Many perpetrators of human rights abuses on the white side did not come forward. It's also true that the African National Congress, which had also been guilty of human rights violations against its own members—there have been horrific stories of torture of people that have been suspected of being spies for the apartheid regime—did not come clean.

"And the whole question of reparations was not taken seriously enough. The new government explicitly refused to consider the matter of paying financial reparations to people who had suffered. So, I think people who were cynical about it were probably correct to be cynical. I think it has not succeeded in drawing out this poison of the past. I think it was extremely important politically at the time as a part of the process of transition, but I think it fell short of its aims."

Du Toit says white South Africans, like many Americans, have decided that the best path forward is to simply start from zero, as if they and their black countrymen are now on a level playing field. To wipe it all clean as if nothing bad ever happened. Such a path rarely leads to true reconciliation. I will never forget a nationally prominent member of the black clergy in America telling me after the Mother Emanuel massacre that black people have had enough of "Amazing Grace." We have a right to be angry, and to seethe at the squandering of our lives by those who are bent on racial destruction.

"By the late 1970s and early 1980s," du Toit says, "most white South Africans were able to decisively enter the urban elite, have university educations, and be sure that their children would have careers as managers, lawyers, doctors, and so on. So, in a way, racial discrimination as such was no longer necessary, and you could demolish that scaffolding of privilege without actually worrying that you were going to lose your sources of advantage."

Du Toit says many white South Africans came to believe that it was enough to simply be color-blind and that black South Africans, "if they just work hard enough, should be able to get access to university and should be able to get a decent income. Therefore, there's a kind of a discourse against 'affirmative action,' which we call 'black economic empowerment' here. And there's a blindness to the reality of white privilege. And in that context, quite a lot of racial resentment has surfaced." As a result, he says, "a lot of particularly young black people in South Africa at the moment are very cynical about white people." It all sounds achingly familiar.

That cynicism extends to views of America, which looms large in the imaginations of South Africans, particularly after Barack Obama was elected president in 2008. "I think in a way Barack Obama and Nelson Mandela stood for a certain kind of tradition of radically democratic and inclusive politics that I think continues to be extremely important in South Africa," says du Toit, though "the picture of Mandela that circulates in the international media is a misrepresentation of who he really was; portraying him as a kind of 'Christ-like' figure of redemption and forgiveness and reconciliation.

"He was that," Du Toit says, "but it's important to remember that the reason Mandela could end the armed struggle was because he began it." It's an echo of the postcard rendering of Dr. King, who is remembered in death as much less militant than he was in life. Like King, Mandela was a transitional figure, whose historical role was to make it possible for South Africa to move from horror to hope. Du Toit believes that Obama's role was to show America, and the world, a glimpse of what a multi-racial future could be.

So what about Trump?

Perhaps he is a transitional figure, too. He has certainly re-minded us of our vulnerabilities—of the ways in which our un-solved racial tribalism and mutual suspicion can be easily roused and used against us, by an American demagogue and by a for-eign adversary. Racial resentment, xenophobia, and nativism fueled Trump's candidacy and allowed the Russians through the doorway.

Nelson Mandela was South Africa's warrior who became a statesman so that his country could become a nation. He saw racial reconciliation as a national security imperative. America has no Mandela now. We have the opposite in power—a presi-dent who stokes racial and cultural division almost daily. So what are we to do?

CHAPTER 8

The Media in the Trump Age

*"Publicity, publicity, publicity is the greatest moral factor
and force in our public life."*

— Joseph Pulitzer

OF DONALD TRUMP'S MANY FRAUGHT RELATIONSHIPS—WITH
women, Latinos, African-Americans, our European allies, to
name only a few—none has been as frayed, or as complicated, as
his interactions with the media.

The New York media arguably created Donald Trump as a
larger-than-life character. During the 1980s and 1990s, he was a
staple of the New York *Daily News* (at the time owned by businessman Mort Zuckerman) and the Rupert Murdoch–owned *New
York Post*. They covered his real estate exploits and his battles with
characters like the irascible mayor Ed Koch, over Trump's bid to
redevelop the Central Park skating rink, and the gossip pages had
regular updates on his liaisons and exploits with women.

"He knew the movers and shakers to hit, to keep himself in
the media, like [the *New York Post*'s gossip column] Page Six,"

said Rev. Al Sharpton, who battled the New York establishment over racist incidents that left young black men dead at the hands of white mobs in Bensonhurst, Brooklyn, and Howard Beach, Queens. "He didn't come down the main highway to fame. He came through the side ramps." Trump was portrayed in the New York papers as an almost "Great Gatsby–esque" figure, Sharpton says.

David Dinkins's election in 1989 tore New York City in two. Black voters were thrilled to have a first black mayor after eleven tumultuous years of cantankerous Mayor Koch, but Dinkins's arrival came at a time of vicious racial tumult in the city's five boroughs, which became national news with a 1984 incident in which a white subway rider, Bernhard Goetz, shot four black teenagers aboard a New York City subway train; he claimed self-defense and was acquitted on all but unlicensed firearm charges. When five black and Hispanic teenagers were accused in the beating and gang rape of a twenty-eight-year-old white jogger in 1989, Trump used his penchant for media exposure to get involved.

Yusuf Salaam, one of the teens who was goaded by police into signing false confessions and put in prison for between seven and thirteen years in the "Central Park Jogger case," wrote decades later that "though we were innocent, we spent our formative years in prison, branded as rapists. During our trial, it seemed like every New Yorker had an opinion. But no one took it further than Trump. He called for blood in the most public way possible. Trump used his money to take out full-page ads in all of the city's major newspapers, urging the reinstatement of the death penalty in New York."[1]

Sharpton recalls that Trump "was like the guy we marched against in Bensonhurst and Howard Beach. He wasn't a Bill Buckley kind of conservative." He wasn't exactly doing politics on an intellectual scale. Sharpton believes Trump was so determined to weigh in on the Central Park Five incident because "he was playing to the police unions and his buddies in the NYPD because he came out of Queens."

With former U.S. attorney Rudy Giuliani on the rise and poised to lead a pro-cop crusade against Dinkins in the next mayoral election, Trump was simply choosing his natural side. "The construction guys on his sites were anti-Dinkins and the police union guys were his friends," Sharpton said. "That was his social circle. He wasn't exactly hanging out at Sylvia's" soul food restaurant in Harlem.

Some of the reporters covering Trump as president go back to that era, like the *New York Times*' Maggie Haberman, who covered City Hall for the *New York Post* and the New York *Daily News* as "The Donald" was climbing the local ladder, and many consider her a "Trump whisperer" for her unique ability to get her calls returned by Trump, to land exclusive interviews, and to allow the public to peer inside Trump's head through her active and popular Twitter feed. *Vanity Fair* writer Joe Pompeo called Haberman "the queen of political journalism at a time when Trump's reality-television administration has supercharged the news business, with hundreds of thousands of new subscribers flocking to legacy publications like the *Times* and *The Washington Post*, TV ratings through the roof, and a refreshing bump in public trust, according to a new Reuters survey, for the 'fake-news media,'"[2] as Trump has dubbed the mainstream, non-Trumpian press.

Haberman, for her part, notes that part of her access stems from Trump's fundamental need. "He wouldn't talk to me as much as he does if I wasn't at the *Times*," Pompeo recounts the reporter telling a political podcast. "That's just the reality. He craves the paper's approval."

Indeed, Trump has a long-documented obsession with the *New York Times* that has carried over to the White House.

While Trump granted the conservative Fox News Channel

more interviews than any other outlet—forty-one in his first two years as president[3]—and denounced the adversarial press as "fake news," he has definitely not shunned mainstream outlets like the *Times* (which he called "failing"). He has given the paper multiple lengthy, rambling interviews, flattering Haberman and chief White House correspondent Peter Baker and imploring the newspaper's publisher, A. G. Sulzberger, to give him positive coverage.

"I came up from Jamaica, Queens, Jamaica Estates, and I became president of the United States," he pleaded in a session intended to address his frequent attacks on the press. "I'm sort of entitled to a great story from my—just one—from my newspaper."[4] According to the published transcript, he asked an aide who was attempting to end the interview, "What's more important than the *New York Times*?"[5]

Trump was a perfect media candidate for president. His rallies were raucous and entertaining. He shared a talent for wry wit even in the course of threatening violence against protesters, with progenitors like Huey Long or George Wallace. The coordinated chanting: "Lock her up!" and "Build the wall"—"Who's gonna pay for it . . . ? Mexico!" made for great television. And great ad revenue, too.

In a moment of perhaps too-much candor, then-CEO and executive chairman of CBS Les Moonves (who would later be driven out in a sexual harassment scandal) called Trump's presidential bid a "circus" that he dearly hoped kept coming to town. At a Morgan Stanley technology conference in February 2016, Moonves all but gushed, "Man, who would have expected the ride we're all having right now? . . . The money's rolling in and this is fun."[6] Moonves told the conference that "Donald's place in this election is a good thing." The ads may not be about issues, he said, and Trump's run was "full of bomb throwing," but on the upside, "there's a lot of money in the marketplace."[7] Moonves's blunt conclusion would make headlines: "It May Not Be Good for America, but It's Damn Good for CBS."[8] He admitted that it was all a terrible thing to say.

As spectacle, Trump delivered the ratings. When he bragged that the TV networks "loved" him because the people were tuning in, he wasn't wrong. And in pure dollars and cents, the "Trump for President Show" got back as good as it gave.

The show Trump put on during his run for president earned him between $2 billion and $6 billion in free media, depending on the estimate. The tracking service MediaQuant estimated that Trump received "$4.96 billion in free earned media in the year leading up to the presidential election," and "$5.6 billion throughout the entirety of his campaign, more than Hillary Clinton, Bernie Sanders, Ted Cruz, Paul Ryan and Marco Rubio combined."[9] That was money he didn't have to spend out of his own pocket—something campaign aides said he was loath, or perhaps unable, to do.

Trump may not be the most sophisticated man, but he is a savvy media player. One former *Apprentice* contestant recalled that during the auditions process, which included hundreds of aspirants all gathered at rows of tables at once, Mark Burnett controlled events, but Trump commanded the room. He lacked discipline on the show set, but he knew what he wanted to get out of a scene. He could be eminently charming in person, as well as utterly calculating, remembering aspects of a contestant's life or career that could benefit him in future business deals. The "boardroom" was a set Burnett built in Trump Tower, and the show was filmed just a few floors from Trump's apartment. He used the show to hawk everything, and even made the contestants drink Trump water (the former contestant said it was "terrible"). He had real-life business executives, some from well-known companies, parade through the set, sometimes with their families, in what looked like a soft pitch (or a hard sell) to do business with Trump.

Despite his long-running success at navigating the media, Trump complains constantly to his core supporters that he is disrespected by the media's upper echelons. When he ran for president, just two major U.S. newspapers out of the hundred with the largest circulations endorsed him over Hillary Clinton. (Even third-party candidate Gary Johnson got twice as many newspaper endorsements as Trump.[10]) Of the two newspapers to endorse Trump for president, the *Las Vegas Review-Journal* is owned by his largest donor, Sheldon Adelson, and the other, the *Florida Times Union*,[11] was in his second-home state, where lots of men like Trump, determined to escape the cold, the high taxes, and the liberal sensibilities of the Northeast, go to retire, turning that state redder and redder with every election cycle.

Trump reflects the portion of the country that has long believed the media looks down on them and their values. They echo the southerners who chafed at northern newspaper coverage of lynching in the decades after black newspaperwoman Ida B. Wells and her fellow antilynching crusaders cajoled and shamed the nation's press for their matter-of-fact treatment of the hangings, shootings, castration, burnings at the stake, and draggings of black men, women, and even children, including black soldiers returning from World War I.

Robert A. Gibson, author of *The Negro Holocaust: Lynching and Race Riots in the United States, 1880-1950*, wrote that the bloodless coverage of southern carnage, which sometimes included advance word of the extra-judicial killings to come, occurred because "many white people believed that Negroes could only be controlled by fear."[12] Besides, the premise of the vigilantes' rage was rarely challenged in the newspaper stories published, and all of the dead were deemed guilty.

Over time Wells and civil rights organizations like the NAACP persuaded newspapers to change their coverage, and to confront the horror of what they saw. By the 1950s, when northern newspapers sent reporters south to cover desegregation efforts led by civil rights activists, the narrative included villains, who were white, and victims, who were black. Many white southerners believed this more empathetic coverage was "riling up" otherwise docile and compliant "Negro" citizens as surely as were the civil rights leaders and other "outside agitators." Southerners viewed their own resistance to desegregation as merely protecting their way of life, not some proof of their moral monstrosity, and the northern interlopers were unfairly scrutinizing communities they knew nothing about.

This view was reinforced by the Ku Klux Klan's messaging that blacks would have remained quiescent if not for a mythical cartel of international, communist Jews, who controlled everything from the banks to the federal government to the burgeoning civil rights movement and the media, too.

Northern newspapers at that time were also competing for black readers with black-owned newspapers like the *Baltimore Afro-American* and New York's *Amsterdam News*, and with national magazines like *Jet*, which during its heyday in the 1950s was the "*Newsweek*" of Black America. *Jet* was where Emmett Till's mother went to display pictures of her lynched fourteen-year-old boy's ruined body, laid out in a casket with his bludgeoned face shown to the world, and where the first images of Martin Luther King Jr. were seen as he lay in a hospital bed after a 1958 stabbing attempt in Harlem by a deranged black woman who approached his book signing. If the mainstream press wanted to earn black dollars, they simply had to change.

Once coverage of civil rights, race relations, and desegregation shifted north, to places like Chicago, Detroit, and New York, the notion that the media favored black rights over white freedoms took hold there, too. When Boston erupted in race riots over the busing of black students into the suburbs' predominantly white schools, a September 25, 1974, *Harvard Crimson* reported, "Many busing opponents on Sixth Street said they blamed the liberal press for the state of affairs. After all, it was the press, they said, that had made busing a momentous issue initially."

After describing incidents in which a reporter and photographer were attacked, the article said, "Thomas Winship, editor of *The [Boston] Globe*, acknowledged the significance of press accounts by issuing a directive to all reporters . . . The memo largely instructed journalists to keep level heads and to make special efforts to report the news fairly. It said, for instance, that headlines, which 'many of our readers will not get beyond,' should be written with 'delicacy.'" [13]

The right's view that the media was biased against traditional, conservative values was exacerbated by critical coverage of the Vietnam War, and what was seen as overly sympathetic takes on those who refused to serve in it. When the popular heavyweight boxing champion Muhammad Ali became a face of black resistance to the war, it created a huge ripple among his young fans, black and white. Ali had joined the Nation of Islam and was a friend and mentee of Malcolm X, the outspoken devotee of Marcus Garvey–ite black self-determination. Malcolm was a counterweight to Dr. King, and he was a particularly frightening figure to white Americans. Ali, like King, was young, attractive, and expert at using television, the new dominant media force.

The civil rights movement was made for the TV age, filled with images of impeccably dressed black schoolchildren being fire hosed by remorseless uniformed sheriffs armed with German shepherds and nightsticks, of burnt buses and shaken white and black "freedom riders" giving emotional interviews in front of bus stations with garish "white" and "colored" signs overhead, of bespectacled black collegians having cups of water hurled at them at the local Woolworth's by scowling young white men in dress shirts and polos, and of figures such as James Baldwin and celebrities like Harry Belafonte and Sydney Poitier appearing regularly on talk shows, offering devastating critiques of America's system of racial apartheid, including in debates with conservative stalwarts like *The National Review*'s William F. Buckley.

Television amplified the civil rights era as a national morality play.

A 1961 CBS report featuring a white-gloved, hatted lady of southern high society, Mrs. George Bridges of Birmingham, Alabama, exemplified the challenge. Mrs. Bridges told Howard K. Smith (in a segment produced by Edward R. Murrow) how little prejudice her community held by recounting the story of a "Negro" boy, "from the Negro schools," who surprisingly won an art contest she sponsored as the Alabama representative for UNICEF. The boy, she explained, had been refused entry to the "white library" to receive his accolade—a situation she remedied with a phone call so that he and his family could gain "special permission to enter the library"[14] just that once. The segment must have made Mrs. Bridges seem like quite an anachronism to the rest of America, even in 1961.

White suburbanites watching the coverage on the three networks would have seen southern and northern parents who looked and sounded a lot like them, shrieking at frightened black children and teenagers as National Guard troops enforced school desegregation. The Hollywood stars at the March on Washington, and the telegenic Democratic president and his glamorous first lady were all on one ideological side. The moral asymmetry of the peaceful marchers on the Edmund Pettus Bridge and the dogs, fire hoses, and batons unleashed on them by white sheriffs and policemen was amplified by the moving images.

If television and the dramatic images it carried were unhelpful to those hoping to slow down a changing culture, they would prove even more damaging to prosecutors and supporters of America's war in Vietnam, belying a long history of media-government collaboration.

The media—newspapers and newsreels—had been among the most powerful tools in the government's quiver during the nation's prior wars. The modern White House press corps was born in the 1890s, during the era of President William McKinley, who led the nation into the Spanish-American War. In the run-up to the conflict, which was driven by America's designs on the former Spanish colony of Cuba, Americans thrilled to the jingoistic "yellow journalism" of Joseph Pulitzer's *New York World* and William Randolph Hearst's rival *New York Journal*. The papers used wry comics and sensationalized coverage of alleged Spanish atrocities in Cuba to whip up war fever—and sell lots of papers. When America had its eye on Hawaii, the newspapers' overwrought coverage of the plight of white planters and ugly, racialized stereotyping of the island's congenital queen helped popularize the land grab. The Spanish-American War was considered the country's first "media war."

At that time, before radio broadcasting, the White House wasn't able to communicate with the entire nation. Newspapers were Americans' primary source of information, which made the New York tabloids that much more powerful. In Washington, reporters hoping to offer more sober coverage had to stand outside the White House, grab visitors who were leaving, and ask what the president had said to them. Jay Rosen, media critic and New York University journalism professor, said an official in the McKinley White House eventually "had the bright idea of saying, 'well, why don't we just invite them in and give them a room, so they can work.' It sounds like a nice thing to do, from the point of view of the reporters out in the rain. But when you're inviting them in, that's the first step in taming them."

With radio technology expanding its reach, journalism found itself with greater influence, but under tremendous stress. As the nation entered World War I, the Woodrow Wilson administration and Congress passed speech-chilling laws against not just espionage but also "sedition." Wilson created a Committee on Public Information that, in media historian Christopher Daly's words, "elevated propaganda and censorship to strategic elements of all-out war." The president, Daly wrote, "waged a campaign of intimidation and outright suppression against those ethnic and socialist papers that continued to oppose the war. Taken together, these wartime measures added up to an unprecedented assault on press freedom." [15] Americans were expected to speak with one voice—one that supported the war and the government.

The media was equally compliant during World War II, with the press playing a vital role in the war effort. America got its news during the war not just from the radios in nearly every home and newspapers, which by then numbered more than 11,000 nationwide, but also in newsreels that preceded popular films in movie theaters. Hollywood was "all in" for the war—with famous actors heading to the front, and famed comedians and actresses participating by entertaining the troops. And the press was, too. War correspondents were embedded with the troops and experiencing the fight firsthand.

The FDR administration exerted strict control over the news through direct censorship by the Office of War Information (OWI), through which all news reports had to pass, via a "Code of Wartime Practices for the American Press," which was adopted voluntarily by every American news organization,[16] and through an unwritten code of patriotic coverage that every journalist who wished to work followed to the letter.

The moral clarity of the war's mission—defeating Nazism and the Axis powers—and the day-by-day coverage gave reporters clear marching orders. And so, as then-reporter John Steinbeck later recalled, "There were no cowards in the American Army, and of all the brave men, the private in the infantry was the bravest and noblest. The reason for this in terms of the War Effort was obvious. The infantry private had the dirtiest, weariest, least rewarding job in the whole war. In addition to being dangerous, a great many of the things he had to do were stupid. He must therefore be reassured that these things he knew to be stupid were actually necessary and wise, and that he was a hero for doing them . . . A second convention held that we had no cruel or ambitious or ignorant commanders." [17]

As Steinbeck recalled, reporters understood that they were "all a part of the War Effort. We went along with it, and not only that, we abetted it. Gradually it became a part of all of us that the truth about anything was automatically secret and that to trifle with it was to interfere with the War Effort. By this I don't mean that the correspondents were liars . . . [but] it is in the things not mentioned that the untruth lies." [18]

When in February 1968, CBS *Evening News* anchor Walter Cronkite used his perch as the most trusted man in America to declare that the Vietnam War was all but lost, supporters of the conflict felt he had breached a fundamental trust. Although the OWI was long gone, Cronkite had been among the journalists who dutifully covered the war with patriotism in mind, and who repeated the fictions offered by the Johnson administration about why the war began and whether we were winning.

As the conflict dragged on, journalists began to bring the war's nightmare into America's living rooms and the protesters shifted from "unwashed hippies" to former soldiers, including decorated officers like Navy lieutenant John Kerry, the articulate, patrician spokesman for Vietnam Veterans Against the War. As Vietnam became an anvil around Lyndon Johnson's neck—so much so that he would choose not to seek reelection—the narratives beaming directly to Americans via their morning newspaper and during the dinner hour truly sank in. For decades, Republicans blamed the media for meddling and negativity that caused America to lose its first war—a war they believed it could have won.

By the 1980s, TV news found itself competing with conservative AM talk radio stations that freed their listeners from having to hear from the "mainstream media" at all. By the late 1990s, the

Fox News Channel provided an alternative to Ted Turner's Cable News Network (CNN). Fox News was launched by veteran Republican communications strategist Roger Ailes, under the growing umbrella of Australian media baron Rupert Murdoch, whose company, News Corporation, had already purchased the *New York Post* and part of the movie studio 20th Century Fox.

Under Ailes, Fox News, using its primary color graphics and its slogan "fair and balanced," plugged into decades of discontent and conservative viewers' sense of victimization by the mainstream press. It gave their viewers a parallel reality where sympathy accrued in their direction, where the world was portrayed the way they believed it to be, and where the people they most feared or loathed could be "exposed" as the *true* villains in the American story.

Fox News' mix of news and Republican messaging called on Ailes's specialties as Richard Nixon's TV "executive producer" and as communications consultant to Ronald Reagan and George H. W. Bush, for whom he took the Lee Atwater "southern strategy" prime time. Fox News shared with conservative talk radio programs hosted by high-voltage performers like Rush Limbaugh a determination to find the "truth" the mainstream media was "hiding" about the "dangers" of illegal immigration, "unpatriotic" kneeling by NFL players, and "lawless" Black Lives Matter activists who "hate police." Fox News was programmed to keep its core viewers exercised.

A January 2017 Pew Research study found that 40 percent of Trump voters name Fox News as their main source of information, versus 19 percent of the general public and just 3 percent of Hillary Clinton voters. Only 8 percent of Trump voters listed CNN as their main source of news, followed by Facebook at 7 percent, NBC at 6 percent, and local news at 5 percent.[19] When political scientists Matt Grossmann and Dave Hopkins compiled five years of Public Policy Polling data, from 2010 to 2015, on viewer trust in the major broadcast and cable networks by party, the results were stark: Republicans were as distrustful of the broadcast television networks as they were of MSNBC, while Democrats tended to be distrustful of Fox News, but roughly equally trusting in mainstream media outlets and MSNBC.

And Fox News' influence is not just a matter of who viewers trust to give them information. A September 2017 study for the *American Economic Review* by researchers Gregory J. Martin and Ali Yurukoglu found that even though Fox News was a relatively small part of the overall media universe, it was significantly more influential on actual voting behavior than CNN or MSNBC. The study determined that Fox News had influenced presidential election outcomes between 2000 and 2008 through "a combination of increasing viewership and increasingly conservative slant on Fox News," and that a desire by their viewers for "like-minded news" had caused political polarization to increase between 2000 and 2012.

Political and racial polarization existed long before Trump or Fox News, of course, but today only 7 percent of respondents in a December 10, 2018, *Washington Post* Fact Checker poll said that Democrats and Republicans are more likely to agree on basic facts than they were ten years ago, and 68 percent said they are less so.[20] Increasingly, where you get your news determines what you believe is true, and Americans hold wildly divergent beliefs about the plain facts of well-documented events, driven by ideology and political tribe. The rise of Fox News has played a significant part in our disagreements about what is, and is not, true.

Jay Rosen dates this trend back to the Barry Goldwater era in the early 1960s, when the Republican Party, facing an increasingly fractionalized political base, made up of social, economic, and national security and "national greatness conservatives," found it first profitable and then necessary to make hating the press a common theme in order to hold the party together. "Those factions were growing apart," Rosen says, "but there was a need to still win elections and have conventions and candidates that everybody could agree on. Instead of being unified at the level of interests and ideas, they began to be unified by culture war and hate objects and other-ing."

With the mainstream media seen as part of one political tribe, the other tribe has created its own, alternative reality. A result is that Trump's overall approval ratings hover at the bottom for any president in modern history, but his supercharging distrust of the press keeps his numbers among his Republican base stable at record highs. His supporters simply don't believe what we in the press are saying, and they believe what Trump's campaign manager turned advisor Kellyanne Conway called "alternative facts." Some Watergate veterans have speculated, as John Dean, former Nixon White House adviser and star witness in the televised Watergate hearings in 1973, told *Politico Magazine* in January 2018, that "there's more likelihood [Nixon] might have survived if there'd been a Fox News."[21]

And Fox's influence came not just from the ways it mirrored White House messaging. Fox News hosts such as Sean Hannity enjoyed personal influence too, acting as a near-daily sounding board for the president, according to journalists Gabriel Sherman, who wrote the definitive book on Roger Ailes, and the *New Yorker*'s Jane Mayer, who in February 2019 wrote an exhaustive article on the "making of the Fox News White House."[22]

Bill Shine, Hannity's former executive producer and Fox's onetime co-president, became Trump's communications director after being ousted in a massive shakeup triggered by serial sexual harassment allegations against the network's former prime-time star, Bill O'Reilly, and Roger Ailes.[23] Hannity appeared at a rally with Trump ahead of the midterm elections and was one of three alleged clients (though Hannity denied it) of Michael Cohen, from whom Hannity said he merely received occasional real estate advice. No fewer than twelve former Fox News contributors landed in the Trump White House in the first two years of his presidency.[24] And Fox hosts and contributors were influential in Trump's rejection of a budget deal he'd previously endorsed, which triggered the longest government shutdown in U.S. history.

Trump's presidency "is as good as it will ever be for" the network's stars and contributors, former Breitbart consultant Kurt Bardella said. "They will never have more influence over a president than they do right now. We have frankly never seen any media entity or personalities have as much influence over a president."

Trump, as a candidate and as president, took full advantage of what Fox News offered. He had long cultivated ties to Ailes and Murdoch (who Mayer reported was also close to Trump son-in-law Jared Kushner),[25] and he actively sought to benefit from Fox News' manipulations of reality. The cable network had a strong bond of trust with its audience—through the stories it covered and the ones it ignored. In the world as Fox News imagined it, the FBI and Robert Mueller were part of a "deep state" conspiracy conducting a "witch hunt" against Trump, while the real criminals like Hillary Clinton, "illegals," and black radicals got away with their crimes, and Democrats allow Central American gang members to commit murders and rapes while Muslims infiltrate the country bent on terrorist destruction.

In December 2018, Fox News prime-time host Tucker Carlson expressed indignation on his nightly show, saying "we have a moral obligation to admit the world's poor, they tell us, even if it makes our own country poorer, and dirtier, and more divided."[26] The rant cost Carlson nearly two-dozen major advertisers, and the cable giant denounced its advertisers' actions as "censorship." But it perfectly reflected the deep-seated resentments of Fox's loyal audience.

Donald Trump was not only taking advantage of Fox News' presentation of the world; he seemed to be living in it. Reports from inside the White House, including tell-all books by reporters and former staffers, said the president regularly spent hours of unstructured "executive time" watching Fox News programs and tweeting in response. Trump even appeared to take policy and communications advice directly from Fox News programs, particularly the morning show *Fox & Friends* and shows hosted by Carlson, Hannity, and former New York judge Jeanine Pirro. Matthew Gertz, a senior fellow at the liberal media watchdog group Media Matters for America, monitored Trump's Twitter feed for the final three months of 2017 and concluded that the president was essentially "live-tweeting the network's coverage."[27]

Trump's cries of "fake news" weaponized the idea that the media is inherently biased against conservatives, and when they did their jobs, which are to scrutinize and question the president, he cast them in the role of scornful, biased haters and called them "the enemy of the people," an idea most often associated with Joseph Stalin.[28] "His method has been to say, 'they're tough on me, because they hate you,'" Rosen says. "For a certain percentage of the people in his coalition, it works."

Rosen believes this "has become central to what the Republican Party is, so much so that if the media dropped out as a hate object, I don't know if there would be a Republican Party. I don't think the journalists reporting on Trump have quite understood that hating them is a basic tool of the Trump coalition."

Fox News had been formulated to appeal to disaffected white Americans and organizing them around issues, such as racial anxiety, immigration, and religion, that mirrored the post-Reagan party. Former RNC chair Michael Steele said this also helped Republicans win back those "Reagan Democrats who went home to 'Bubba'—Democrat Bill Clinton—in 1992." Fox News launched the year of Clinton's reelection, and its ratings exploded, as Republicans, led by Newt Gingrich, and backed by determined right-wing financiers like Richard Mellon Scaife,[29] relentlessly rode a Clinton sexual scandal to impeachment.

Years later, in 2005, with George W. Bush in the White House and Republican voters feeling demoralized by the Iraq

War and the Bush administration's mishandling of Hurricane Katrina, Fox News host Bill O'Reilly took a book by a conservative radio host named John Gibson and turned it into TV gold. The book was called *The War on Christmas: How the Liberal Plot to Ban the Sacred Christian Holiday Is Worse Than You Thought*.[30] As one former senior producer at Fox News said, "with 'the war on Christmas,' the bosses realized that religion rates like crazy. So, they just kept doing it."

Fox News is just one in a constellation of right-wing outlets serving as Trump's media echo chamber. Others include the Christian broadcasting networks; online right-wing websites like Redstate, the *Washington Examiner,* The Federalist, the Drudge Report, and Hot Air; web-cable hybrids like Newsmax and the Tucker Carlson–created *The Daily Caller*; fringe outfits like Alex Jones's Infowars and Jerome Corsi's "birtherism" progenitor World Net Daily; and particularly as Trump became a popular figure on the right, the anti-immigrant vehicle turned into a "home" of the white nationalist "alt right" by Steve Bannon: Breitbart News.

After Roger Ailes was ousted amid a sex scandal (and then soon died), Murdoch's sons seemed to see into the rearview mirror. Over time, the network's content became "more Breitbart than Breitbart ever was," according to Bardella. "You look at the things that come out of Fox programming every night with Laura Ingraham and Hannity, and the things they're saying are what you used to see as headlines on Breitbart." Back then, "people would roll their eyes and go, wow, they're nuts," he says of the onetime Bannon site. Now, he says, Fox News has "effectively neutralized Breitbart's impact."

And Fox News' reach—2.5 to 3.3[31] million viewers in prime time on an average night in 2018—while significant, is smaller than that of the three broadcast networks, whose nightly news broadcasts pulled in 6 to 8 million viewers on a given night in 2018.[32] Those networks, and rivals like CNN and MSNBC, also reach a more diverse set of Americans, while Fox News' viewers are on average the oldest cable news viewers[33] and approximately 94 percent white.[34]

Meanwhile, as politically powerful and influential as Fox News has become, its reach is dwarfed by another conservative media player: the Sinclair Broadcast Group, the nation's largest broadcaster, which owns or manages 193 television stations nationwide, and in 2018 was seeking to purchase Tribune Media, in a $3.9 billion deal that would have given Sinclair access to 73 percent of U.S. households. (The deal fell apart in 2018 amid a failure to win approval from the FCC, cheering anti-monopoly advocates.)

Founded in 1971 by a Baltimore electrical engineer named Julian Sinclair Smith and managed by his sons, principally longtime chairman David Smith, Sinclair first caught public attention in 2004 when the company announced that its stations would run a documentary critical of Senator John Kerry (who was then the Democratic nominee for the presidency) two weeks before the presidential election. Sinclair Broadcast made headlines again in 2018 when a reporter at the website Deadspin discovered that the network had begun forcing its local news anchors to read a script accusing "some members of the media" of "us[ing] their platforms to push their own biases" and decrying "the sharing of biased and false news" on social media.

The Deadspin mash-up of local TV anchors reading the identical words, in what appeared to be an attack on media criticisms of Donald Trump, quickly went viral, prompting Democratic members of Congress to call on the FCC to reject the proposed merger, which Trump publicly, and in unprecedented fashion for an American president, had supported.

"There is nothing like Sinclair in the media system," Jay Rosen says. "It's really not comparable to Fox. You know you're watching Fox. Even though it says, 'fair and balanced,' or used to, you pretty much know what you're getting. You don't know you're watching Sinclair, because they hide behind the logos of the three broadcast networks. They present themselves as local broadcasting. They market their anchors as local people who have trusted relationships with their communities, and they are turning themselves into a megaphone for a national, political agenda that is synthesized at headquarters in Baltimore. Why the three broadcast networks allow this and don't make a fuss about it, I don't know."

IF TRUMP'S LOVE OF FOX NEWS WAS HELPFUL TO HIM POLITICALLY, his hostility to the rest of the media, and its primary, democratizing function was ominous.

Trump refused to condemn Vladimir Putin for ordering the killings of journalists who challenge the Kremlin, telling MSNBC host Joe Scarborough, who had asked him to issue such a condemnation during a December 2015 call-in to his morning show, that Putin is "running his country, and at least he's a leader, unlike what we have in this country," adding, "I think our country does plenty of killing also, Joe, so you know."[35] When Scarborough gave him a second opportunity, saying, "you obviously condemn Vladimir Putin killing journalists and political opponents, right?" Trump responded dismissively, saying, "Oh sure, absolutely." Days later, he told ABC's George Stephanopoulos regarding Putin, "you're supposed to be innocent until proven guilty, at least in our country. It has not been proven that he's killed reporters."[36]

At an October 2018 rally in Oregon, Trump praised a Republican congressman, Greg Gianforte, for body-slamming a reporter who was trying to ask him a question. Gianforte later pleaded guilty to assault.[37] That month, 211 current and retired journalists signed an open letter condemning what they called Trump's "un-American and utterly unlawful and unseemly" attacks on a free press.[38]

In February 2019, after a Trump supporter wearing a "Make

America Great Again" baseball cap shoved and cursed at a BBC News photographer during an El Paso rally, the White House Correspondents' Association issued a condemnation. "This time, no one was seriously hurt," the release said, but, "the president of the U.S. should make absolutely clear to his supporters that violence against reporters is unacceptable." White House press secretary Sarah Huckabee Sanders, in a rare rebuke, said in a statement, "President Trump condemns all acts of violence against any individual or group of people—including members of the press. We ask that anyone attending an event do so in a peaceful and respectful manner."

Twice during Trump's first two years as president, white male fans of the president, one a self-described white nationalist, targeted his "enemies" for violence, including journalists. CNN's Manhattan offices were evacuated multiple times because of bomb threats. On February 20, 2019, the Program on Extremism at George Washington University revealed that five days earlier, a self-proclaimed white nationalist, forty-nine-year-old Lieutenant Christopher Paul Hasson, had been arrested in Silver Spring, Maryland, for plotting the mass murder of senators, presidential candidates, and major media personalities from CNN and MSNBC.[39] And incidents such as the 2018 mass shooting at the *Capital Gazette* in Annapolis, Maryland, even when not tied to Trump's rhetoric, rattled members of the press who felt increasingly targeted during a time when the president of the United States was turning them into a hate object.

When Trump and his administration looked the other way after *Washington Post* columnist Jamal Khashoggi walked into the Saudi consulate in Istanbul, Turkey, in October 2018, and, according to U.S. intelligence services, was murdered by a group of Saudi men at the behest of the Crown Prince, Muhammed bin Salman, it sent a chill through journalists across America and around the world. Bin Salman, or "MBS," had become a close friend and ally of Trump and his son-in-law Jared Kushner, and Trump seemed determined to protect the family relationship. Khashoggi had once advised the Saudi royals before fleeing the country and moving to the Washington, D.C., area. He had found a sense of liberation in writing about Saudi repression from the safety of the United States under the auspices of a major news organization.

"He lived here," said Khashoggi's editor at the *Washington Post*, Karen Attiah, who had recruited him as one of several international voices. "He'd come in for meetings and coffees and lunches with us. He was a part of the 'Washington scene' when it came to Arab and Gulf affairs, and discussions about Saudi Arabia. So, I think he definitely felt like he had this powerful platform that would not only give him a voice but that would protect him. And I know I felt that way. Actually, I had writers that I worked with that I was more afraid for than for him."

Attiah was stunned when Trump's reaction to Khashoggi's disappearance, then to the undeniable fact of his murder, veered from silence to excuse-making to repeating Saudi denials, including their claims that the journalist may have been an " 'enemy of the state' " and a member of the Muslim Brotherhood extremist group. "It was infuriating and frankly quite scary to see the blatant carrying of the Saudi line," she said. "I realized, wow, okay: if something like this can happen to Jamal, somebody who's arguably one of Saudi Arabia's most famous journalists, someone with a million Twitter followers—a *Washington Post* columnist—if he could be eliminated in this way and have the president look the other way, what chance do the rest of us stand if we happen to fall prey to Saudi Arabia or some other so-called ally? It just told us that they can really get away with anything."

No president is ever a "friend" to the media, but Trump acted as if he did not understand or support the role of the press in a free society. His authoritarian approach appealed to his supporters who shared his suspicion of the media. And the more he kept up his contempt for reporters by treating them disrespectfully, the more thrilled his supporters became. When he didn't like a question, he simply barked at the reporter and demanded that he or she sit down. He was particularly vitriolic with black women journalists. He once snapped at CNN reporter Abby Philip and dismissed as "stupid" her question about the special counsel investigation.

Trump publicly called American Urban Radio's April Ryan a "loser" who "doesn't know what the hell she's doing." During a White House press conference, he cut off a question by PBS correspondent Yamiche Alcindor about his use of the word "nationalist" in connection to racist factions in America by saying, "that's such a racist question . . . excuse me, but to say that, what you said, is so insulting to me. It's a very terrible thing that you said." [40]

Trump's habit of lying to the press and the public was so breathtaking and relentless that the *Washington Post* tracked 6,420 "false or misleading claims" over 649 days ending October 30, 2018. [41] He consistently refused to take in factual information, and used his Twitter feed to toss out falsehoods that the media dutifully turned into headlines, often putting the fact check into the body of stories, where in the bustle of social media sharing, it was never guaranteed to be seen.

Rosen explains that since the formal Washington press corps came into being, it was common practice to treat what the president says as news. "You didn't have to explain it to your editor. You didn't have to explain it to the readers and users. That's just the way it was."

In a presidency that is frequently "misstating facts, making things up, and lying to the American people," Rosen says that model no longer makes sense. "It should be relatively easy to ditch that rule," he says, "but it's not. That's why you still have these headlines that say, 'Trump Accuses Democrats of Stealing the Election in Florida,' as if the accusation itself was somehow news whether there was any evidence or not behind it."

Jeff Jarvis, a former journalist and media critic who has worked for the *Chicago Tribune, People* magazine, and *TV Guide*, believes that "at a tactical level, the fact that news outlets all write a story every time Trump tweets is absurd. It's an indication of how we're being used." Jarvis, who holds the endowed chair of the City University of New York Graduate School of Journalism's program in journalism innovation, focuses on the future of the news business. He sees Trump's aggressive lying and the media's relative normalization of his presidency as a dangerous combination.

Eric Boehlert covered the 2000 Florida recount for *Rolling Stone* before writing two books on what he called the media's tendency to "roll over for Republicans." He spent about a decade working for the liberal watchdog group Media Matters for America, founded by former Republican operative David Brock, before returning to writing at the liberal site Shareblue. He says that even though individual journalists have excelled at reporting on Trump's outrages, he compares much of the mainstream media's take on Trump to the "frog in a pot of boiling water."

"I think journalists realize this is an epic, crazy, historic time," he says, "but so much of the coverage day to day, doesn't reflect that."

The mainstream media has certainly covered Trump as an outré president, but outside of prime-time cable news, he is rarely portrayed as a dangerous one. "There's just not the acknowledgment that [Trump has created] a breakdown in democracy," Boehlert says, "and that we are careening towards an inevitable crisis. There just seems to be an unwillingness to sound the alarm on a daily basis."

Every day, cable news shows depicted the ways in which Trump crashed through the constitutional guardrails set for the presidency. Still, there seemed little media appetite to "go to war" with Donald Trump. Most journalists see their job as delivering accurate information about the administration and letting the public decide what all of it means. And so, Trump was treated with the deference afforded any American president. His and the administration's statements were transmitted as valid presidential pronouncements, and his policies analyzed for their probability of success or impact on his poll numbers, as any president's would have been. Reporters accompanied him overseas and took their seats at his and his team's press conferences, even though they had no reasonable expectation of honest answers to their questions, and sometimes were excluded by the administration from official events they would be allowed to cover under any other president.

The rules and norms of presidential coverage benefited Trump, even if he didn't play by them. The only constraints were on those who believed in the rules, which Trump most certainly did not.

Almost immediately after Trump took the oath of office, then–press secretary Sean Spicer, in his first briefing, pronounced that Trump's inaugural crowd was the largest in history, even though photographic and the U.S. National Park Service evidence plainly showed far fewer people in attendance than President Obama had in 2008 or 2012. Things did not get better from there.

Many traditional media outlets were initially loath to use the word *lie* and referred instead to Trump's *misstatements, erroneous claims,* and *falsehoods.* This allowed these organizations to avoid the question of intent. John Daniszewski, the standards editor at the Associated Press, said in response to criticism of this, "We feel it's better to say what the facts are, say what the person said and let the audience make the decision whether or not it's an intentional lie."[42]

Not everyone in the media maintained the euphemisms. Daniel Dale, the Washington correspondent for the *Toronto Star,* and Aaron Rupar of Vox.com were among the journalists who relentlessly catalogued Trump's lies on Twitter. The *Washington*

Post's David Fahrenthold dug deep into Trump's past business dealings, the Trump Foundation, and Trump University, and he strictly held Trump to account for facts. Journalists in the briefing room remained relentless in their refusal to back down or to stop asking questions in the face of Trump's taunts.

Polls showed that even as some of the finest investigative reporting since Watergate was uncovering Trump scandals at a breathtaking pace, none of it undid the president's iron grip on just over a third of the American electorate. If anything, this reporting reinforced the sense among the president's supporters that the mainstream media were out to get him. In reaction to this, some in the media became determined to counter that mistrust with "balance," which involved presenting "both sides," even if the sides weren't weighted equally.

Rosen says professional journalists feel a powerful incentive to prove "they have no politics themselves, no views of their own, no side, no stake, no ideology and therefore no one can accuse them of . . . political bias."[43] Just as the "objective school," in the early years of the twentieth century, with its scientific method of reporting, prevented reporters from confronting the horrors of lynching, the drive to prove that journalism is a "non-ideological trade" has made it challenging for the media to fully synthesize what the Trump presidency means in real time.

After an election result that surprised the media along with the country, many outlets sought to tamp down the "coastal biases" of an increasingly "big urban" press by having reporters spend time in "Trump's America." Strenuous debates were held on cable and broadcast news shows over whether Trump voters, who pulled the lever for a candidate who put racism, xenophobia, Islamophobia, and misogyny on gaudy display during the campaign, could be called racist, xenophobic, Islamophobic, and misogynistic themselves.

When *Christian Science Monitor* editor David Grant tweeted that a 2019 Pew poll showed seven in ten Republicans feeling misunderstood by the media, the backlash was swift. Ian Mill-hiser, the justice editor at ThinkProgress, replied: "The more I think about this tweet, the more it enrages me. Our job as journalists is not to make sure everyone feels good. Our job is to tell the truth. That means that, if one party has become an anti-intellectual white nationalist movement, they aren't going to like the truth."[44]

Some critics argued that the media was normalizing Trump's most extreme supporters, through profiles of "the neo-Nazi next door" and matter-of-fact coverage of alt-right figures like Steve Bannon and Stephen Miller.

Boehlert believes this anthropologizing of Trump's political base sprang from the stunned media reaction to his elevation to the White House. Before Trump, Boehlert says, "it had never dawned on any newsroom that we should just keep interviewing supporters of the president over and over again." For Trump, he says, "the press just concocted out of thin air a whole new standard and a whole new area of reporting."

Boehlert is concerned that this new standard applies only to this one president. "If you go back to the Obama rollout out of the healthcare law, that was an awful story for them," he says. "They couldn't fix [the ACA website] for a couple weeks." Coverage from conservative, mainstream, and liberal media was scathing. But "there weren't headlines saying, 'Democrats rally around Obama,'" Boehlert points out, adding that if you had said " 'hey, let's get a panel of Obama voters together and see how much they still love him,' you would have been laughed out of any newsroom."

For media critic Jeff Jarvis, the main trouble is the media's reluctance to acknowledge that there is a disconnect between a press whose most influential members live and work in the large urban centers on the East and West Coasts, and the bulk of what is often called "flyover country." When it comes to modern social values like women's rights, civil rights, and immigration, "we are liberal," Jarvis says of the media writ large. "We did a terrible disservice to the country by not admitting that and by giving in to the myth of objectivity. Conservatives used that to set us up."

Jarvis believes this fundamental cultural disconnect had caused the media essentially to bypass half of the country for decades, and not fully examine its views. "We left a void and vacuum that was filled entirely by Rupert Murdoch. And, I think more than any single individual on Earth, the blame falls to him for the destruction of American, British, and Australian democracy," he says. "I know it sounds hyperbolic, but I believe it."

Meanwhile, the *Washington Post*'s Karen Attiah sees another disconnect. She pointed out that while the new Congress in 2019 was the most diverse in history, with "more women, more black and brown" members, when "we look at newsrooms across the country, they're still very stubbornly white, very stubbornly male." The latest survey by the American Society of News Editors (ASNE), which has examined diversity in America's newsrooms since 1978, found that "31 percent of the *Washington Post*'s newsroom [consisted of] minorities compared to 54 percent of the people who lived in the Washington-Arlington-Alexandria metropolitan statistical area. The *New York Times*'s newsroom [was] 78 percent white and 22 percent minorities, while the New York–Newark–Jersey City metro area [was] 53 percent minorities."[45] And as the *Washington Post*'s Paul Farhi pointed out in September 2018, the White House briefing room remains overwhelmingly white, drawing from a pool that has grown its nonwhite cohort only marginally since the Kerner Commission called on American media companies in 1967 to expand their demographic pool.

Attiah worries that "we in national media are not putting ourselves in a position to adequately (a) cover the damage to marginalized communities" that's taking place in the Trump era, and "(b) really be able to just reflect where our country is going."

In 2013, years before Trump was considered a serious presidential candidate, Rosen asked if it was even possible for journalists to provide what has been called a view from nowhere. "What if you have to risk the appearance of being partisan in order to describe accurately what is going on in a hyper-partisan situation?"[46] he wrote.

In many ways, Trump's bizarre and scandalous behavior had been "priced in" to his celebrity and to his status as a "political outsider" who drew the poker hand of a century in 2016 and played for the win. Media watchdogs and experts on authoritarianism warned the press and the public not to be lulled into a false sense of normalcy, or to become numb to Trump's constant outrages. But that advice could sometimes prove hard to take, as Trump warped what it meant to be a "normal" president and rewrote the rules to suit himself.

"There is no way if a President Hillary Clinton had done one hundredth of what Trump has done, that the press wouldn't be in overdrive," Boehlert says, citing the relentless coverage of Hillary Clinton's use of a private email server and the document dump of emails from WikiLeaks, which were eagerly disseminated by the mainstream press, and what he calls a long record of Republican attempts to intimidate the media.

"Even before Trump," Boehlert says, "being tagged as part of the 'liberal media' had real-world consequences" for the perceived value of a journalist's reportorial voice, and even for their ability to be at peace online or, in the worst cases, confident of their physical safety. "If you get targeted by the right-wing mob, whether it's Breitbart or Fox News," it can mean vicious attacks and threats on social media, including from the armies of trolls and automated bots unleashed to boost Trump during the presidential campaign.

The left has its share of online trolls that can prove to be as vicious and relentless as those on the right, but with Trump, public hatred of journalists, per Boehlert, has been "magnified and put on steroids." Trump, he says, "is swinging the sledgehammer like no one has ever swung it before."

THE MEDIA STOOD AT THE CROSSROADS IN A COUNTRY EXPERI-encing what many experts believed was a threat of autocracy not experienced since the 1930s. During that era, prominent Americans like Charles Lindbergh and Henry Ford offered praise for Adolf Hitler, and the *New York Times* ran mundane articles on the Nazi leader's policies toward the arts, his oratorical skills, and the "simple Bavarian chalet" where "Hitler dreams and plans,"[47] while often playing down his threatening language toward Jews.[48] The U.S. government after World War II made a concerted effort to repel fascism in America, through propaganda films and newsreels, which urged citizens to resist the suspicions of others that could easily cause division and violence.

The power to cajole Americans toward our better angels no longer rested in the hands of the government, in a nation so beset by partisanship, let alone with a president bent on divisiveness sitting in the White House. Nor did it abide with the press, given the deep mistrust of a plurality of Americans, and the complete fragmentation of the sources where people get their news.

Platforms like Facebook and Twitter have been reluctant to view themselves as content providers—even though, increasingly, that's what they have become.

Pew Research in 2017 found that 68 percent of American adults reported getting their news regularly from social media, though nearly as many—57 percent—said they expected that news to be inaccurate and subject to deliberate fakery. Users said those concerns were outweighed by the convenience of the platforms, which they said was their favorite attribute.

Rosen believes that "the most devastatingly powerful effect of Facebook" is probably how easily like-minded people can find each other and connect, and also how vulnerable objective truth is to being weakened. People on the political and ideological extremes can use Facebook to locate each other. "People who all hate the media in the same way can now find each other and start developing not just alternative sources, but campaigns to discredit the press."

Donald Trump clearly loves Twitter, tweeting an average of seven times a day during his first year in office.[49] Many of those tweets quickly turned into headlines, to the horror of media watchdogs who view it as a way of co-opting and manipulating the legitimate press into transmitting Trumpian propaganda. Twitter was also where Russian and American trolls relentlessly attacked Trump's opponents during 2016 and boosted his candidacy.

The memes generated on online platforms including Reddit and 4Chan, where users are younger, whiter, and more often male, were recycled onto Facebook and Twitter, featuring vicious attacks on women, Jews, and African-Americans. This grew from the wave in 2014 and 2015 of misogynistic attacks on women in the online video gaming space, which were collectively dubbed Gamergate. Yet even before Gamergate, there had been an online surge of systematic harassment, directed specifically at black women.

Technology analyst Shireen Mitchell was among the black women who endured relentless racist and sexist online attacks beginning in 2013, a year before Gamergate. She said black women active on Twitter and Facebook began noticing an uptick in hostile interactions with users who presented themselves as black men, but who were more likely automated bots and trolls. When these women called this out at a technology conference, they were harassed, and some were hounded out of their jobs. Mitchell and other black women technologists created a hashtag—#YourSlipIsShowing—in 2014 to call out the trolls.[50]

They requested intervention from Twitter and Facebook, but the companies did nothing.

Gamergate entered the national lexicon that same year. It began as one male gamer's attempt to punish his game developer ex-girlfriend by "doxing," or publicly releasing private, sensitive information about her and directing other gamers to harass her and any woman who defended her. It soon morphed into a frenzy of online abuse by mostly young, white men online, directed at women whom they accused of imposing "political correctness" on a gaming culture long defined by misogynistic storylines, scantily clad female digital characters, and extreme violence. The abuse, which dovetailed with a growing "man movement," which blamed women's liberation for the inability of some tech-savvy young men to find partners, and sometimes violently threatened women as a result, quickly spiraled to include death and rape threats, doxing, and purportedly comedic but viciously offensive "memes" designed to humiliate and even chase women off social media platforms altogether.

These online movements harnessed the anger and frustrations of young, mostly white men who soon became eager recruits for a larger project: electing Donald Trump.

Some of the same actors who participated in or egged on the Gamergate attacks, including then–Breitbart contributor Milo Yiannopoulos, eventually emerged as online fans and enforcers of Trump's 2016 campaign. They trafficked in racism, sexism, anti-Semitism, and even Nazism to harass female supporters of Hillary Clinton on Twitter. And their tactics were soon picked up by foreign attackers aligned with the Kremlin, such as Russia's Internet Research Agency, a St. Petersburg–based "troll farm" whose operatives hacked into dormant Twitter and Facebook accounts, mimicked the identities and vernacular of the users they targeted—including black women and even Black Lives Matter activists—while unleashing armies of automated, robotic social media accounts or "bots" to attack young, female, and particularly black voters in order to discourage them from supporting Hillary Clinton, or from voting at all. Special prosecutor Robert Mueller would ultimately indict thirteen Russian nationals and three Russian companies, including the Internet Research Agency, on conspiracy and identity theft charges, along with the Putin-linked Russian oligarch, Yevgeny Prigozhin, who allegedly financed the operation.

During congressional testimony in November 2017, former FBI special agent Clint Watts called the social media swarm attacks like Gamergate a "dry run" for Russian social media manipulation during the campaign. Author and expert on authoritarianism Sarah Kendzior wrote on the NBC News THINK website in November 2017, "the trolls were hiding in plain sight." [51] Russian troll farms studied what American online harassers had done and adapted the techniques to help elect Donald Trump.

Mitchell is convinced that the big tech companies could solve the problem of user impersonation and manipulation if they wanted to. She says that Facebook and Twitter could easily discover which of their users are real and which are bots, but she believes these companies avoid that conversation because "their growth is user based." In other words, the more users they have, the more their companies are worth, regardless of whether those users are human.

The tech giants have also been adept at lobbying against legislation that would force them to disclose the sources of money behind the political ads on their platforms, which during the campaign were weaponized by Russian trolls to pump false information and anti-Clinton propaganda into the news feeds of American voters on the right and on the left, targeting those thought to be open to Trump's messaging, and progressives who might be disappointed by Bernie Sanders's loss in the 2016 Democratic primary.

The Trump campaign bragged about having Facebook representatives working with them, practically as an arm of the campaign. There were also shady organizations like Cambridge Analytica, which was bankrolled by the billionaire Mercer family, whose previous projects included funding Breitbart under Steve Bannon and Trump campaign manager and White House senior adviser Kellyanne Conway's polling company. Cambridge Analytica facilitated the theft of Facebook users' data without their knowledge, enabling the Trump campaign to target potential supporters based on what they revealed about themselves online, which in their minds had been only to their family and friends.

Mitchell doesn't believe much will change about this landscape that's ripe for information warfare, as long as the men who run Facebook and Twitter remain indifferent to the suffering their platforms can facilitate. And she sees little hope in the extreme libertarian views espoused by these tech leaders, who are more concerned with government censorship than with providing their users a safe online experience.

As the 2020 primary season began in earnest in 2019, online trolls began attaching themselves to an obscure pocket of black nativists calling themselves "American Descendants of Slaves" (ADOS), a "blood and soil" movement designed to stoke anti-immigrant fervor among black voters, and targeting in particular the candidacy of Democratic senator Kamala Harris of California, who announced her run for president on Martin Luther King Day 2019.

The daughter of a Jamaican immigrant father and an Indian immigrant mother, the former state attorney general was born in Oakland, California, and attended historically black Howard University, where she pledged the Alpha Kappa Alpha black sorority. Yet the attacks centered on the authenticity of her claim on African-American identity—a version of the "birther" attacks on Barack Obama, including by Donald Trump. Any tweet or post by or about Harris triggered a flurry of "bot" and troll activity, even as federal authorities began to track a resurgence of the Internet Research Agency's meddling online.

Trumpism had fulfilled the fondest wishes of men like John Tanton, founder of the Federation of American Immigration Reform, and whom the Southern Policy Law Center considers the founder of the modern anti-immigration movement. Tanton, a eugenicist and retired Michigan ophthalmologist whose principal benefactor was an heir to the Scaife fortune—of the Mellon family tree[52]—had long sought avenues into the mainstream, through bland-sounding organizations like FAIR and the Center for Immigration Studies.

A former member of the Sierra Club, he "green washed" his nativist movement via faux-liberal organizations like Progressives for Immigration Reform (PFIR).[53] Tanton's network, though steeped in "race science" and "European-only" immigration restrictionism, even tapped into a small but enduring tradition of black nativism through FAIR offshoots like the Black American Leadership Alliance (BALA). BALA's leadership included conservative African-Americans like T. Willard Fair, the longtime president of the Urban League of Greater Miami; FAIR board member Frank Morris, whose ties include the Carrying Capacity Network, whose former chairman Virginia Abernathy was a self-declared "ethnic separatist" with ties to the "neoconfederate Council of Concerned Citizens"[54]; and conservative religious/media figure and Fox News favorite Jesse Lee Peterson. BALA's founder Leah Durant was an attorney with FAIR's legal arm and served as PFIR's executive director when the group ran a national ad campaign in 2012 calling for the country to "reduce mass immigration until all Americans are back to work."[55]

The ADOS co-founder, Yvette Carnell, was herself a former PFIR board member and onetime staffer to two Democratic members of Congress. The #ADOS social media–based anti-immigration online push focused on steering black voters toward an all-or-nothing ultimatum to Democrats: commit to a multi-trillion-dollar reparations package for American slave descendants or black voters should withhold their votes or support Donald Trump's reelection. Ann Coulter was among the push's social media supporters.

Jarvis worries that all of this will produce a backlash that limits the unprecedented freedom offered by the Internet and social media. "I get worried that there's a moral panic going on about the Internet," he says. "Yes, there are bad guys there. And yes, the Russians are there, and yes, the trolls are there. All of that's a problem. But the people who say that we should control the net and control social media are in a position of privilege. They are the people who were always covered by big media. But, without social media, we wouldn't have had 'Me Too,' we wouldn't have had 'Black Lives Matter.' We wouldn't have 'Living While Black' that has taught me huge lessons about the utter banality of the causes of white people calling police on black people, even for barbecuing. That kind of coverage has never come out in mainstream media. It is able to come out now, because more communities are enfranchised" via the powerful image transmitters in their phones. Those organizing and democratizing tools should not be allowed to go away, or to be buried by larger outlets.

The 2020 election seemed poised to be even more racially and culturally divisive than 2016, featuring a historically diverse Democratic field, with no fewer than five women running, including three of Harris's fellow female senators. Also declaring for president were an Hispanic former Texas mayor, Julián Castro; openly gay Indiana mayor Pete Buttigieg; and two black candidates, Harris and New Jersey senator Cory Booker. There were contentious issues such as reparations for slavery, immigration, Trump's racism, and the potentially divisive candidacies of Bernie Sanders (the Vermont independent whose most extreme followers had been known to wage vicious attacks on Clinton supporters and members of the media in 2016) and Tulsi Gabbard (an iconoclastic former social conservative and sometime apologist for the regime of Bashar Assad in Syria who ran for Congress as a progressive Democrat and emerged as a favorite of Russian media). In April 2019, former vice president Joe Biden also joined the race, hinging his launch on the outrage over Trump's dismissal of the neo-Nazism in Charlottesville two years before. Biden's run sparked fresh debates about whether the Democratic Party would spurn its diverse base in pursuit of the restless white working class, risking diminished turnout among black voters just as they were being targeted for disenfranchisement in Republican states as well as online.

Trump faced an uncertain future two years into his presidency. Even with the Mueller probe completed, more than half a dozen of his former business and campaign associates had been indicted, including his onetime campaign manager. His former lawyer and fixer Michael Cohen delivered his devastating, live testimony in front of Congress about what he described as Trump's racism and cruelty, his disloyalty and selfishness, and, more important, the crimes Cohen says he committed on Trump's behalf, both during and while he was president. And unlike even John Dean during Watergate, Cohen came to Congress bearing documentary evidence: checks to him for reimbursement of the payoffs to women, signed by the president while in office.

There would be more testimony to come. House Democrats subpoenaed more than eighty Trump associates as part of ongoing investigations, including former Trump business associate turned FBI informant Felix Sater, and Trump's new attorney general, who would deliver a crushing blow to the resistance in an act that many would deem the ultimate cover-up. It was one Richard Nixon could only have dreamed of as an ending to Watergate.

CHAPTER 9

"Mr. Barr Goes to Town"

"Therefore, thus saith the LORD, Behold, I will bring evil upon them, which they shall not be able to escape; and though they shall cry unto me, I will not hearken unto them."

—Jeremiah 11:11

NO ONE IS COMING TO SAVE YOU. THE ABOVE BIBLE VERSE, FROM the Old Testament, is referenced throughout the Jordan Peele horror film, *Us*, which was released in March 2019, the same weekend Special Counsel Robert Mueller sent his long-awaited report on Russian interference in the 2016 election to Attorney General William Barr.

In the film, long-deprived, underground-dwelling clone doppelgangers emerge from the sewers to terrorize their above-ground matches, eliminate them, and steal their lives. The Bible verse—a rebuke of the Israelites by their God for their descent into apostasy and idol worship—is meant to explain the hopelessness of waiting for saviors to stop a determined and ruthless adversary. Americans who were disturbed by two-plus years of politics that *New York Magazine* writer Eric Levitz called akin to running the White House like the Mafia would soon learn a similar lesson: that Mueller was not going to save them from Donald Trump.[1]

On March 22, 2019, the "Mueller report"—the product of twenty-two months of investigation by some of the top prosecutors in areas from national security to money laundering—was submitted to Barr, who had been in place for just over a month. Forty-eight hours after receiving Mueller's work, Barr had distilled nearly two years of investigative and grand jury efforts, resulting in thirty-four indictments and more than a half dozen convictions and five people sent to prison, into a four-page letter claiming, "the Special Counsel's investigation did not find that the Trump Campaign or anyone associated with it conspired with Russia in its efforts to influence the 2016 U.S. presidential election."[2] It quoted only snippets from the actual report, including a truncated sentence stating, "The investigation did not establish that members of the Trump campaign conspired or coordinated with the Russian government in its election interference activities"[3] related to an indicted Russian troll farm and the hacking of the Democratic National Committee and dissemination of Democratic emails.

Barr's letter outright cleared Trump of obstruction of justice, a decision Barr claimed Mueller left to him, rather than to Congress, as the Watergate investigators had done or Independent Counsel Kenneth Starr had before President Bill Clinton was impeached. Barr's letter contained one other key quote, purportedly from the Mueller probe: "While this report does not conclude that the President committed a crime, it also does not exonerate him." But "exoneration" is precisely how the Barr letter was received, by most of the media, by the public, and most especially, by Donald Trump and his supporters.

Democrats were stunned.

They shouldn't have been.

Barr had been nominated to become attorney general on

December 7, 2018—one month to the day after Trump finally pushed out Jeff Sessions, whom he had relentlessly abused and ridiculed for the sin of recusing himself from oversight of the Mueller probe. Barr would succeed the sycophantic "acting" attorney general, Matthew Whitaker, who was never confirmed in the Senate. Barr's confirmation finally delivered Trump what he wanted when he asked his then–White House counsel, "Where's my Roy Cohn?"[4]

Cohn, of course, was the vicious "red scare" prosecutor during the McCarthy hearings, described by NPR as "a legendary and controversial attorney who pushed legal tactics to the limits for a dazzling array of clients—from senators to mobsters and high rollers in sports and entertainment."[5] Cohn also had once been Trump's lawyer and fixer. Long dead, he was discarded by Trump, according to *Vanity Fair*, when he fell ill with complications from AIDS.[6] But before that, he helped pad Trump's seedy rise through the world of New York real estate.

The *New York Times* said the special counsel learned in January 2018 that Trump had ordered his then–White House counsel to stop Sessions from recusing himself from oversight of Mueller's investigation.[7] Trump believed Sessions should have protected him the way, in his mind, Robert Kennedy protected JFK, and President Obama's attorney general, Eric Holder, shielded him. (Neither the Kennedy nor Obama administration was hit by criminal investigations or racked with scandal like Trump's tenure had been, and it is not the job of the United States attorney general to "protect" the president.) Trump made no secret of his intention to rid himself of Sessions, despite the attorney general's doggedness in pursuing Trump's malicious policy of removing non-white immigrants from the United States—and to replace him with a political fixer.

In June 2018, Barr auditioned for the job, doing so via an unsolicited memo[8] that was addressed to Deputy Attorney General Rod Rosenstein and Assistant Attorney General Steve

Engel. Barr's memo, with the subject line "Mueller's 'Obstruction' Theory," expressed "deep concern" about the Mueller probe and its potentially deleterious impact on the presidency. It stated, "Mueller should not be permitted to demand that the President submit to interrogation about alleged obstruction." It called the entire theory underpinning Mueller's obstruction probe "fatally misconceived," despite admitting that Barr himself was not versed in the facts. (He later said he gleaned what he did know from media reports.) His memo also called the entire enterprise potentially damaging to the power and prestige of the presidency, while asserting that, in his view, the president of the United States "*alone* is the Executive branch," and "as such, he is the sole repository of all Executive powers conferred by the Constitution." Barr was clear in his view that Donald Trump had the absolute right to fire then–FBI director James Comey, or indeed anybody he wished.

The June 2018 memo cast Barr as a man who had made up his mind. As far back as the late 1980s, when he served as an assistant attorney general, his memos and written opinions indicate that he believed in an almost monarchical executive at 1600 Pennsylvania Avenue—with powers so sweeping they could barely be checked by Congress.[9]

Barr, as the ACLU warned[10] during his confirmation, had as a Justice Department lawyer during the 1980s sought to justify everything from FBI interrogations of innocent Arab-Americans in the lead-up to the Persian Gulf War, to indefinite detention of Haitian asylum seekers at the U.S. naval base in Guantanamo Bay, to secret military tribunals after bombings in Lockerbie, Scotland in 1988, and again after 9/11, when Barr testified as a private citizen and expert witness before the Senate Judiciary Committee.[11] Now he was essentially broadcasting his agreement with Trump that the probe into whether the Trump campaign conspired with Russians to swing the election and afterward obstructed inquiries into that interference was little more than a dangerous "witch hunt" that the president could sweep aside at will.

Barr sent his memo expressing his distaste for the Mueller probe to a raft of Trump attorneys, including White House special counsel Emmet Flood, Solicitor General Noel Francisco, and Pat Cipollone, who previously served with Barr in the Justice Department and succeeded Trump's first White House counsel, Don McGahn. He made sure his views got around Washington, discussing his opinion on the Mueller probe with Trump lawyers including Jay Sekulow and Marty and Jane Raskin and with Jared Kushner's attorney, Abbe Lowell.[12] He was determined to have the letter seen by the right people surrounding the president, as well as the president himself. William Barr wanted very much to be the next attorney general of the United States. According to one Republican source, Barr also saw himself as a potential future justice on the Supreme Court.

Despite his obvious conflict of interest in pre-judging the Mueller investigation, Barr was confirmed by the Senate on Valentine's Day 2019, by a vote of 54 to 45. There were clear reasons why Barr should recuse himself from overseeing the Mueller probe, just as Sessions had done, but he refused.

Barr, a 69-year-old New Yorker, was a graduate of George Washington University School of Law. He served as deputy attorney general under President George H. W. Bush from 1990 to 1991. When in August 1991, Attorney General Richard Thornburgh resigned to run for the U.S. Senate, Barr served first as acting attorney general and was confirmed to the position in November, serving until Bush's tenure ended. Among those who reported to him at that time was Robert Mueller, then the head of the Justice Department's Criminal Division.

As attorney general, Barr would prove to be a reliable partisan. In the summer of 1992, during the heart of the presidential campaign, he pushed to accelerate an FBI investigation into allies of his boss's political rivals, Bill and Hillary Clinton.[13] Local FBI officials in Arkansas reportedly believed the probe had no merit, but Barr and other Republicans apparently hoped had to get in front of the American public amid the presidential election. That investigation later flowered into the Whitewater affair, which ultimately found its way to sexual scandal and President Clinton's impeachment.

In 1992, Barr refused to appoint an independent counsel to investigate a scandal dubbed "Iraqgate," involving Reagan-era agricultural loans to Iraq, used to purchase weapons for their conflict with Iran. With a month to go before the election, and with congressional Democrats bearing down, Barr appointed a special counsel—who reported to him, and could be fired by him, rather than reporting to Congress. The maneuver led conservative columnist William Safire to label Barr "the Coverup-General," in a scathing October 19, 1992, column in which he concluded that Barr was blocking an independent probe into the Iraqgate scandal, "Because he knows where it may lead: to Dick Thornburgh, James Baker, Clayton Yeutter, Brent Scowcroft and himself." [14,15]

As the Bush administration drew to a close, Barr supported the president's decision to pardon six leading figures in the Reagan-era Iran Contra scandal, including former defense secretary Caspar Weinberger, who was set to go on trial for lying to Congress about what he knew regarding the plan to sell arms to Iran in order to fund Nicaraguan rebels—a scheme Bush had supported as Ronald Reagan's vice president, per Weinberger's notes. [16] The pardons obstructed the efforts of Independent Counsel Lawrence Walsh, who had obtained three guilty pleas and one conviction, and had two remaining cases pending.

In short, Barr seemed the ideal man to take on the job of ridding President Donald Trump of the Mueller probe.

On March 24, 2019, he showed his worth. As *Esquire*'s Charles P. Pierce wrote the next day: "William Barr on Sunday did what he was hired to do. He summarized Robert Mueller's report in the most favorable light possible to the administration and, where he couldn't do that—specifically, on the crime of obstruction of justice—he just decided to turn Mueller's own conclusion completely upside down." If Barr's summary could be taken at face value, Pierce wrote, "Paul Manafort et al. got caught up in a criminal conspiracy in which the only crimes were their own."[17]

Much of the media rushed to declare Trump's vindication, as did his allies. None of them, however, had seen the Mueller report—just Barr's four-page summary, which highlighted his decision to toss aside any legal claims against the president. Barr's benign conclusions about the Trump campaign's repeated contacts with Russians—and their repeated lies about them—flew in the face of what Americans had seen and heard with their own eyes and ears for three years.

Legal experts expressed deep skepticism. Barr's argument "suggests that if a subject of a criminal investigation avoids indictment for the underlying offense—whether it be insider trading, burglary, or election interference—he should not be charged with criminal liability for efforts to obstruct the investigation of the potential offense, either," attorney David R. Lurie wrote in Slate. "That is simply not the law."[18] Lurie cited domestic doyenne Martha Stewart's conviction for obstructing an insider trading investigation, in which she went to jail, despite never having been charged over her stock trades. And Lurie pointed out that Barr's reasoning was not just wrong, but dangerous: providing an incentive for alleged criminals to obstruct investigations in order to prevent prosecutors from obtaining sufficient evidence to prove an underlying crime.

On CNN, former Nixon White House counsel John Dean speculated that Barr's letter "put a little lipstick on something that might've been fairly ugly"[19] inside the Mueller report. In a New York Times op-ed, former U.S. solicitor general Neal Katyal, who wrote the special counsel regulations under which Mueller served, questioned how Barr could have concluded, in just forty-eight hours, that Trump did not act with corrupt intent without even trying to interview him.[20]

Not everyone was surprised.

On the weekend the Barr letter was released, Trump was at Mar-a-Lago, golfing and dining with friends, including Senator Graham, former South Carolina congressman Trey Gowdy, and others. According to one party guest, the atmosphere was giddy. Those around Trump already knew what Barr's letter would say. They were confident that Barr would keep any embarrassing or damning material from ever becoming public. For Trump, his family, and his cronies, getting away with it all would be the best revenge. The Republican Party intended to ensure Trump remained in power, by whatever means necessary, so that his immunity from the reach of federal law would continue. And the Kremlin, having succeeded beyond their wildest dreams in perhaps the boldest information warfare and campaign intrusion operation ever launched against the United States, was free to do it again, as were other foreign governments who could look upon the Trump administration like a movable feast.

Appearing with me on MSNBC, the day before the Barr letter dropped, defense attorney and AboveTheLaw.com editor Elie Mystal asked: "Is Trump's flunky going to release a report that might be damaging to his sugar daddy? I don't think so." Mystal wondered aloud whether Barr had stepped in to halt Mueller's investigation before sentences were handed down to major figures like General Michael Flynn, or before Roger Stone's trial had even begun. "This is a 22-month-long investigation," Mystal said. "Barr's been on the scene for a month, and now we're done? That doesn't strike anybody as odd? No, I have absolutely no confidence that Bill Barr will do anything other than what is in the best interest of Donald Trump."[21]

Speaker Nancy Pelosi told her House caucus in the days after the Barr letter's release that there was no reason to trust an attorney general who had already declared, in writing, that the president is above the law, and that the public would need to see the full report.[22]

Still, Trump's Republican partisans crowed about the president's "complete exoneration" and demanded that his critics apologize to him and bow down. California congressman Devin Nunes, the fiercely Trumpist former chairman of the House Intelligence Committee (and who was in the process of suing parody Twitter accounts for mocking him and his fervent obedience to Trump), suggested on Fox News that the Mueller report could simply be "burned."[23] Trump and his allies, hailing what they viewed as the cloud being lifted from his presidency, began hinting that the Department of Justice should now target and investigate Trump's enemies, starting with Hillary Clinton and anyone involved in launching investigations into him. It was the kind of behavior that often happens in autocratic countries around the world.

Within two days of Barr's letter, Trump's 2020 campaign sent a memo to TV news producers, instructing them that "the only way to interpret [Barr's] conclusions is as a total and complete vindication of President Trump." It also named six prominent Democratic members of Congress who had spoken of collusion while on air, telling producers they ought to ask themselves: "Does this guest warrant further appearances in our programming, given the outrageous and unsupported claims made in the past?"[24]

With pressure mounting from congress, and polls showing Americans overwhelmingly wanted to see the Mueller report for themselves, on April 18, Barr released a redacted version of the report.

The report contained stark differences from Barr's summary. Far from clearing the president of potential criminality, Mueller's report simply restated the Justice Department rules against indicting a sitting president and said that had the investigators been able to clear Trump and his campaign of wrongdoing, they would have. But they very pointedly did not.

"We recognized that a federal criminal accusation against a sitting President would place burdens on the President's capacity to govern and potentially preempt constitutional processes for addressing presidential misconduct," the report stated. But it added, "while the Office of Legal Counsel (OLC) opinion concludes that a sitting President may not be prosecuted, it recognizes that a criminal investigation during the President's term is permissible. The OLC opinion also recognizes that a President does not have immunity after he leaves office." [25]

The report further "concluded that Congress has the authority to prohibit a president's corrupt use of his authority in order to protect the integrity of the administration of justice." [26]

Mueller's more than four-hundred-page report differed starkly from Barr's presentation of its findings, both in his March letter and in a terse press conference held hours before he released the report to Congress or the public, which reporters in attendance questioned as "spin" in favor of the White House.

Where Barr portrayed a frustrated president trying in earnest to cooperate with an investigation he viewed as unfairly tainting his election and impeding the conduct of his office, the Mueller report states that "In this investigation, the evidence does not establish that the president was involved in an underlying crime related to Russian election interference. But the evidence does point to a range of other possible personal motives animating the president's conduct. These include concerns that continued investigation would call into question the legitimacy of his election and potential uncertainty about whether certain events—such as advance notice of WikiLeaks' release of hacked information or the June 9, 2016, meeting between senior campaign officials and Russians could be seen as criminal activity by the president, his campaign or his family." [27]

The report established definitively that Russia had interfered in the 2016 election to help elect Trump, "identified numerous links between the Russian government and the Trump campaign," and confirmed that the campaign sought to benefit from Russia's meddling. It reiterated reports that Paul Manafort shared polling data and strategy information with a Russian oligarch, detailing the campaign's plans to target Michigan, Pennsylvania, Wisconsin and Minnesota—three out of four of which Trump narrowly won on his way to an Electoral College victory. It established that the Trump campaign eagerly accepted Russia's help, that the Trump children openly courted Russia ties, and that Julian Assange of Wikileaks solicited hacked material from the Russian intelligence services who stole them, even smearing a dead DNC staffer, Seth Rich, to obscure Russia's role in disseminating the material Wikileaks helped to spread, including to traditional news media.

And where Barr parsed Mueller's findings to find only the most exculpatory ones, the actual conclusions in the report were damning. The report found ten distinct instances of potential obstruction of justice, including Trump pressuring James Comey to end the investigation of General Michael Flynn, Trump's pressuring of cabinet members to publicly deny he had any connection to Russian interference, the firing of Comey and Trump's attempts to force his subordinates to remove the special counsel, and the editing of Donald Jr.'s press statements, encouraging Michael Cohen to not cooperate with the Mueller probe and attempts to hide information from the public. Mueller's report concluded that only the refusal by members of Trump's administration, including the White House counsel to accede to his demands, prevented Trump from succeeding in carrying out that obstruction.[28]

And the Mueller report came to a damning conclusion on the potential crimes of the president of the United States: "if we had confidence after a thorough investigation of the facts that the president clearly did not commit obstruction of justice, we would so state. Based on the facts and the applicable legal standards, however, we are unable to reach that judgment. The evidence we obtained about the president's actions and intent presents difficult issues that prevent us from conclusively determining that no criminal conduct occurred. Accordingly, while this report does not conclude that the president committed a crime, it also does not exonerate him."

But it hardly seemed to matter. Barr had done the job Donald Trump hired him to do. He had thrown enough sand in the gears to allow Trump and his supporters to claim the Mueller report as both total vindication and a sham. After two years of scandal and investigations, Americans seemed exhausted. Barr's actions left the country to face the daunting prospect that an American president could indeed place himself above the law, by simply remaining president, and raising the political stakes for impeachment so high that an opposition House dared not act. Even if they did, the partisan Senate was unlikely to act in the way Republicans did with Richard Nixon by supporting conviction.

"Barr has grievously betrayed his oath to support and defend the constitution of the United States by repeatedly lying to the American people about the findings of the legally authorized probe into the Russian attack and Trump's obstruction, as conducted by special counsel Robert Mueller," Professor Laurence Tribe said on April 19, the day Congressional Democrats issued a subpoena for the full, unredacted Mueller report. "I'm hoping Mueller will soon break his silence when responding to the congressional invitations to testify publicly."

Tribe believed the report had provided a clear roadmap to the president's impeachment—a question that would weigh heavily on Democrats as nearly two dozen candidates barreled toward the 2020 election. They included former vice president Joe Biden, who entered the race in April 2019, bringing with him Obama nostalgia and the freight of more than forty years traveling the distance between the conservative, blue collar Democratic ethos of 1970s anti-busing politics, 1990s "tough on crime" Bill Clintonism and a new era in which Anita Hill had gone from accused "scorned woman" in the Clarence Thomas hearings Biden once chaired, to heroic template for the "Me Too" era. All of that American baggage would be on the table in 2020.

ROBERT MUELLER HAD NOT SAVED THE DAY. THERE WERE NO superheroes coming—no "Deus ex machina" ending to the Trump saga. Donald Trump, according to Republican sources, was feeling invincible, demanding that all federal aid to hurricane-ravaged Puerto Rico be halted, that the southern border be sealed and fresh cruelties doled out to helpless migrants seeking sanctuary in the U.S. Trump had fully unleashed Stephen Miller to shut down all asylum claims and all but close the doors to immigration. He was embracing his full inner autocrat, even demanding that his aides monitor Fox News to ensure they "stay loyal to me."[29]

Trump had already ordered Barr's Justice Department to stop defending the Affordable Care Act from a surprise and many believed partisan federal court ruling that the entire law was unconstitutional—a decision that if upheld by the Supreme Court could strip tens of millions of Americans of their healthcare. Sources around Barr made it known through leaks to *Politico* that he opposed the unprecedented idea[30] of refusing to defend a duly enacted federal law. And yet, the job was his to do.

Barr seemed destined to live in infamy as the attorney general who occupied the place in the administration that Michael Cohen once served in the Trump Organization. Barr would even be accused by Speaker Pelosi of lying to Congress. As Cohen had warned and numerous discarded members of the Trump administration had learned, to sign on with Donald Trump was to hand over your honor, your dignity, and your reputation. *Washington Post* columnist Paul Waldman wrote in April 2018: "there may be no precedent for the degree of ruined reputations that President Trump is leaving in his wake," adding: "Is there a single Trump aide or official who will leave the service of this president with their reputation enhanced, or at least not diminished?" As Waldman pointed out, it was partly down to the quality of men and women Trump managed to attract to his administration, which Waldman described as "the most morally repugnant people," and the way he "actively forces people to behave unethically."[31] Barr was set on a course, and it seemed unlikely he could change direction, so long as he chose to remain as Donald Trump's attorney general.

"Did you think Trump was a bad, dangerous president before March 24, 2019?" *Philadelphia Inquirer* columnist Will Bunch wrote in the days following the Barr letter. "You ain't seen nothing yet. Emboldened by the Barr-fed Total Exoneration Myth, an energized Trump is acting exactly like the autocrat so many feared on the night he was elected." Indeed, despite still facing more than a dozen ongoing investigations at the federal and state level, including pending matters in his home state of New York, and an open question of whether a counterintelligence investigation of the president remained ongoing, Donald Trump's appetite for destruction and revenge was only growing. What would he order his "Roy Cohn" to do next? Investigate Hillary Clinton? Literally "lock her up"? Jail those who contributed to the investigation of his campaign? Surely, he was now free to openly bond the United States to Russia, North Korea, and the other authoritarian states he admired. What Republican in Congress would dare oppose him now?

If the American people wanted to end Trumpism, and to seize back the country from the man seemingly determined to tear it apart, they would likely have to do it themselves, in the next presidential election.

CHAPTER 10

Un-Democratic America?

"Democracy should not mean the leveling of everyone to the lowest common denominator. It should mean the possibility of everyone being able to raise himself to a certain level of excellence."

—James Baldwin, in a public conversation with
Margaret Mead, later published as *A Rap on Race* (1971)

IF DEMOCRATS WERE GOING TO PREVAIL IN 2020 AND STOP Trumpism's destructive romp across the American political and social landscape, it would require a Herculean effort. They would need to reverse the apathy and cynicism that saw reduced turnout among key voting groups in 2016. They would need to counter what would surely be an accelerated interference effort by foreign powers emboldened by Russia's success in 2016, and the impunity they had been handed by Republicans. They would have to fight what would surely be a voter suppression effort on a scale unprecedented even by the standards of the last election. And they would have to do it all while wading through a primary field of almost two dozen contenders, each representing different components of the country's most diverse political party.

And they would have to do it all while fighting not just Donald Trump, but also Mitch McConnell. The Senate majority leader stood foursquare in the way of passing any legislation that would ease voting for those groups that tended to favor Democrats. He had long made his priorities clear: winning reelection in 2020, remaining majority leader, and seating conservative judges who would remain on the bench for decades and cement his legacy as a legislative hero of the Christian far right. For that, he needed a Republican president. And whatever McConnell's private thoughts about Donald Trump, the forty-fifth president was working out for the Senate leader just fine.

When Democrats opened their House majority in 2019 by proposing sweeping legislation to make voting easier, McConnell called it a "power grab." Speaking on the Senate floor on January 30, a week before the president's rescheduled State of the Union speech, he lambasted the bill that would make voting a national holiday. Speaker Nancy Pelosi had announced weeks earlier that HR1, the "For the People Act," was her party's first priority—before it got derailed by the record-setting government shutdown.

HR1 would create nationwide automatic voter registration, provide a path to restoring the right to vote for those who have completed federal prison sentences, expand early voting, and streamline the absentee ballot process.

The bill would put Congress to work restoring Section 5 of the Voting Rights Act, which the Roberts Court gutted in 2013 based on the false premise that race-based disenfranchisement no longer exists. This work is already being undertaken by groups like the NAACP Legal Defense and Education Fund, led by Thurgood Marshall's heir to the presidency of the organization, Sherrilyn Ifill, and by Stacey Abrams, the defeated Georgia gubernatorial candidate who continued to lead an organization dedicated to reversing voter suppression.

If passed into law, the "For the People Act" would outlaw

the voter purges that took place in Georgia at the hands of now-governor Brian Kemp, and that have alarmed election integrity experts for decades, from the "caging" of thousands of Florida voters in 2000 under then-governor Jeb Bush, to the voter restrictions in states like North Carolina, Texas, Wisconsin, and Ohio, to the "crosscheck" system unleashed on the 2016 election by then–Kansas secretary of state Kris Kobach, targeting millions of voters with Hispanic surnames in multiple states. The bill would also seek to roll back partisan gerrymandering by encouraging every state to use independent redistricting commissions and to bolster election security nationwide to keep foreign hackers out of state voter rolls. And it would provide federal support for switching election systems from penetrable electronic voting machines to more secure paper ballots.

The act would subject justices of the Supreme Court to the same ethics rules as every other government official. In addition, it would target "dark money" and its pervasive influence on American elections, for the first time legally requiring presidential and vice presidential candidates to release their tax returns. It would strengthen campaign finance laws, forcing the wealthy who donate to "super PACs" to reveal themselves to the public, while reaffirming that Congress, not the billionaire-friendly Supreme Court, is the body invested with the power to regulate money in politics. It would also bring about nearly every recommendation made in the past decade by advocates of full democracy.

And yet it had almost no chance of passing a Republican-majority Senate.

McConnell, the gravel-voiced Kentuckian, called the ideas a "Democrat [*sic*] power grab." Snarling from the Senate floor, he charged that Democrats "want taxpayers on the hook for generous new benefits for federal bureaucrats and government employees," by creating a "new paid holiday for government workers."[1]

"So, this is the Democrats' plan to 'restore democracy,'" he sniffed, deriding the legislation as "the Democrat Politician Protection Act" and claiming federal workers would use the paid holiday to "go out and work on [Democratic] campaigns." Mc-Connell's remarks were quite a reveal of his true intentions, and he was roundly denounced. How, after all, could making it easier for American citizens to vote be a "power grab"? And a power grab by whom—voters who might take advantage of increased access to the polls? McConnell seemed to be acknowledging that the only way his party can win elections is if fewer people vote, and if billionaires are allowed to spend unlimited money on campaigns.

The United States has become what elections experts call a "non-participatory democracy." Between 40 and 60 percent of Americans either skip voting in midterm and presidential elections each cycle or are rendered unable to vote through suppressive tactics. Millions more are barred from the ballot by laws, remnants of the postslavery southern resistance to Reconstruction, that strip former felons of their right to vote.

Statistics compiled by the nonpartisan United States Elections Project found that midterm turnout set a record in 2018, at just 50.3 percent of the "voting eligible population" (VEP).[2] That was lower than the 60.1 percent of the VEP who participated in the 2016 presidential election or the 58.6 percent who voted in 2012. Turnout was at a seventy-year low in 2014 at just 36.7 percent. In non-presidential elections, participation typically drops by an average of 20 points compared to presidential years, with older, more rural Republicans taking part in these elections more so than diverse Democratic voters in the out-years, leading the Republican Party to seize back state and federal legislative power even after the election of a Democratic president.

American voter participation has been anemic for decades, particularly among younger Americans, unmarried women, and Hispanics (who tend to be young relative to the rest of the population), as well as those of lower incomes. Research has found a direct correlation between household income and voting likelihood.[3] A 2012 study by the largest private salary survey company, Payscale, found that the 70 percent of Americans earning less than $70,000 were significantly more likely to vote Democratic, while the 30 percent earning more than $70,000 were more likely to vote Republican.[4]

The National Assessment of Educational Progress has determined that people with low scores on understanding basic civics from eighth through twelfth grade are less likely to vote.[5] America's high levels of non-participation in elections place us near the bottom of developed countries. U.S. voter turnout in 2016 was in the lowest third of developed countries: below Estonia, Ireland, Slovakia, Spain, Portugal, and Canada, and above only Luxemburg, Slovenia, Poland, Chile, Latvia, Switzerland, Iceland, Japan, and Turkey.[6]

That seemed to suit Donald Trump's party just fine.

Nancy MacLean, in her book *Democracy in Chains,* chronicles the generations-long quest by the superrich to hobble democracy in their own interest. She said the Republicans who lined up behind Trump, their paymasters, and even some socially liberal members of the financial elite have used their wealth to bend the levers of government to their will, to reduce taxation on themselves, and to strip as many benefits from ordinary Americans as politicians will bear. And they've used a pointed, often racialized communications strategy to convince nonwealthy, white voters to go along.

MacLean traces the strategy for selling this view of guarding wealth as almost a moral and even racial imperative among those on the right to the work of James McGill Buchanan, an influential Tennessee economist particularly active during the 1960s as a professor at the University of Virginia and considered one of the architects of the modern right. Buchanan "understood how much white people depended on government," MacLean said to me. The white farmers and working poor in the southern states didn't need to be political scientists to recognize that the government had brought them electricity and farm subsidies when the crop yield was low, and provided Social Security, Medicare, and Medicaid, which made growing old bearable.

In her book MacLean revealed the contents of Buchanan's papers and said the economist was determined to find ways to undermine people's faith and confidence in government, and to replace it with skepticism and even hostility as a means of convincing those rural, working-class people to vote against their own interests and in favor of reducing the taxes on the wealthy.

Buchanan's work, she said, "systematically tried to show government failure as opposed to market failure," when things go wrong in the economic lives of citizens. Buchanan pioneered the stigmatizing of people who rely on public assistance that became a staple of the "welfare queen" politics Reagan deployed and that Donald Trump has revived as a way of demonizing undocumented immigrants. "Even in his academic work," she says, "Buchanan used language like, 'parasites on the productive,' or 'predators and prey.'" In this formulation, the "predators" were senior citizens who wanted a prescription drug benefit, red state teachers trying to save their schools, or the working poor, and the "prey" are the wealthy taxpayers who don't want to commit the resources. "The 'takers versus makers' rubric," which became common among Republicans, "comes from this," MacLean says.

Even Trump's language about "draining the swamp" had a pedigree in these divisive politics. It was a theme of the "southern strategy" deployed by Republican politicians like Barry Goldwater, Richard Nixon, and Ronald Reagan. It underpinned the notion of stripping away parts of the New Deal and LBJ's Great Society simply because they represented the overreach of "big government," no matter how much they helped people.

MacLean describes researching in Reagan's presidential library and viewing his advice to female aides joining the federal government. The archives revealed how Reagan instructed the newly minted public servants never to speak of the federal government, for which they were now working, as "we." Rather, Reagan said that in all public pronouncements to refer to all government agencies, even their own, as "they," lest they "lose the fight to 'drain the swamp' "—the phrase Reagan first popularized in 1983 to describe his goal of limiting government's reach.[7] "He was supposed to be inspiring people who were going into the federal employment," MacLean said, "and he was saying, never say, 'we.' Say 'they' and making government the enemy will help drain the swamp."

Three decades later, Mitt Romney, the former Massachusetts governor and presidential candidate whose net worth was estimated by *Forbes* at $230 million in 2012, was secretly recorded telling a small group of wealthy donors during a Boca Raton, Florida, fundraiser, that there are "47 percent" of Americans "who are dependent upon government, who believe that they are victims, who believe the government has a responsibility to care for them, who believe that they are entitled to healthcare, to food, to housing, to you-name-it. That that's an entitlement. And the government should give it to them. And they will vote for [President Obama's reelection] no matter what . . . These are people who pay no income tax."

Romney's dismissal of those Americans as voters he could never win was of a piece with the same philosophy of "makers and takers" that had long animated his party. "[M]y job is not to worry about those people," Romney told his well-heeled audience. "I'll never convince them they should take personal responsibility and care for their lives."[8] When the statement was exposed by *Mother Jones*, it proved fatal for Romney's campaign. What received less attention was his unsubtle appeal to white grievance, when he quipped that had his father, who was born in Mexico, where the family lived with other Mormon exiles, "been born of Mexican parents, I'd have a better shot of winning this."[9]

"Ultimately, it means economic eugenics," MacLean said. "It's not the overtly racial eugenics of the early 20th century, but it is a language to say that some people are, not only disposable, they must be controlled and shamed and pushed away from those who are deemed more productive. It's slowly eating away like acid at our sense of connection to one another."

That acid is getting stronger. A January 2019 National Bureau of Economic Research study by Gabriel Zucman found that income inequality has reached levels not seen since the Gilded Age, with the top 1 percent income earners in the United States taking home nearly a quarter of the earnings from the U.S. economy. Zucman found that in the years leading to the Great Depression, the top one-tenth of the 1 percent of richest Americans gobbled up a full 25 percent of household wealth. Starting with the Depression through the 1970s, the share of wealth held by America's superrich declined until it bottomed out during the 1970s, and then it began rising during the Reagan era, when the top 1 percent controlled between 25 and 30 percent.[10] By the time Donald Trump was elected president, the figure had ballooned to 40 percent.

The average member of the top 1 percent of income earners, who earns $421,926 before taxes, takes home about 8.4 times the average income of the other 99 percent, who have average incomes of $50,107. And depending on which state a person lives in, the threshold for getting into the 1 percent is getting higher, requiring $744,426 in earnings in New York, $1.7 million in Jackson Hole, Wyoming (home to former vice president Dick Cheney), and $1.32 million to make the classification nationwide.

As of 2019, Amazon founder and *Washington Post* owner Jeff Bezos, America's richest man as of 2019, with a net worth of $137 billion, earns nearly three times the average American wage earner's income *every minute of his life*, even while he's asleep.[11] And wealth in America, defined as a total value of net assets, is even more concentrated at the top than income.

Zucman also found that the top 0.1 percent—men, for the most part, like Bezos—control nearly 20 percent of the nation's wealth, more than the bottom 80 percent of Americans combined. Zoom out to the top 10 percent, and the share of the wealth they control balloons to 70 percent. The concentration of wealth in America is reaching historic highs. A February 2019 report for *Fortune* noted that "the 400 richest people in the U.S., or the top 0.00025 percent, have tripled their share of wealth since the 1980s. Meanwhile, the 150 million Americans in the bottom 60 percent have seen a decline from a 5.7 percent share in 1987 to a 2.1 percent share in 2014."[12]

Internationally, America is ranked fortieth (out of 150 countries) with the highest levels of income inequality, about the same levels of inequality as Russia. The rich in both countries control approximately equal shares of the wealth and income. America, in a very real sense, has its own oligarchs.

In the United States, the states with the highest levels of income inequality tend to be high-population states and the states in the South.[13] The central and western states, where Republicans have held near-absolute power for decades, and those in the South, where the party seized total control in the midterm election routs of 2010 and 2014, are characterized by low wages, broken or non-existent unions, low or even no state taxes, and paltry funding for public schools.

After the *Brown v. Board of Education* decision in 1954 desegregated public schools, followed by the bold transgressions against southerners' "traditional way of life" by black schoolchildren, backed by the federal government and the National Guard in Little Rock, Arkansas, and Selma, Alabama, many white parents pulled their children out of the newly desegregated schools, leaving many of them almost entirely black. Once their children were no longer in the public school system, defunding of those institutions at the state level was easy for conservatives to achieve.

Civil rights leaders continue to fight the gutting of public schools in places such as Florida, North Carolina, and Mississippi, which along with western states like Arizona, Idaho, and Oklahoma are among the states that spent the least money per pupil on public education in 2016, the latest year for which the Census Bureau has provided data. The state that spent the least on public education in 2016? Utah. And the state that spent the most: New York, followed by the District of Columbia, Connecticut, New Jersey, and Vermont.

Hatred of taxation is particularly strong in the South, as demonstrated on the extreme end by a shocking Valentine's Day 2019 editorial in an Alabama newspaper, *The Democrat-Reporter*, that during the 1990s had attracted Pulitzer Prize talk and widespread praise for its coverage of local corruption. The editorial, written by Goodloe Sutton, publisher and editor and the son of the newspaper's founder, who was hailed in a 1998 congressional citation as "one of Alabama's finest and most ethical journalists," [14] called for "the KKK to night ride [*sic*] again," seeming to call for a Klan raid on Capitol Hill in Washington, D.C., and warning that "Democrats in the Republican Party and Democrats are plotting to raise taxes in Alabama." The editorial was bizarre, even alleging that some freed slaves "borrowed their former masters' robes and horses and rode through the night to frighten some evildoer" [15] as would-be Klansmen themselves. And Sutton blamed Democratic presidents for getting the United States into World War I, World War II, and the Korean War, darkly warning of the creep of socialism.

Sutton concluded by saying that, "Seems like the Klan would be welcome to raid the gated communities up there" in Washington, D.C., adding, "truly they are the ruling class." Asked by the *Montgomery Advertiser* to defend his written comments, Sutton said, "If we could get the Klan to go up there and clean out D.C., we'd all been better off," adding that if not, "we'll get the hemp ropes out, loop them over a tall limb and hang all of them." [16]

When the editorial drew national attention, Alabama politicians roundly condemned Sutton, and there were numerous calls for his resignation. He ultimately stepped down, even handing over control of the paper to a black woman. But this kind of talk didn't sound much different from what David Duke said when he ran for governor of Louisiana.

The spurning of taxation by red states—even when it was more mainstream than Goodloe Sutton's rant—advantaged the wealthy by shifting the burden of taxation away from their income and assets, and toward regressive forms of taxation that most heavily burden the poor. According to the Institute on Taxation and Economic Policy, of the ten states with the most regressive tax policies, seven (Florida, South Dakota, Nevada, Tennessee, Texas, Washington, and Wyoming) levy no broad-based personal income tax at all, and two (Pennsylvania and Illinois) use a flat tax that falls on rich and poor with equal percentage weight but vastly different shares of disposable income, and the last (Oklahoma) attaches a top rate to its graduated income tax that is so low, at $12,000, that it might as well be a flat tax.

The institute's 2018 report on the distribution of tax systems nationwide pointed out that these "terrible ten" states, which rely heavily on sales and excise taxes, tolls, and other fees paid day by day, "tax their poorest residents—those in the bottom 20 percent of the income scale—at rates up to six times higher than the wealthy. Middle-income families in these states pay a rate up to four times higher as a share of their income than the wealthiest families." Income inequality in the states with regressive tax systems was far higher than in high-income-tax-rate states like California, which the ITEP determined has America's least regressive tax system, followed by the District of Columbia, Vermont, Delaware, and Minnesota.[17]

It's hard to see how this could be sustainable. Despite historically low unemployment, more than 110 months of consecutive job growth dating back to the Obama administration, and even some wage growth in recent years, the average American has only about the same purchasing power that they had forty years ago.[18] Real wages, after inflation, haven't grown in decades.

The wage gains that have occurred have mainly gone to the highest income earners.

The 2019 government shutdown drove home the fact that most Americans can't long outlast a single missed paycheck. Pushing more of the tax burden onto middle- and low-income workers, including restaurant and fast food workers, nurses, and public school teachers, in an economy where employees of companies like Walmart are forced to supplement their incomes with food stamps, amounting to a huge taxpayer subsidy to one of the most profitable companies in America, feels like a recipe for social breakdown.

Writing in the *Atlantic* about his launch of a modern-day reboot of Dr. King's "Poor People's Campaign," Bishop William Barber of North Carolina stated that, "In the richest society in human history, nearly half of the population lives in poverty or is struggling to make ends meet. More than half of African-American workers and nearly 60 percent of Latino workers are paid less than $15 an hour. In the South, half of all jobs pay less than $15 an hour. During the past five years, state legislatures have stepped in to override many of the municipalities where the 'Fight for $15' has succeeded." [19]

Noting that America's economic growth, particularly since the Great Recession of 2007 and 2008, had delivered its overwhelming benefits to the very rich, and that "Wall Street got bailouts while working Americans saw their jobs shipped overseas or outsourced to contractors," and that "the top 400 taxpayers earn an average of $97,000 an hour, while people are arrested for protesting because they can't survive on $7.25 an hour, the minimum that Washington requires," Barber named what he called the "four diseases, all connected, [that] now threaten the nation's social and moral health: racism, poverty, environmental devastation, and the war economy—sanctified by the heresy of Christian nationalism." [20]

Indeed, five years after the financially beleaguered city of Flint, Michigan, switched its taps from the pristine water of Lake Michigan to the polluted Flint River, the city's residents had still not been made whole. The interim move to take water from the Flint River had been designed to save money while the city, under the control of an unelected "emergency manager,"[21] prepared for a permanent switch to a newly created, potentially lucrative county water authority outside of big-city Detroit's control. The "emergency manager"[22] law was the brainchild of the state's Republican governor, Rick Snyder, a venture capitalist swept into office with the Tea Party wave in 2010. When residents complained about the water—and as sickness and hair loss and lead poisoning spread—the manager refused to stop the Flint River water flowing. The priority was the $5 million the city could save.

In Detroit, when other reporters and I arrived to cover the crisis, residents and activists spoke darkly of different motives: gutting Detroit financially by robbing it of its biggest water customer while enriching a new set of water barons, or outright racism against the largely black residents of Flint. In the end, a dozen people died and more than eighty were sickened by an outbreak of Legionnaires' disease.

Although more than a dozen people were charged with crimes related to the switching of the taps and the outbreak of disease, as of January 2019, no one had gone to jail. Of the fifteen people charged with crimes related to the sickening of Flint, seven pleaded no contest to misdemeanors, with the promise that their records would be expunged in exchange for their cooperation, and four of the five people on the front lines of the crisis, including the head of the state's drinking water authority, accepted plea deals, leaving residents—many still living on bottled water—furious.[23]

A 2017 lawsuit filed by the Center for Constitutional Rights and others on behalf of residents and elected officials in cities such as Detroit, Flint, Benton Harbor, and Pontiac charged that the 2011 law creating the emergency managers, pushed through by Snyder and the Republican legislature upon his election, repealed during the higher-turnout presidential race in 2012, and then reinstated by Snyder and the legislature in a different form, was applied unequally against the state's black residents, 56 percent of whom were living under "emergency" control at the time.[24] In all, seven cities and school districts were at one time or another placed under the unreviewable control of the state.

The battle for fair treatment of America's working classes reached far outside of struggling urban centers in the Northeast and the Rust Belt. Around the country, teachers from West Virginia to Colorado to California went on strike in 2018 and 2019 to demand decent wages so they could afford to live where they taught.

Meanwhile, the one area where Trump's Republican chorus in Washington was willing to oppose him was on drawing down our military presence around the world. Trump, having hired John Bolton and Elliot Abrams, hawkish remnants of Reagan-era and Bush II military adventurism, knew when to get back on script. He routinely bragged on the campaign trail that under his watch, the military had never been so flush with taxpayer dollars. "Our problem isn't that we don't have enough money. It's that we don't have the moral capacity to face what ails our society," Bishop William Barber wrote in *The Atlantic* for a 2018 issue celebrating the legacy of Dr. Martin Luther King Jr.

America's moral crisis was deeply spiritual and cultural, but, according to activists like Barber, it was also economic, and steeped in the unending quest for a small, wealthy few for absolute power. The one thing Dr. King, during the first Poor People's Campaign, might have found unimaginable was that the man who would become the perfect avatar for the plutocrat chorus's war on the working class, the poor, the social safety net, and America's quest for human decency would be a pure, carnival showman like Donald Trump, who turned out to be the finest ally the Republican establishment—men like Mitch McConnell—ever had.

PETER GEORGESCU WAS BORN IN ROMANIA JUST AS THE SECOND World War began. He touts his novel birthday, "3-9, 3-9," saying, "if you believe in numerology, that has to be a great number." His British-educated father ran Romania's Ploesti oil fields for Standard Oil of New Jersey, one of the companies spun off from Standard Oil, the oil behemoth founded by John D. Rockefeller and Henry Flagler in 1870, after the company was broken up as an illegal trust by the Supreme Court in 1911. Georgescu says that when he was a child, Romania was the "Saudi Arabia of Europe," and its oil fields were a particular focus of bombardment by Allied war planes.

Though Romania sided with the Nazis until near the war's end, Georgescu's father ran afoul of the Axis power. "My father was arrested by the Germans and put in prison along with many other potential threats to the Nazis." While in prison, he says, his father became a kind of "governor" among the incarcerated businesspeople, professors, and other dissidents while his mother became a courier, passing messages between his father and the Office of Strategic Services, the forerunner of the CIA.

After the war, in 1947, his parents flew to New York on business for a two- or three-week trip on behalf of the oil company, leaving eight-year-old Georgescu and his older brother with his grandparents. While they were gone, the Iron Curtain came down, and his parents couldn't return, for fear the communists would kill them. The regime executed 300,000 people during this period. Others were put to work in labor camps, including Georgescu, his brother, and his grandfather, a former governor of Transylvania, who was eventually murdered in prison. Georgescu describes the labor camps as dismal: "ten-hour days, hard labor, cleaning sewers, digging holes for electric poles, working high-tension wires, obviously no schooling. Six days a week we worked. Sundays we slept."

Georgescu's parents, thousands of miles away, grew increasingly desperate. They were approached by Romanian diplomats and offered an ultimatum. "They said to my father, 'you want to see your kids alive again? Then spy for us.'" Instead, his father went to U.S. authorities for help.

"He went to the FBI the next morning and said, 'What do we do?'" Georgescu said. The FBI suggested he become a double agent. Georgescu says his father had "seen that play before. It never ends well." So he asked for an alternative, and the agents suggested he go public with the story of their children's incarceration. They told his father, "That'll put the Russians on notice, that [we know] they have you and you had better be alive." The agents offered to use the FBI's media contacts to make the story go big. At that time, "the communists wanted the world to know that they were civilized," he says, as part of the "PR gamesmanship between America and the Soviet Union."

The gambit worked. In 1954, the Georgescu brothers were freed and reunited with their parents, with the help of President Eisenhower and Frances Payne Bolton, a Republican socialite and the first female member of Congress from Standard Oil's founding state of Ohio. The brothers went on a U.S. media tour, being photographed with the president and congresswoman in Washington and appearing on the *Today* show. Georgescu was fifteen years old, and he was given a full scholarship to attend elite Phillips Exeter Academy, provided he could learn English by the first year. He went on to lead a storied life, earning degrees from Princeton and Stanford Business School, and eventually rising to the chairmanship of Young & Rubicam, the advertising agency from which he eventually retired as chairman.

Now an author, public speaker, and U.S. citizen, Georgescu is among those who fear that the Trump era, coming on top of decades of expanding economic inequality and growing tribalism, could lead to an American lurch toward the extremism he witnessed in Romania in his youth.

His native Romania, he says, had "an absurdly authoritarian, totalitarian system on the extreme right" under Nazism, "and on the extremist left" when communism, which he calls "an aggressive form of socialism," took over.

Georgescu says, comparing it to the modern day, "Bernie Sanders and Donald Trump were kissing cousins," in 2016, "because their campaigns were almost identical" in their cries of a "rigged system" that only they could overturn.

Georgescu thinks the way to prevent the country from lurching to either pole is a fundamental reinvigoration of American democracy. "Extremism cannot operate in a truly democratic environment," he says. Instead, the power of extremist movements "comes from the disadvantaged; from the folks who are frustrated and angry."

That anger, he says, is rooted in America's yawning, and growing, economic inequality. "When inequality gets to be too large, there are two ways the problem gets solved," he says. "You either redistribute wealth through taxation or formal government action or you redistribute poverty. My grandmother and I, when we were in Romania, we went to the city hall with everybody else, and we were told, 'Bring all the money you have.' Some people would empty their mattress, with all the cash that they were holding, because there was new paper, new coins. Your old money was no good, and you brought all of your millions [of leu, the Romanian currency], or hundreds of thousands, or a thousand, whatever you had. The only small point was that you only got back a maximum of two hundred leu. So, that's it. That's redistributing poverty."

Georgescu worries that inequality is pulling America apart, weakening its fabric through a combination of defunded public schools, reduced wages exacerbated by globalization, union overreach during the 1970s, and the decimation of labor organizing power during the 1980s through the combined might of government and business. "Basically, employees—and I call them employees, not just workers, because 'workers' sounds like I'm just talking about blue-collar workers, when I mean most the employees outside the C-suite—are seeing their wages flat and growing at below inflation." He says that rising inequality has created two Americas, echoing the theme of Senator John Edwards's aborted 2004 presidential campaign. "And it's absolutely devastating."

"If you go around and ask people, 'What's inequality mean?'" says Georgescu, who has made income inequality the focus of his writing and public speaking, they'll say, "Maybe it's really poor people—people making less than $30,000 a year; that's inequality. Well, it isn't. The median wage now in America is about $54,000. But even at $75,000 a year, people with three and four kids can't make ends meet." Georgescu says a better way to look at inequality is to talk about households.

"Every household has a 'kitty,'" he says. "You know what's coming in, you know what's going out, and what's left goes into a metaphorical kitty. So, what goes into the kitty?" He says that for six in ten American households, the answer is nothing, and that nearly 60 percent of American households "have to borrow money," by dipping into overdraft funds, taking out payday and other short-term loans, or even using high-interest-rate credit cards to put food on the table.

"For 20 percent of us, life is as good as it gets," Georgescu says. But for the rest, the amount of spendable or savable cash left at the end of the month—after rent or mortgage and food and utilities and kids' college tuition, even for those classified as middle class—is much too small. "God forbid the roof leaks, your car gets broken into, and you're not fully insured, you get sick or get fired."

That sense that everything about our society is unfair, and someone has to be blamed or made to pay is a breeding ground where fascism, nativism, and racism can fester. Fixing that, Georgescu says, has to be a top priority, not just of the U.S. government, but of the business community as well.

"This other America is frustrated," he says of the two countries living within our borders. "They're unhappy, they're angry, they have lost hope. That's the worst part. They have lost hope that anybody in this country is willing to listen. And they found in 2016 two people who spoke to them directly: Trump and Bernie Sanders, who both said, fundamentally, 'We hear you. The establishment has let you down.' And, by the way, that's true, both Democrats and Republicans alike have not really addressed the plight of those folks."

These voters "are not policy wonks," he says. "They don't spend their days listening to the news, though they do listen to Fox. They want to make sure that the establishment that has let them down for forty years goes away. That's the only thing that they know: that what is, is bad. So that means anarchism. They want to destroy. They don't know how to fix it."

Georgescu says American business should do its part by paying their employees a decent, living wage as a first step toward reducing economic inequality, and by mitigating against the inevitable march of automation, which he says should be used, not to "get rid of people," but to make people's work easier and more productive. He calls employees "the secret sauce for the twenty-first century," saying "only employees can increase innovation and productivity." And they, not just company shareholders, should be compensated for it.

He points out that today we have "shareholder primacy," in which "ninety cents out of every dollar of operating profit goes to the shareholder. Which means that the workers don't get paid much, which means that you don't invest in your own business, which means that you don't do basic research for the future. So, we're becoming less competitive over the years, and we're going to become a poorer nation, economically and in every sense." He fears that if America continues down its present course, "we'll become another mediocre country in this world."

"Poverty has improved dramatically because of the principles of democratic capitalism, which today we don't have" in America, Georgescu says. "We have democratic capitalism for us, the plutocrats. But it's not 'inclusive capitalism,' and that's got to change. We need capitalists, we need their principles, but not the capitalism that started in 1980 under Reagan and Milton Friedman. That's not the capitalism we want. We need inclusive capitalism where all the boats are all lifted because the tide is coming. So we have to find the ways to do that."

It seems easier said than done.

As Anand Ghirdadas, author of *Winners Take All: The Elite Charade of Changing the World*, has frequently noted on Twitter and the cable airwaves that the global elite have erected an intricate system that preserves their own wealth and power, festooning it with philanthropy to keep the Bastille stormers at bay.

Ghirdadas is among those who say the first step toward finding a solution to wealth and income inequality is the one voiced by a Dutch historian named Rutger Bregman, who stunned a panel on inequality at the World Economic Forum in Davos, Switzerland, in February 2019: raise taxes on the rich.

"This is my first time at Davos," Bregman told the audience during the annual gathering of the well-heeled to discuss solutions to global problems. "And I find it quite a bewildering experience, to be honest. Fifteen hundred private jets are flown in here to hear Sir David Attenborough speak about how we're wrecking the planet. I hear people talk in the language of participation, and justice, and equality, and transparency. But then, almost no one raises the real issue of tax avoidance and of the rich just not paying their fair share. It feels like I'm at a firefighters conference and no one's allowed to speak about water, right?"

Some in the audience seemed stunned, and other panelists chimed in, including Oxfam International executive director Winnie Byanyima, who recited a litany of first world sins: jobs that don't pay a living wage, American women working in chicken-plucking factories where they were forced to wear diapers due to limited bathroom breaks, and a breathtaking concentration of wealth among a handful of the world's wealthiest people, such that, according to Byanyima, "last year alone, the wealth of billionaires was rising by $2.5 billion a day," while "the wealth of the bottom half of humanity, 3.8 billion people, was declining . . . by $500 million a day."[25]

"Something needs to change here," Bregman said. "Ten years ago, the World Economic Forum asked the question, 'What must industry do to prevent a broad social backlash?' The answer's very simple; just stop talking about philanthropy and start talking about taxes, taxes, taxes." Bregman recalled a challenge by tech billionaire Michael Dell, who during the forum challenged those gathered to name a single country where a top marginal tax rate of 70 percent had produced results.

"I'm a historian," said Bregman. "The United States, that's where it has actually worked, in the 1950s during Republican president Eisenhower, the war veteran. The top marginal rate in the U.S. was 91 percent for people like Michael Dell and the top estate tax for people like Michael Dell was more than 70 percent. This is not rocket science. We can talk for a very long time about all these stupid philanthropy schemes. We can invite [rock star and human rights advocate] Bono once more. But, come on, we gotta be talking about taxes."[26] A video of the exchange quickly went viral.

A solid majority of Americans agree, favoring taxing the wealthiest among us by large margins. A February 2019 *Politico/Morning Consult* poll found that 76 percent of registered voters wanted the superrich to pay more in taxes, with 61 percent favoring the kind of "wealth tax" proposed by Massachusetts senator Elizabeth Warren, who launched her run for president that month. That tax would levy a 2 percent surcharge on those with a net worth of $50 million or more. A smaller plurality, 45 percent, favored a plan proposed by New York congresswoman Alexandria Ocasio-Cortez that would restore a 70 percent top income tax rate on incomes above $10 million—the top rate when Ronald Reagan took office, before the first of two massive tax cuts he signed slashed the top rate first to 50 percent in 1981, then to 28 percent in 1986. Income and wealth inequality ballooned every year thereafter.

The reversion of American society to a nation of the superrich and the rest—compounded by an economy that has permanently shifted away from the industries that built the Rust Belt and toward information-technology-based jobs in coastal and urban centers, and automation in the fields that once employed millions of Americans, mostly men, without college degrees—is straining the country in ways that go beyond economics.

London-based author and management expert Umair Haque put it bluntly in a Valentine's Day 2019 Medium essay: "Capitalism is imploding into fascism," he wrote. "It is doing so at light speed, with a vicious fury, and there's no certainty that it's going to stop before it burns the house down."[27]

Haque, a sharp critic of capitalism in general, appears to believe that such a collapse is inevitable. He writes that after "having concentrated too much money in too few hands, a collapsing middle class—enough of it, at least—is reverting to tribalism, racism, hate, and violence as the primary modes of social organization. This was especially easy in America because unlike most other rich countries, it was an apartheid state until the 1970s. White Americans dislike hearing that—but in Virginia, where I grew up, 'intermarriage' was illegal until 1973 or so. America's had roughly 30, maybe 40 years, to attempt something resembling a modern democracy of genuine equals. But it didn't try nearly hard enough, didn't invest in democracy nearly enough—and now it's imploding into fascism."[28]

Indeed, the Trump era was rife with dire warnings, with bestselling books carrying ominous titles like *How Democracies Die* and former secretary of state Madeleine Albright's *Fascism: A Warning* flying off the shelves. In Texas, I met a Holocaust survivor named Margaret, who pulled me aside as we waited to enter the military-style detention camp the Trump administration set up to hold unaccompanied Central American children in custody. Margaret said she feared the warning bells that should have been going off for Jewish intellectuals and shopkeepers in Europe in the 1930s could be sounding again.

Meanwhile, some moderate Democrats and "never Trump Republicans" and former Republicans who had abandoned the party over Trump feared a lurch toward socialism, as well as a backlash that would send the superrich fleeing right back into the arms of Trump, to avoid confiscatory taxation of their wealth on behalf of an angry public.

Even some wealthy Democrats were beginning to view their party's backlash against plutocracy as a threat to their personal wealth, and they were growing increasingly nervous as 2020 loomed. Sanders returned to the presidential stage, and new, young, and boldly progressive political figures like congresswomen Alexandra Ocasio-Cortez, Ilhan Omar, Rashida Tlaib, and Ayanna Pressley strode to prominence. Progressive politicians were proffering ideas like a "Green New Deal" and taxpayer-subsidized college.

The small but vocal pool of "third way moderates" feared that the same toxic brew of extreme income inequality, stagnating heavy industry, outsourcing, and racial conflagration that produced a President Trump would cause the party left standing, the Democrats, to lurch too far to the left, leaving their core values adrift.

The choice as the 2020 election loomed was increasingly between a president many former Republicans could not abide, over his ugly rhetoric, flouting of American ideals, and fidelity to

Vladimir Putin, but whose totems of old-line Republicanism—like tax cuts, deregulation, a conservative Supreme Court, and a hawkish foreign policy, they hoped to preserve.

Steve Schmidt, who ran John McCain's presidential campaign in 2008 and played a key role in promoting an early iteration of the Trump circus, in the form of vice presidential nominee Sarah Palin, became one of Trump's most eloquent detractors. In 2019, however, Schmidt signed on, along with Barack Obama campaign veteran Bill Burton, to the potential third-party candidacy of former Starbucks CEO and once-prolific Democratic donor Howard Schultz.

Many political watchers feared a Schultz run would help Trump win a second term, something Schultz vowed he would never knowingly enable. But Schultz framed his potential campaign not around a critique of Trump, but on his disdain for a lurch toward socialism, with its threats to raise taxes on the superrich, like him. He seemed to be pitching a more mannerly plutocracy.

Former moderate Massachusetts governor Bill Weld entered the race, launching a primary bid against Trump. He was potentially offering a return to a kinder, gentler version of Trumpism: retaining the hyperlow taxes for the rich, the deregulation and the friendliness to Wall Street, without the crudeness, vulgarity, subservience to foreign leaders, and moblike corruption that Trump had foisted on the party. Maryland governor Larry Hogan signaled he might join the fray as well.

Bruce Bartlett, the former Reagan-Bush official, believes that in a fundamental way, the rich have always feared democracy. "Their fear is the de facto French Revolution where the people are in control. Of course, they're quite right when they point to the Founding Fathers as sharing this view. The Electoral College, for example, is the most anti-democratic institution you can think of next to the U.S. Senate," which until 1913 and the Seventeenth Amendment to the Constitution, was elected by state legislatures.

Perhaps Howard Schultz was laying the groundwork for a new political party to compete with both the Grand Old Party Trump had so altered and a Democratic Party that some feared was answering Trump's indecency with socialism. The challenge, of course, was that Donald Trump had revealed, in stark terms, that the old, "small government" mantra of the donor class had no real voting base. Were there enough "low taxes on the rich, little government support for the poor" social moderates like Schultz (or the billionaire Koch brothers, who declined to support Trump and married progressive ideas including criminal justice reform with their libertarian push for dramatic deregulation of their core energy businesses) to form a viable third party? Ross Perot tested that proposition in 1992, and again in 1996, and came up short. Even then, the anger Perot tapped into was on the same anti-government, populist right where Trump lives now.

The voters who kept Republicans in power, and who stood foursquare behind Donald Trump, were making it clear, in poll after poll, that they cared more about preserving the prerogatives of white, Christian Americans than about tax cuts for the rich or more foreign wars. They had inaugurated Trump and the right-wing media complex as their new leaders.

And elected Republicans clearly feared them.

"I just cannot believe how wrapped up we have become in this idea of just winning an election," said former RNC chairman and current NBC News/MSNBC contributor Michael Steele, expressing incredulity at Trump's rambling performance at the 2019 Conservative Political Action Conference in Maryland (the state where prior to his Barack Obama–era party chairmanship, Steele served as lieutenant governor). "Could you imagine the first black president standing on a stage, cursing and ranting for two hours? Every Republican I know would have been out of their minds. Donald Trump is doing and becoming everything Republicans accused Barack Obama of being and doing. He is acting like the autocrat he's always wanted to be."

Steele, who was a Catholic seminarian before entering Republican politics as county, state, and then national chairman, frames his party's dilemma in biblical terms. "I call it the 'idolatry of Trump,'" he says. "Trump has become the 'golden calf' that the tribe now worships. And the various Moseses of the party, those of the past like McCain, the Jeff Flakes [who have left office rather than battle Trump] and the Kevin McCarthys [who remain] have gone off to a mountaintop somewhere. We have reached the point where you have people talking about Trump the way they *never* talked about Reagan—and you *know* how people in the party felt about Reagan."

Steele traces his party base's veneration of Trump to "a reactionary politics [stimulated by] almost 50 years of benign neglect by the political institutions." Those institutions, including the leadership of the Republican Party in the years starting with the "southern strategy" deployed by Richard Nixon to bring white southern Democrats into the party, followed by Reagan and George W. Bush's pitches to white Christians, "made promises they knew they weren't going to keep"—from ending legalized abortion and appointing a Supreme Court that would overturn *Roe v. Wade*, to reversing federal intervention in southern and northern schools. "They bilked their base of their money and their opportunities for years, for their own political aggrandizement," Steele says.

"Trump, and Bernie Sanders, represent the antithesis of that," says Steele. When Trump promised to drive Central American migrants and Muslims out of America, he implemented it. He has gone to extremes to make good on "building a wall," even if as a practical notion it is impractical, impossible, and unsanctioned by Congress. He has called on his Justice Department to make good on his vows to "lock up" Hillary Clinton and to refashion federal law enforcement as his protectors, and labeled them the "deep state" when they refused to comply, signaling his agreement with his base's anti-government stance.

Even as he runs the executive branch, Trump has made good

on the Reagan mantra that government is "them," not "us." He has launched the trade wars with China that he vowed on the campaign trail, and while he didn't end NAFTA, he renamed it, which for his base is good enough to call a "fix." Even when his policies hurt his base's bottom line, the point is that he has kept his promises, which makes him something other than a politician.

Steele worries that Democrats fail to understand how powerful that is, and how much it augurs the real potential for Trump's reelection, no matter how low his poll numbers go. Even if he made good on his vow to extinguish Obamacare and take the health coverage of tens of millions of Americans—including his own followers—down with it, there seemed to be little chance that many of the Trumpist faithful would vote against him. And if he is reelected in 2020, Steele says, "Trump will conclude that, wait, you [in the media and 'the establishment'] threw everything at me, and the people didn't buy it, and they reelected me anyway? In his mind, at that point, he's unstoppable. So that episode at CPAC will be a daily occurrence. That's one of the hallmarks of an authoritarian," says Steele. "They love the sound of their own voice."

What has Trump done to America's voice? And can the country get it back once he is no longer in power, whether after four years or eight, or in the nightmare scenario of those who fear his reign most, more?

Nancy MacLean believes America needs more than just an adjustment to its capitalist system or to its rates of taxation if it hopes to pull itself back from the brink Trump has driven us to. She says the nation needs a new "story"—a narrative that can bind together our disparate parts into a cohesive whole, and that will give every American a stake in the success of this experiment in multiracial democracy.

"The philosopher Richard Rorty wrote this book called *Achieving Our Country*, that kind of stuck with me," she said. "It basically says you can't win the support of a majority in America if you don't have a good narrative of who we are as a people, and a story of where we came from and where we're going. That was one of the things that I admired so much about Barack Obama." MacLean says that from the first time she heard Obama speak, as he ran for the U.S. Senate from Illinois, where she lived at the time, she thought, "Whoa, that is the narrative we need. We can be proud to be Americans if our history is Frederick Douglass, and the women's suffrage movement, and the labor movement, and all these transformations. It's a narrative that at least says there was," and is, "a 'we.'"

MacLean fears that the country, with Trump as its avatar, is in danger of "losing the American narrative with nothing to replace it." She worries that Trump will leave behind an America that few beyond his fervent base can take any pride in.

The American story has a hopeful narrative if we can find the parts that sing over the chorus of pain. And while no president on his (or one day, her) own can end voter suppression and gerrymandering; end racism, nativism, and xenophobia; loosen the grip of the billionaire class on our economy and government; or restore democracy at home and American leadership abroad; and no one occupant of the White House can impose fairness and equity on a capitalist system that is hurtling toward a future that bodes ill not just for the American worker but for the global workforce, too, we can hope that the next one, if we're lucky, will try.

EPILOGUE

After Trump, Who Are We?

"When you get to know a lot of people, you make a great discovery. You find that no one group has a monopoly on looks, brains, goodness, or anything else. It takes all the people—black and white, Catholic, Jewish and Protestant, recent immigrants and Mayflower *descendants—to make up America."*

—Judy Garland

MARIA TERESA KUMAR, AN NBC NEWS/MSNBC CONTRIBUTOR, has spent a lot of time recently in El Paso, Texas. As the CEO of Voto Latino, which focuses on civic engagement and voting rights for America's 52 million Latinx citizens, she has immersed herself in the fight for human rights for the undocumented. She recalled one El Paso trip to address the United States' detention of unaccompanied minors—more than 14,600 at last count—up from just over 9,000 when Trump took office.

Most of the children had come to the country alone, sent on the perilous journey by their desperate parents in hopes they could join relatives already in the United States. Thousands had been separated from their parents by the Trump administration beginning in October 2017.

"I spoke to a volunteer at one of the nonprofit shelters," she said, emphasizing "nonprofit," because the detention of migrant children has become a multimillion-dollar business. Since Donald Trump's inauguration, two private prison companies—GEO Group and CoreCivic—have taken in approximately $400 million in contracts from the Department of Homeland Security.[1]

At the same time, thousands of allegations of sexual abuse have been logged at shelters around the United States.[2] Kumar said the volunteer recounted the story of an eight-year-old Guatemalan boy being housed at a shelter. "He asked if there were coffee vines there," because, he said, "I can pick really fast. I'm really good.'"

The idea of taking the world's labor on the cheap and devaluing the laborers—even of stealing children from their parents—is not new to America. This was built into America's founding, through slavery and indentured servitude, "Indian removals," and more. Cruelty and exploitation have accompanied waves of migration from all over the world, making sure our vegetables and wine get to the table, our hotel rooms get cleaned, our children are cared for, and our standard of living stays high.

The genius of this country, and its redemption, is in how those migrants, and indentures, and enslaved folk, have become a part of the American fabric, even if sometimes they had to fight and bleed to get there. No other country has, in so short a time, absorbed the sheer breadth of humanity and called that Tower of Babel a country. Kumar was born in Colombia, raised in Sonoma, California, and educated in California and at Harvard. She is an American, in the most classic sense of the word.

Karine Jean-Pierre, the national spokeswoman for the activist group MoveOn.org and an NBC News/MSNBC contributor, was a regional political director for the Barack Obama campaign in 2008, and in 2012, she served as his deputy battleground states director. Her parents—her cabdriver dad and home healthcare worker mom—migrated to the United States from Haiti to give their kids a better life. Their daughter wound up working in the White House, for America's first black president. Jean-Pierre's wife, Suzanne, is a descendant of Louisiana Creoles and a successful journalist. They are raising their daughter in an America that was unimaginable when their parents were born.

Jean-Pierre believes that when Obama was elected, the part of America that jealously guards that progress went to sleep, awakening only in time to ensure his reelection. "There was this feeling that, 'We have Obama, we're safe,' " she said. "And I think in many ways we were complacent, and kind of sat on our laurels." Those who said, "I never thought I'd see a black president in my lifetime," weren't off base, she said. "But I think people kind of saw [Obama] as the savior, like he would save all of us."

She believes that Obama was one person who never saw it that way. "I remember him saying, even on election night, that he couldn't do it alone. Like, 'Yes, this has happened, and we've made history,' but that he needed everyone to help him be successful. And I don't think we listened." Instead, too many people just reveled in the magic and the miracle, never fearing that monsters could be at the gate. "There were eight years of thinking, okay, we have a black man in the presidency, I think we're good," she said. "He's decent, he's our guy. We got him reelected. . . . And then you get Donald Trump."

Leah Daughtry grew up in Brooklyn, the daughter of the legendary Rev. Dr. Herbert Daughtry, who came from Savannah, Georgia, with his family as a child, had a religious conversion while serving time for armed robbery, and emerged to follow his father into the ministry; during the 1970s, he fought school segregation and led boycotts against businesses who refused to hire black employees. Leah, a Pentecostal minister, entered Dartmouth College in 1980. She was there at the same time as Laura Ingraham and Dinesh D'Souza, and said the meanness and divisiveness of right-wing politics is nothing new.

Daughtry sees Trump's core followers as an expression of one part of America's DNA that has always been there, and probably always will be. The fear of the "other," the resentment of "the new immigrants," and the jealous guarding of what each American tribe believes to be "their place," their things, their piece of the pie, is just part of a multiracial democracy. There never will be a way to stamp out all of the division.

"We have to decide who we are and what kind of country we want to be inside and outside our borders," she said. "Who do we want to be in the world? What are the values that define us? What image do we want to have and how do we play on the world stage? Who are we to each other, and who are we with our partners in the world?"

Daughtry believes the Donald Trump era is forcing those questions on all of us.

"Trump's presidency is the quiet part out loud," said Faiz Shakir, who was an aide to Democratic majority leader Harry Reid until the senator retired. Shakir, who was born in Florida to Pakistani immigrant parents, agreed that Trump is unearthing the sentiments many on the right have quietly harbored for decades, but never felt "it was politically smart to talk about." Trump "opened that door wide, and said, 'I'm going to talk about [those things] loudly and proudly. I'm going to bash Muslims. I'm going to bash immigrants. I'm going to bash the trans community. I'm going to bash low-income women who go to Planned Parenthood.' It was just explicit. And given that he was rewarded for it politically and feels like his base actually loves and enjoys that, it doesn't surprise me that he has moved so aggressively, policy-wise."

"You've got a certain strain in the country that is susceptible to demagogues," says Nick Akerman, who hails from Springfield, Massachusetts, and was an assistant U.S. attorney for the Southern District of New York, prosecuting bank fraud and other white-collar crimes before signing on to the Watergate investigation to work with fired special prosecutor Archibald Cox and his successor, Leon Jaworski. Akerman sees Trump heading down the Nixon road.

"We actually were lucky to not have to go through it during the Depression," Akerman said. "[Populist Louisiana politician] Huey Long could have very well been elected president in 1936. His style was very similar to Trump's. He was somebody who didn't really know much about the issues, didn't really focus on policy as much as appealing to people through promising things and demagoguery."

During the Depression, "people were more frightened than ever. The world economy collapsed, the economy in the United States collapsed. So that would have been the time that we were probably most vulnerable as a country to somebody like a Donald Trump. It was just a quirk of history that it turned out differently."

Trump exposed weaknesses in American democracy that were never anticipated by the country's founders. "His very election underscores the danger that the dysfunctional Electoral College presents, and might present with increasing frequency," professor Laurence Tribe says. He sees that danger as, "the selection of presidents who are not really supported by a majority of the people, but who manage, in this case with the help of foreign adversaries, to work the system—which has new and newly exposed weaknesses as a result of social media." The founders "clearly believed the Electoral College would filter out dangerous characters who managed through guile and demagoguery to win their way into the hearts of enough people" to gain positions of enormous power, like the presidency. Instead, the system they built proved to be incredibly fragile.

Equally fragile, it turns out, is the idea that a larger American idea can hold our disparate factions together and survive the temptations toward tribalism and factionalism that Trump, and our foreign adversaries, so deftly exploited.

Whatever becomes of Trump—whether he is impeached and removed or serves out his term; whether he is ever held to legal account by prosecutors in Washington or New York; whether his family business survives and grows, or the Trump brand withers; and whether he can build up another wave of anger, resentment, and fear and ride it to four more years in the White House, the Trump era's danger signs are sure to outlast him.

"He rose to the highest level of power by dividing Americans and pitting one against the other," says Kumar. That won't be easily forgotten. "Meanwhile, the biggest challenge is that my children are now part of the most diverse generation America has ever seen. And instead of being thoughtful about how we use the strength of our diversity to move forward and continue being a global leader, he's making it so we can't actually identify and solve the problems that lay ahead."

America stands on the brink of a massive economic upheaval, in which technology and artificial intelligence, not immigration, will be what Kumar called "the true disruptor of our workforce." Yet instead of planning for that future, Trump is leading a third of the country on a crusade against America's youngest population, Latinos.

The youth bulge among America's nonwhite and immigrant populations will have to pay for an aging America's Social Security benefits, keep our safety net afloat and our tax base flush, and could, or should, power our high-tech future. Right now, rather than figuring out how to emerge into that future as a stable, functioning, participatory, multiracial democracy, we're arguing about whether gangs of rapists are storming our southern border and fighting among ourselves in serial episodes of the Trump Show.

The good news—if there is good news—is that most Americans know it.

"Donald Trump in the White House has caused us to stand up and say no," Jean-Pierre said of the American majority who consistently disapprove of Trump by wide margins. The sense that "there's a madman in 1600 Pennsylvania Avenue," particularly among the marginalized communities that feel they are under attack, has sparked a tremendous level of political engagement, inspiring a wave of new aspirants to office who might have sat out the process with a more conventional president in the White House.

In 2020, America will decide what story it wants to tell about itself, when the country chooses between keeping the Trump Show going or fundamentally changing the script.

AFTERWORD TO THE PAPERBACK EDITION

The Bell Tolls

"It is midnight in Washington. . . . How did we get here?"

—Rep. Adam Schiff, February 3, 2020

DEMOCRATIC REPRESENTATIVE ADAM SCHIFF OF CALIFORNIA began his closing argument at the impeachment trial of President Donald J. Trump by thanking Chief Justice John Roberts, who was presiding over the Senate chamber. Schiff then quoted Abraham Lincoln: "Senators, we are not enemies but friends. We must not be enemies," adding that "if Lincoln could speak these words during the Civil War then surely, we can live them now, and overcome our divisions and our animosities." He proceeded to declare that America's democratic system had reached its darkest hour: "It is midnight in Washington." Two months earlier, on December 18, 2019, Donald Trump became the third American president to be impeached by the House and tried in the Senate.[1] Schiff was appointed by Speaker Nancy Pelosi as the lead impeachment manager, and the answer to the riddle Schiff posed on the floor of the Senate—"How did we get here?"—involved a birth, and a death.

The Republican Party was born in 1854 out of a visceral opposition to the expansion of slavery to the American West. The party acceded to presidential power with the inauguration of self-taught lawyer and former Illinois congressman Abraham Lincoln in 1861. Lincoln came to the White House with a fiercely antislavery Radical Republican from Maine, Hannibal Hamlin, at his side as vice president. The two men agreed that the human breeding and bondage that powered the southern economy was incompatible with the notions of liberty the United States was founded on; however, unlike Hamlin, who favored both emancipation and the arming of black Americans, Lincoln never believed in racial equality. Still, the war to preserve the union over which he presided forced America to face its deepest moral rot, through the bloodiest war ever on American soil.

The Republican Party that achieved that physical and moral victory died on February 5, 2020, with Donald Trump's Senate acquittal. Republicans left the legacy of Mr. Lincoln in shambles, along with their own dignity, as they bowed to Trump's disdain for the constitutional balance of power and his open corruption of the office of president. Those who had quit the party when Trump arrived in Washington, or as his behavior became more erratic and unhinged, grieved not just for the end of the party they knew but also for the cause of its death. Their former colleagues benighted themselves in exchange for whatever power they thought they could cling to in a racially changing America.

"Republican leaders in Congress believe—and privately say— that they fear the country is quickly changing in ways that may soon deprive them of power, and that they must use the power they have now to delay it as long as possible, even by harming the Republic if necessary,"[2] Evan McMullin, the former CIA officer–turned 2016 Independent presidential candidate tweeted to explain why the once Grand Old Party had allowed itself to be devoured by Donald Trump.

Another reason was fear.

"For the stay-in-office-at-all-cost representatives and senators," Democratic Senator Sherrod Brown of Ohio wrote in a February 5 op-ed in the *New York Times*, "fear is the motivator. They are afraid that Mr. Trump might give them a nickname like 'Low Energy Jeb' [Bush] and "Lyin' Ted [Cruz]," or that he might tweet about their disloyalty. Or—worst of all—that he might come to their state to campaign against them in the Republican primary. They worry: 'Will the hosts on Fox attack me?' 'Will the mouthpieces on talk radio go after me?' 'Will the Twitter trolls turn their followers against me?' My colleagues know they all just might. There's an old Russian proverb: The tallest blade of grass is the first cut by the scythe. In private, many of my colleagues agree that the president is reckless and unfit. They admit his lies. And they acknowledge what he did was wrong. They know this president has done things Richard Nixon never did. And they know that more damning evidence is likely to come out."[3]

Whether due to cravenness or cowardice, the Republican Party had fully become the Trump Party. Impeachment would not elevate them as it had the Republicans of the Richard Nixon era, many of whom stood up to the criminal president in the end, or the Republicans of the 1860s, who launched this country's first presidential impeachment against Lincoln's successor, Andrew Johnson.

Like Johnson, a Democrat Lincoln unwisely replaced Hamlin with for the 1864 reelection, hoping to appease the treacherous southern states and who inherited the White House after Lincoln's assassination in 1865, Trump was impeached for defying Congress and ignoring its constitutional authority. Like Johnson, Trump had built his political power on a bedrock of rage, rallies, and petty racial hatreds.

Johnson made it clear from the moment he became president that while he had supported keeping the Union intact—a belief that got him on that bipartisan ticket—he wanted no part of making full citizens of the formerly enslaved. He vetoed

America's first Civil Rights Act in 1866 and fired the Secretary of War, whose charge it was to protect black men, women, and children from the violent white insurgents in the renegade southern states whose goal it was to brutalize or lynch any black man, woman, or child who resisted remaining in their prewar condition of servitude and subjugation. Johnson resisted the Radical Republican congressional majority's attempts to repay the blood of 620,000 dead American soldiers by creating a nation of equals that Lincoln, though no egalitarian, had died for. And he was impeached for it.

"Our government may at some time be in the hands of a bad man," Frederick Douglass said of Andrew Johnson in a speech entitled "Sources of Danger to the Republic" in 1867. "When in the hands of a good man it is all well enough. . . . [W]e ought to have our government so shaped that even when in the hands of a bad man we shall be safe."[4]

It is fair to say that neither Douglass nor any politician of Johnson's era could have conceived of the kind of "bad man" Trump would be as president. He was impeached for something no previous president had ever been so much as suspected of: endangering the national security of his own country, and all but declaring that Congress had no authority to investigate him or his administration, ever. In the summer of 2019, Trump withheld nearly $400 million in congressionally approved military aid[5] to Ukraine, which was desperately fighting off the remnants of Russia's invasion of its Crimea region in 2014. The president, working through state department political appointees and his personal attorney, former New York mayor Rudy Giuliani, plus a pair of soon-to-be indicted Soviet-born freelancers, Lev Parnas and Igor Fruman, made it clear to the Ukrainian government that the aid would not be released unless Ukrainian President Volodymyr Zelensky, who like Trump came from the world of entertainment (he had been a comedian) went on CNN and announced investigations into Joe Biden and his family. Biden had served two terms as vice president to Barack Obama, and now he was running for president in his own right and polling well against Trump, who seemed obsessed with destroying him and his only remaining son, Hunter. (Biden's oldest son, Beau, died of cancer in 2015.) Trump also wanted the Ukraine government to substantiate a Kremlin-sourced conspiracy theory that might remove the shadow of illegitimacy from his presidency, by proving that not only did Russia not help him become president, Ukraine had been the one conspiring to help Hillary Clinton. In the end, Ukraine refused. But the scheme leaked after career diplomatic and national security staff discovered it, and the Trump administration released the aid. And after a House investigation, he was impeached. But despite extensive proof of his guilt, including his own admissions and a partial transcript of a July 2019 call between himself and Zelensky released by the White House, Trump had by then so totally consumed the Republican Party that his acquittal was never in doubt. Mitch McConnell had even guaranteed it in advance in an appearance on Fox News.

Trump's defense counsel was a virtual rogues' gallery. It included Pam Bondi, who years before as Florida attorney general had declined to investigate the fraudulent Trump University after receiving donations from Trump and his daughter Ivanka. There was Jay Sekulow, a lawyer and radio talk show host who also served as chief counsel to the right-wing Christian alternative to the ACLU, the American Center for Law and Justice (ACLJ). And there was Kenneth Starr, who after leading the partisan Bill Clinton impeachment investigation in 1998 was removed decades later as president of Baylor University for seeming to ignore allegations of sexual abuse on campus. Perhaps most controversial was Alan Dershowitz, whose stature as a TV-friendly lawyer who had participated in the legal defense of controversial figures from Claus von Bülow to O.J. Simpson had been overtaken by his association with deceased convicted serial pedophile Jeffrey Epstein, the high-flying financier with ties to celebrities and politicians (including Trump) and even royalty, who in 2019 was charged with trafficking underage girls for sex,[6] but who died in an alleged suicide in federal prison. For a president whose White House had become an extension of Fox News and reality TV, these seemed the perfect cast members for his impeachment drama. They were joined on Trump's defense team by members of the White House counsel's office—paid by American taxpayers—who would compromise themselves in their own ways over the course of the weeks-long Senate trial.

Starr had eagerly pursued President Clinton for years, failing to unearth crimes related to Clinton and his wife's Arkansas real estate investments and belatedly discovering the president's illicit affair with a White House intern, which provided the fig leaf for Speaker Newt Gingrich and his House Republicans to seek Clinton's removal. Yet it was Starr who argued that impeaching Trump was too partisan and disruptive for the country to endure. Sekulow and the White House counsel attorneys argued that the only way witnesses should be permitted in the Senate trial would be if Trump's defense team could interrogate Joe and Hunter Biden, as well as the anonymous whistleblower who had disclosed the Ukraine "aid for dirt" scheme. They and elected Republicans seemed determined to finish the hit job on the Bidens that Trump's rogue diplomatic team never got Ukraine to do.

One deputy White House counsel, Pat Philbin, left Democratic senators speechless after he argued that a president asking a foreign leader for information on a political opponent "is not something that would violate campaign finance laws."[7] Connecticut Senator Chris Murphy told reporters afterward that "there were audible gasps on the Democratic side" during Philbin's statement. "That's a pretty extraordinary message to put on the record in the middle of an impeachment trial about that very kind of corruption," he said.[8]

But it was Dershowitz who took his arguments for the president's supposed impunity to the greatest extreme. He argued in the well of the Senate that since every public official he had ever encountered deemed their own reelection to be in the public interest, if a president "did something that he believes will help him get elected—in the public interest—that cannot be the kind of quid pro quo that results in impeachment."

This argument stunned the Senate gallery, and perhaps even Trump's other legal defenders, who raced to distance themselves from Dershowitz's extreme arguments the following day, even as Dershowitz rushed to television cameras and social media to clarify himself. Still, he was roundly and widely denounced as essentially having argued that a president, or at least this Republican president, could do virtually anything short of actually breaking the law to try to remain in office. As Schiff warned the gallery, if Dershowitz's argument was taken at face value, Donald Trump could cheat and cheat and cheat until he succeeded in winning reelection, so long as in his own mind winning a second term was in the public interest. It sounded like a red-carpet invitation to tyranny.

Poised for a fight that seemed futile but was a vital stake in the ground, defending the notion that no American president should ever be permitted to act as a king, Schiff and his racially diverse group of House impeachment managers: House Judiciary Chairman Jerry Nadler and House Democratic Caucus Chair Hakeem Jeffries of New York, Zoe Lofgren of California, Val Demings of Florida, Sylvia Garcia of Texas, and Jason Crow of Colorado would each offer compelling arguments, rebuttals, and pleas to the senators, all of whom were required to attend and listen in silence. Schiff would emerge during the hearings and trial as the Thaddeus Stevens to Trump's Andrew Johnson. His eloquent arguments were praised by legal scholars and went viral on social media almost daily as he heaped scorn on the arguments of Trump's legal team and shame on the Republican senators who would ultimately vote to refuse to hear from a single witness or to see a shred of evidence against their president.

Republicans would remain steadfast, even as Trump's former national security advisor, John Bolton, leaked parts of an upcoming book to the *New York Times,* in which he confirmed the testimony his former deputies gave to the House. It would be revealed that a member of Trump's defense team, the White House counsel, may have himself been involved in the Ukraine scheme,[9] which, besides Giuliani, also ensnared former Texas governor–turned energy secretary Rick Perry; Kurt Volker, the envoy to Ukraine; and Trump's ambassador to the European Union, Gordon Sondland, who had donated $1 million to Trump's inaugural before gaining his post. Volker, Perry, and Sondland had even dubbed themselves "the three amigos" as they pursued their assignment to turn Ukraine policy toward Trump's desires.[10] And then there was the evidence from Trump himself: his boasts about wanting not just Ukraine but also China to investigate the Bidens, and the memorandum of the July 25, 2019, phone call— falsely called a "transcript" by Trump and his supporters—that the White House released in which Trump asked the Ukrainian president to "do us a favor, though"[11] before he would discuss selling Ukraine the military equipment they were desperate for.

By withholding critical aid to a country at war with our adversary, Russia, Trump "has betrayed our national security and he will do so again," Schiff said. "He has compromised our elections and he will do so again. You will not change him. You cannot constrain him. He is who he is. Truth matters little to him. What's right matters even less and decency matters not at all." It's something Republican senators all surely knew.

"History will not be kind to Donald Trump," Schiff warned. "I think we all know that. Not because it will be written by 'never Trumpers,' but because whenever we have departed from the values of our nation, we have come to regret it, and that regret is written all over the pages of our history. If you find that the House has proved its case and still vote to acquit, your name will be tied to his with a cord of steel and for all of history. But if you find the courage to stand up to him, to speak the awful truth to his rank falsehood, your place will be among the Davids who took on Goliath. If only you will say 'enough.'"

In the end, only one Republican said "enough." Mitt Romney, the party's 2012 presidential nominee who is now the junior senator from Utah, voted "guilty" on impeachment article one, "abuse of power," making him the first Senator in U.S. history to vote to convict a president of his own party on any impeachment count.

"The president asked a foreign government to investigate his political rival," an emotional Romney told the Senate gallery before his vote. "The president withheld vital military funds from that government to press it to do so. The president delayed funds for an American ally at war with Russian invaders. The president's purpose was personal and political. Accordingly, the president is guilty of an appalling abuse of public trust." Romney called Trump's actions, which had also implicated his secretary of state, Mike Pompeo; his acting chief of staff, Mick Mulvaney; and the attorney general, William Barr, "a flagrant assault on our electoral rights, our national security, and our fundamental values.

"Corrupting an election to keep oneself in office is perhaps the most abusive and destructive violation of one's oath of office that I can imagine," Romney said. He spoke movingly of his Mormon faith as he explained his vote, with just four other senators— all Democrats—in the chamber to hear him. Still, despite his rhetorical rebuke of the president, and his historic vote on article one, on article two, "obstruction of congress," Romney joined his fifty-two Republican colleagues in voting to acquit.

"[T]he corruption that is regularly laughed off in our age of political cynicism makes me shudder—not least as the son of civil rights activists who risked their lives to expand American democracy in the 20th century," Reverend William Barber of the reborn Poor People's Campaign wrote in *The Guardian* US. "The coordinated cover-up we are witnessing as 53 senators conspire to facilitate Trump's obstruction of Congress is deeply troubling to anyone who knows the long history of southern courthouses where district attorneys openly coordinated with all-white juries and corrupt judges to cover up acts of racial terror. With patience and decorum, Mitch McConnell has brought southern justice to the US Senate."[12]

Trump would remain in office, marked with a scarlet "I" for all time, but still in power, and seemingly unrestrainable by Congress. Republicans, by voting to abrogate their own authority as members of a coequal branch of government, might as well have stripped the impeachment clause out of the constitution, Democrats lamented. And they had done it for a president who had long since said publicly that the Constitution's Article II "allows me to do whatever I want."[13]

It was as if Trump was trying to prove Vladimir Putin right, said former U.S. ambassador to Russia Michael McFaul, who served under President Obama, that our democracy is no different than theirs, and no better; that our claims of democratic exceptionalism were a false promise to potential allies, who would be better off with Russia's more honest take on power. McFaul recalls hearing it from Putin himself during his years as a diplomat that "Obama controlled the television stations just like he controls the television stations," and that the United States interfered with elections, including Putin's reelection when Hillary Clinton was Obama's secretary of state. So why not meddle to stop Secretary Clinton from becoming president? Trump must have seemed ideal to Putin. He consistently took the Russian view of history and of the world, and he came without that Obamaian American righteousness. Putin's message was simple, McFaul said. It was "get over it, America. Stop preaching to the world. You're just like everybody else.

"He's not trying to win the argument that he's better," McFaul said of the Russian autocrat. "He's just trying to say we're all the same and there is no truth. He just wants to throw enough disinformation out there so that nobody can believe anything. Trump's behavior just helps that narrative [and] it really does hurt our vital national security interests abroad because it's always been an important part of our diplomacy that we are *not* just like everybody else. We *do* believe in the rule of law. We do believe in democracy and human rights, and it's part of what attracts allies to us. It's what attracts opposition leaders to us and government leaders to us: that they see that we are different from places like Russia or China or Iran."

Or at least we could claim we were, before Donald Trump became president and set about trying to corrupt Ukraine and succeeding in fostering government corruption at home.

Trump's claim of Putin-like authority and impunity "challenges the fundamental principles of the Constitution," said Jill Wine-Banks, who had, as a young lawyer, been one of the investigators of Richard Nixon. "I think it's a dangerous thing when you would have an executive branch that would have no one to be responsible to. If [Trump] doesn't have to answer to Congress, that diminishes how the Constitution envisioned our government would work."

Predictably, Romney's lonely stand on a single impeachment count drew furious attacks from fellow Republicans, Fox News hosts, and the president's namesake son, despite the acquittal. It was fear of those attacks and the fury of Trump's mob of zealous supporters that had softened the spines of Senate Republicans in the first place, causing them to willingly reduce themselves from members of "the world's greatest deliberative body" to courtiers of an erratic and vengeful king. Republicans who voted to acquit were asked repeatedly by journalists what they thought Trump had learned from impeachment. They had few answers, though some lamely expressed the hope that he would be chastened by the experience. Much to the contrary, these senators had essentially taught Trump that he could ignore congressional subpoenas, withhold documents, and force any White House staffer or cabinet member he wished to refuse to comply with House or Senate investigations. And the Democrats' warnings that acquittal would only embolden Trump further would come true almost immediately.

The purge of those who dared to testify against Trump in the House hearings began within forty-eight hours of Trump's Senate acquittal. Army Lieutenant Colonel Alexander Vindman, who had served on the National Security Council and overheard the infamous phone call with the Ukrainian president (a call Trump continued to insist was "perfect") was escorted out of the White House, along with his twin brother, Yevgeny, an Army officer who also worked on the National Security Council staff but played no role in the impeachment inquiry.[14] Ambassador Sondland was unceremoniously ousted the same day, despite pleas from now-helpless Republican Senators to whom Sondland had been a campaign donor that he be allowed to depart on his own terms.[15] Others were already gone. Ambassador Volker, a former ambassador to NATO, became the first player in the Ukraine scheme to resign, in September 2019.[16] Ambassador Marie Yovanovitch had been recalled by the administration the previous May, following what Democratic lawmakers called a "political hit job"[17] that included attacks by right-wing media, veiled threats from the president that she would "go through some things," and allegations that he she had been physically surveilled in Kiev. Trump's secretary of state, Mike Pompeo, had not uttered a word in her defense. Yovanovitch's replacement, Bill Taylor, the U.S. chargé d'affaires, had been unceremoniously returned to Washington as well. And other witnesses who came forward to testify, despite the open or implied threats to their careers from the White House, had left or announced their impending exits, including Fiona Hill, the former director for European and Russian affairs on the National Security Council, to whom Bolton had called the Giuliani-led Ukraine pressure campaign a "drug deal."[18]

The corruption of the federal government, in nearly every arena, had become Trump's principal accomplishment. And perhaps no federal entity had been more desiccated by Trump than the Department of Justice, where Attorney General Barr had fully emerged as Trump's "Roy Cohn." Within two weeks of Trump's acquittal, Barr was openly interfering in the federal court cases of Trump's friends and allies, including Trump's longtime consigliere, Roger Stone, who had been a player in Russiagate, and Trump's first national security advisor, General Michael Flynn.

Stone was awaiting sentencing following his conviction on seven counts, including lying to Congress, obstruction of justice, witness tampering related to Russia's 2016 election interference, and the peddling of Democratic Party emails through WikiLeaks. After prosecutors issued a sentencing recommendation memo, Trump objected by tweet, and in an unprecedented act, Barr intervened, issuing his own memo calling the sentence too harsh, prompting all four prosecutors in the case to resign in protest. Barr would insist in an ABC News interview that aired the day before Valentine's Day[19] that the timing of his intervention was unrelated to Trump's tweets and that his actions as attorney general were independent of presidential or media influence, an assertion that few career prosecutors who spoke out about the memo override believed.

Flynn had held his administration post for just twenty-four days in 2017 and pleaded guilty later that year of lying to the FBI about his secret conversations with Russia's ambassador to the United States. He, too, was awaiting sentencing when Barr ordered an unprecedented review, prompting new howls of protest and calls for his resignation. One Trump insider, who had managed to conceal their disgust with the president and his administration and focus on what good they thought they could do, said Barr's television self-defense had been precleared with the White House and was both an effort to deflect attention from Barr's eager interventions on Trump's behalf, which he preferred to do without Trump shining a light on them, and so he could continue to advance his goal of securing a "unitary executive" presidency, virtually free from congressional or judicial constraint, that would endure long after Trump. Barr was as fierce a neo-monarchist as former vice president Dick Cheney had proved to be. As a former deputy attorney general under President George H. W. Bush, Donald Ayer wrote in a February 2020 piece in *The Atlantic* calling on Barr to resign. He said that Barr's politicized interventions, bad as they were, were actually "more symptoms than causes of Barr's unfitness for office. The fundamental problem is that he does not believe in the central tenet of our system of government—that no person is above the law. In chilling terms, Barr's own words make clear his long-held belief in the need for a virtually autocratic executive who is not constrained by countervailing powers within our government under the constitutional system of checks and balances." And per Ayer, "[G]iven our national faith and trust in a rule of law no one can subvert, it is not too strong to say that Bill Barr is un-American."[20] On Presidents' Day, the day Ayer's piece posted online, a letter calling for Barr's resignation surpassed two thousand signatures from former Department of Justice officials, Democrat and Republican, Ayers included.[21]

And while Barr professed to be disinterested in how history would view him, insiders said he hoped his public statements gently rebuking the president would quell a growing internal rebellion inside the Justice Department, and forestall more resignations that could lead to former DOJ officials speaking out, or even filing bar complaints against him. For all his protestations of modesty, William Barr—the hand of the king—was an ambitious man who could envision a potential seat on the federal bench for himself one day, too, perhaps even on the Supreme Court.

With Barr as his sword, and House and Senate Republicans

as his shield, Trump was a man unleashed. He burned up Twitter, calling for the prosecutions of the CIA and FBI officials who had investigated Russia's outreach to his 2016 campaign, attacking judges and dangling pardons. He even quote-tweeted a two-week-old *New York Times* article[22] that referenced the famed Ralph Waldo Emerson quote: "When you strike at the king, you must kill him,"[23] including the piece's reference to his determination to "take his case of grievance, persecution and resentment to the campaign trail," as if it was a compliment. In Trump's mind, he was now truly the King of the Disunited States of America.

Some former military leaders, and even former members of his cabinet, including Bolton and General John Kelly, Trump's former homeland security director and chief of staff, slowly began allowing their criticisms of Trump to leak out. But they had been active enablers of the renegade president and participants in some of his ugliest abuses; in Kelly's case, against Muslim travelers, migrant children, and a black Florida congresswoman who Kelly defamed for daring to defend the wife of a dead soldier who criticized Trump, so their criticisms fell on largely skeptical ears.

For most observers, the protests and complaints of Republicans, be they civilians or decorated military men, were far too little, much too late. Trump had disemboweled so many corners of the federal government it seemed there was almost nothing and no one left untainted. Many career federal employees whose integrity remained intact had already quit or were leaving. And those who stayed were under tremendous pressure to play ball. By the time impeachment was "last week's news," the Pentagon was siphoning more money from fighter jet purchases and even military schools to try to make Trump's wall happen, and military units had long since been discovered to have paid the Trump family to put U.S. troops in the family's hotels. McConnell was gleefully ramming scores of young, arch-conservative judges onto the federal courts—192 as of February 12, 2020[24]—meaning he had helped Trump to seat nearly one-fifth of the entire federal judiciary, one-fourth of circuit court judges, and two of the nine members of the Supreme Court, after consistently blocking President Obama from filling federal court vacancies. McConnell was practically boasting that he would reverse the "Merrick Garland rule" he imposed on Obama and fill another Supreme Court opening during the election year if he got the chance, even with an election pending. And members of Trump's legal defenders were sniffing around for federal judgeships of their own as a reward for their service, one Republican insider said. Trump seemed not to care who these judges were, so long as they protected him, ruled as he wished, and importantly, kept his tax returns from public view. And he happily reaped the adulation of white conservative voters for whom "appointing conservative judges" was a voting mantra. For McConnell and his fellow Republicans, control of the federal judiciary was one of many tools that could help cement the political dominance of white Christians for generations after Trump was gone, regardless of how the country around them changed. That would be McConnell's legacy. Meanwhile, the Senate majority leader refused to bring House-passed legislation protecting the 2020 election from foreign cyberattack to the floor for a vote. It was as if Republicans were spoiling for foreign assistance as yet another means for Trump and for them to remain in power.

As for Trump, he had become almost a mafioso figure, openly threatening his political nemeses on Twitter and goading Barr to prosecute them, including the former FBI and CIA officials who had led the investigation of Russia's collusion with his campaign, and of course, the Clintons; and few observers were confident that Barr would refuse. One George W. Bush–appointed U.S. District Judge, Reggie Walton, likened White House pressure on a grand jury investigation into former FBI director Andrew McCabe's involvement in launching the Russia-Trump investigation to the actions of a "banana republic."[25] The grand jury chose not to indict. But the White House's involvement in the investigation of McCabe, whom Trump openly taunted on Twitter, demanding he be punished for his part in what Trump considered a "coup d'état, had Barr's fingerprints all over it. Walton would later rebuke Barr in unprecedented terms for his "misleading public statements about the findings in the Mueller Report," in a case where a media organization and a watchdog group sought to view the unredacted version.[26]

For all of Barr's flagrant abuses of his authority, he could not surpass the brazenness of his boss. One day after the impeachment trial ended, the Trump administration locked the entire state of New York out of a federal program expediting international travel over a state law blocking immigration officials from accessing motor vehicle records.[27] On the day of a planned meeting with New York governor Andrew Cuomo two weeks later, Trump tweeted an apparent demand for a trade: that Cuomo somehow halt ongoing state investigations into Trump and his family businesses to get the program back online. "New York must stop all of its unnecessary lawsuits & harassment [*sic*], start cleaning itself up, and lowering taxes," Trump tweeted. "Build relationships, but don't bring Fredo!"—an insult referencing a character from the mafia film series *The Godfather* that was directed at Cuomo's younger brother, Chris Cuomo, an anchor at Trump's nemesis, CNN. The mafia reference seemed eerily appropriate.

Trump's party was equal parts submissive and complicit, as they watched it all happen; though Republicans would face a verdict of their own in November, presuming U.S. elections, which they had essentially thrown open to foreign intervention, could be trusted.

Trump had tormented the nation's psyche for nearly four years, raging like a bat out of hell in the White House and in his near constant political rallies, including the raucous State of the Union address he delivered the night before his Senate acquittal, which played out like a gaudy reality show, complete with a surprise military family reunion and the awarding of the Presidential Medal of Freedom to right-wing radio shock jock Rush Limbaugh. The award had previously been placed around the necks of American heroes like Dr. Martin Luther King Jr., Rosa Parks, and Harvey Milk. Limbaugh had distinguished himself as a gaudily racist broadcaster who had made a career of tormenting the children of Democratic presidents, belittling African-Americans and women and joining Trump as an Obama "birther."

In Trump's diminutive hands, the president of the United States was the separator of migrant mothers and children; the enemy of asylum seekers, Muslims, and liberated women; and the would-be dream-killer for LGBT people who dared to demand free access to American life. He was the greatest friend to white evangelical Christians and white nationalists, whose shared hatred and fear of nonwhite migrants and modernity made Trump a kind of demigod to them: the savior of the faith and the defender of the race. In Trump's America, neo-Nazis marched openly through the nation's capital, unrepentant and even escorted by police.[28]

Trump had succeeded in transforming America, his party, and the federal government in ways almost no one could have imagined in 2016. His administration had aggressively seeded career people throughout federal agencies after driving Clinton- and Obama-era staffers out of every nook and cranny of government. They gutted the Department of State and the National Security Council and left nearly every federal agency associated with the sciences, from the Environmental Protection Agency to the Department of Agriculture and the Department of Health and Human Services, stripped of seasoned experts. He eliminated the pivotal post of senior director for global health security and biothreats—the person charged with coordinating the response to disease outbreaks and pandemics—on the National Security Council, a decision that would prove disastrous. Career officials who chose to remain, including federal prosecutors, were frequently revealed in news reports to be exhausted and demoralized.[29] Cabinet secretaries, like education secretary Betsy Devos and housing and urban development secretary Ben Carson, seemed intent on dismantling their own agencies and undercutting their purpose. And while the administration refused to prepare the country for the devastating onset of climate change–induced natural disasters, they were fattening developers and oil and gas companies with federal subsidies and coughing up millions of acres of pristine federal land,[30] while larding profits on huge corporate ranchers by rescinding Obama-era regulations that sought to limit the fecal matter allowed in American pork products or the pollution permitted to seep into America's rivers and streams.

The Trump era was a boon for the superrich, for the dying extractive industries, and for big corporations who were gorging on the Trump-Ryan trillion-dollar tax cut, which gave more money to the country's four hundred richest families than to all other taxpayers combined.[31] Meanwhile, small farm bankruptcies and farmer suicides were soaring under the weight of Trump's China tariffs, while the administration put hundreds of thousands of mostly white farmers on federal welfare to ensure their continued support.

It was an extraordinary descent. America had often been a deeply divided and volatile country, but under Trump, the notion of equal protection under the law, which had saved the American constitution from its original writ that some people were not quite people and could be made into property, had been traded for caging migrant children, expelling immigrants, and banning refugees. The federal government that was the cavalry during the Civil Rights era, protecting the vulnerable from state-based tyranny and discrimination, now affirmed the idea of open discrimination against LGBT people in the name of conservative Christianity.

And yet, for all his triumphs on behalf of the rich and the

far right, Trump seemed like a tormented man. Insiders reported him to be unraveling, often reduced to screaming incoherencies about Barack Obama, Biden, and the "deep state" during calls with party officials and donors and complaining to advisers that he was being publicly humiliated by Democrats like Speaker Nancy Pelosi, who ripped up the printout of his State of the Union address on live television, drawing right-wing howls on the day before Trump's acquittal. He continued to rail at the mainstream media that refused to give him the adulation he craved, and to soothe himself with boisterous rallies and appearances on Fox News. According to one former loyalist, his golf courses and properties stood to crater financially once he was out of power and no longer able to command foreign and federal government stays. And Trump faced a new fear as the spring of 2020 approached: the brief presidential candidacy of a *confirmed* billionaire, former Republican-turned-Independent New York City mayor Michael Bloomberg, a seventy-eight-year-old Wall Street and media tycoon and the eighth richest man in America with a $62.8 billion net worth, who entered the race as a Democrat and bowed out months later, vowing to spend any amount—perhaps a billion dollars or more—on the campaign to remove Trump from the White House.

It was an outcome that would suit "Never Trumpers" like Stuart Stevens just fine.

Stevens grew up in Mississippi. As a young man, he was interested in politics but not much of a partisan at a time when the southern states were dominated by racist Dixiecrats like Senator James O. Eastland of his home state, Strom Thurmond of South Carolina, and Richard Russell of Georgia. He became a campaign ad man who worked for Republican presidential candidates like Bob Dole and Mitt Romney but quit the party after Trump's election. Instead, he turned to writing and occasional political consultancy. To Stevens, Trump was able to so easily swallow the once Grand Old Party not because he changed it, but because he saw it for what it had long ago become. Many Republicans had simply refused to see it.

"There are Republicans who can't stand Trump who tell themselves that he hijacked the party," Stevens said. "I'd like to think that, but if you go back to the history of the post-war party and I think there's always been this very dark, racist element." Stevens said the Republican Party had become a white grievance party, and it didn't happen overnight or only when Trump came along. "If you go back to the 1950s," he said, "William Buckley now is hailed as sort of the great intellectual. [Conservatives will say], 'isn't it terrible that [today] we have Donald Trump and not William Buckley—someone who's articulate and smart?' But the truth of the matter is when Buckley first emerged, he was a stone-cold racist, and the intellectual roots of the party [have long] had a deeply troubled, white grievance racist element.

"Republicans like me always liked to tell ourselves that *that* element was the minority of the party, and that the party needed to reach out and repair its ability to attract black voters, for example"—to get back to the time when in 1956 President Dwight Eisenhower won 39 percent of African-Americans, a share that dropped to 7 percent with the nomination of Barry Goldwater in 1964 and never came back. It took time for Stevens to realize that the racial grievance wing he once viewed as a fringe had always been a quiet majority, held in check by the success of Republican presidents at winning elections. Now, he said, neither George W. Bush nor Ronald Reagan could have survived in the current Republican Party, saying Bush's conciliatory acceptance speech in 2000, written by fellow "Never Trumper" Mike Gerson, "reads like an artifact from a lost civilization."

And with white grievance politics, of which Trump was an expert, dominating the party, there was little room for Republican politicians to maneuver. And so, said Stevens, the internal rationalizations began. "There are Republicans who believe Trump is an aberration," Stevens said. "He's got some unfortunate characteristics," this rationale goes, "but the greater good is being served" because of the judges he's putting in place. Stevens calls this argument "nonsense," saying he has rarely met any proponent of that idea who can name ten, five, or even two Trump-era Supreme Court decisions that interest them. "It's like saying you like the Catholic Church because of the incense," he said. "Who knows if it gets you closer to God, but it makes you feel better.

"And then there are those who pretend, although I don't really see how an intelligent person can believe this, that there is an evil out there that we'll call 'socialism' and Donald Trump is the necessary evil to fight it," he continued. And yet, "if you go back to the post-war Republican Party, Ronald Reagan in 1963 made an album about the evils of Medicare, calling it 'socialism' and [saying] the country as we know it would end if we had Medicare. But now I look at the Republican Party and it seems to me that it's pretty much the socialist party. I don't know what giving farmers $28 billion in welfare payments[32] [to reimburse farmers hit by Trump's China tariffs] is but socialism. In my home state of Mississippi, 40 percent of its budget is from the federal government. Why don't we call *that* socialism?" And since few of these proponents can even name a socialist country on demand besides Cuba or Venezuela, "my feeling," Stevens said, "is that that they are [just] looking for reasons not to have to confront Trump.

"I think if [today's] Republican Party was in charge in 1776, we'd still be celebrating the Queen's birthday," he said. "You can just hear them [saying]: 'What are we going to do? Fight the king? The most powerful army in the world? Are you crazy? We just have to work this out.'" He likened the Republicans' excuses for yielding to Trump as akin to the arguments made by the Vichy government in France in the 1930s: "You can always argue it's better to work with the current evil."

Anthony Scaramucci grew up in a middle-class household in a blue-collar neighborhood on Long Island, New York, the second-generation American son of a construction worker father and his wife. He was the first in his family to make it to college, attending Tufts University and Harvard Law School, ultimately becoming a successful investment banker and political consultant. He joined the Trump finance committee after initially supporting Wisconsin governor Scott Walker and then Jeb Bush for president. And for just ten days in 2017, he served as Donald Trump's White House communications director, after the departure of Trump's first press secretary, Sean Spicer. Like many who fell out of Trump's orbit, Scaramucci would become an ardent opponent.

He said Trump's success in overtaking and reshaping the Republican Party had a lot to do with Trump, but also a lot to do with America. "We can pretend otherwise, but we are by and large a patriarchal society . . . and a racially charged society," he said. "We've made it better from 1865 to today, but we are still in a racially charged, patriarchal society. Trump uses those two things masterfully."

Trump, per Scaramucci's observation, "uses his age and his physicality to intimidate and bully people. He [did so] prior to being president, but I just want you to think about how much easier it is to do as president." The intimidation tactics often worked in Trump's business life since "people get nervous because they believe he's worth more than he actually is [and] because of the litany of lawsuits [he'd file], and they didn't want to get ensnared in a way that he could potentially hurt them."

Trump as president has "played off of the Fox News idea that at some point there existed in the heterography of America a very pristine, white America that Norman Rockwell used to paint. And when you're shooting facts through that prism, you have a group of older, white people [who] have not done well in America and feel disenfranchised and they're angry about it, and they need scapegoats. Trump has played that incredibly well, and he does it in a way where there's something in there for everybody. When he says 'there's good people on both sides,' he can get somebody like Scott Adams, who invented Dilbert, saying 'oh no, read the transcript, he's not a racist.' And so his supporters can clutch onto the idea that he's not a racist.

"Trump is a moral test that no one wanted," said Stevens. "Most moral tests are that way. You're walking down the street you see someone mugged, you didn't want that but it's a test. And I think as an institution, the Republican party has decidedly failed." They have refused to "pull the circuit breaker on Trump."

It would be America's turn to take the moral test in November. And as the primary whittled down from nearly thirty diverse Democrats to two septuagenarian white men: Vermont senator Bernie Sanders and former vice president Joe Biden and then to one, it became clear by March 2020 that Trump would face Biden, the very man he had tried to induce Ukraine to investigate, prompting impeachment. Trump's dream of running against Sanders, the Democratic socialist, evaporated after Biden, with no money in the bank and barely a campaign, routed the moderate field with the help of black voters across the South and white working-class voters in places like Massachusetts, Minnesota, and Michigan. Biden had outlasted a Democratic field that began with multiple women, people of color, and a thirty-eight-year-old former mayor, Pete Buttigieg, who became the first gay man to win a primary or caucus. And it was Biden who was reforming the Obama coalition.

It was an election increasingly driven by a combination of exhaustion and fear. And as winter turned to spring, Americans would come face to face with what it meant to be led by a man like Donald Trump during a crisis.

By February, the world began to be gripped with a flu-like pandemic called coronavirus, which emerged first in Wuhan Province, China, and spread quickly throughout Asia and Europe, causing Italy to quarantine its entire population of 60 million and Ireland to shut down its famed St. Patrick's Day parades, while members of governments in Iran and Britain became infected. With the spread of the virus to the United States quickly overwhelming Trump, who had gutted the federal government, the United States found itself without sufficient testing capabilities and with no federal plan. The outbreak quickly destabilized the economy and shook the stock market as the failed federal response laid bare, once again, Trump's narcissism and the extent to which he had demolished the willingness of those around him to tell the truth to the American people, even when it could save lives. Trump began by claiming that news of the coronavirus spread was a hoax created by his "enemies" in the media and the Democratic Party. He brushed it off as less deadly than the flu, an idea unsupported by science and belied by the rapid transmission rate and growing death rate among vulnerable populations such as the elderly. Unfortunately, many of his supporters believed him, making the further spread of the virus all but inevitable.

By March, nearly a half dozen Republican members of Congress had gone under voluntary quarantine, including some who had attended a conservative political conference in Maryland and come in contact with both an infected man and the president and vice president. Those under quarantine soon included Trump's fourth announced chief of staff, Congressman Mark Meadows of North Carolina. And there was Florida congressman Matt Gaetz, who had joined Trump in mocking the seriousness of the outbreak by wearing a gas mask on the House floor. The head of the New York Port Authority tested positive, while a ship with at least twenty-one infected people on board languished off the coast of California, with Trump pushing not to let it dock, lest the infected passengers' entry increase the official American toll.[33] As the number of U.S. patients grew into the hundreds, and threatened to grow much larger, Trump seemed increasingly paranoid, worried that the virus spread was a media fiction designed to harm his reelection; and—ever the germaphobe—he even fretted that members of the media would try to contract coronavirus on purpose so they could ride on Air Force One and infect him.[34] And the cable channel that had become his avatar, Fox News, followed his paranoid message to a tee.

For many Americans, nothing short of the fate of America as a democratic republic rested on the outcome of the November elections, assuming those elections would take place uneventfully at all. For Democrats and Republicans, the question at hand was who would hold the power to shape the next decade of American life—2020 was an election year and a census year, political Armageddon for the party of white Christian America, or for the party of multicultural America. And no one—no one—knew what was to come.

ACKNOWLEDGMENTS

IF THERE IS ONE TRUE THING ABOUT WRITING, IT IS THAT IT's always better with the help of a good editor; better yet—a great one. I have been twice blessed with a great one. Thank you, Henry Ferris, for keeping me succinct (as succinct as is possible with me) and on task. Thanks also to the great Peter Hubbard and his excellent team at William Morrow: Nick Amphlett, Anwesha Basu, and the entire HarperCollins family. And because I am that lucky, I have not one but *two* Henrys to rely on: Henry Reisch, my agent and big brother, thank you. And there would be no books, and a lot less fun, without the wonderful Suzanne Gluck. Thank you! Thanks also to my amazing fact-checker, Sharon Gaffney, who has been an invaluable partner in this process. Also, Shauntay Hampton-Prewitt, without whom I could do nothing at all. Thanks also to all the amazing people who allowed me to take advantage of their knowledge, expertise and stories: Heidi Beirich, Kurt Bardella, Whitney Dow, Timothy Wise, Bruce Bartlett, Nick Akerman, Edward Price, Andries du Toit, Zainab Salbi, Tom Nichols, Nancy MacLean, Jeff Jarvis, Eric Boehlert, Shireen Mitchell, Karen Attiah, Sisonke Msimang, Michael Steele, Paul Butler, Judge Stephen L. Reed,

Naveed Jamali, Tony Schwartz, Jay Rosen, Peter Georgescu, Professor Laurence Tribe, my big brother Rev. Al Sharpton, Karine Jean-Pierre, Maria Teresa Kumar, Faiz Shakir, Leah Daughtry, and those who generously spoke with me on background. Last but not least: thank you to my ever-patient family, for putting up with the madness of my book writing schedule, and with me.

NOTES

Introduction: Welcome to Gotham

1. "Donald Trump Clung to 'Birther' Lie for Years, and Still Isn't Apologetic," Michael Barbaro, *New York Times,* September 16, 2016.
2. "Donald Trump Campaign Offered Actors $50 to Cheer for Him at Presidential Announcement," Aaron Couch, *The Hollywood Reporter*, June 17, 2015.
3. Ibid.
4. "Remember That Time Trump Was Allegedly Cheered by Paid Actors?" Laura Bradley, *Vanity Fair*, January 20, 2017.
5. Testimony of Michael D. Cohen, Committee on Oversight and Reform, U.S. House Of Representatives, February 27, 2019.

Chapter 1: How Trump Happened

1. "Donald Trump's Long, Strange History of Using Fake Names," Michael D'Antonio, May 18, 2016.
2. "An Examination of the 2016 Electorate, Based on Validated Voters," Pew Research Center, August 9, 2018.
3. "What Really Happened in 2016, in 7 Charts," Matthew Yglesias, Vox .com, September 18, 2017.
4. "FBI Clears Clinton—Again," Eric Bradner, Pamela Brown, and Evan Perez, CNN, November 7, 2016.
5. "Russian Hacks on U.S. Voting System Wider Than Previously Known," Michael Riley and Jordan Robertson, Bloomberg, June 13, 2017.
6. "Biden: McConnell Stopped Obama from Calling out Russians," Edward-Isaac Dovere, *Politico Magazine*, January 23, 2018.
7. 2016 presidential campaign, exit poll data.

8. "How John Podesta's Email Got Hacked, and How to Not Let It Happen to You," Tara Golshan, Vox.com, October 28, 2016.

9. "Status threat, not economic hardship, explains the 2016 presidential vote," Diana C. Mutz, *PNAS* (*Proceedings of the National Academy of Sciences of the United States of America*), May 8, 2018, vol. 115 (19) E4330-E4339; published ahead of print April 23, 2018, https://doi.org/10.1073/pnas.171815 5115, edited by Jennifer A. Richeson, Yale University, New Haven, CT.

10. "Beyond Economics: Fears of Cultural Displacement Pushed the White Working Class to Trump," Daniel Cox, PhD, Rachel Lienesch, and Robert P. Jones, PhD, PRRI/The Atlantic Report, May 9, 2017.

11. Ibid.

12. "Why 41 Percent of White Millennials Voted for Trump," Matthew Fowler, Vladimir E. Medenica, and Cathy J. Cohen, *Washington Post*, "Monkey Cage," December 15, 2017.

13. "An Analysis of Trump Supporters Has Identified 5 Key Traits," Bobby Azarian, PhD, *Psychology Today*, December 31, 2017.

14. "The Peculiar Populism of Donald Trump," Thomas B. Edsall, *New York Times*, February 2, 2017.

15. "White Riot: How Racism and Immigration Gave Us Trump, Brexit, and a Whole New Kind of Politics," Zack Beauchamp, Vox.com, updated January 20, 2017.

16. "Trump's Family Fortune Originated in a Canadian Gold-Rush Brothel," Natalie Obiko Pearson, Bloomberg, October 26, 2016.

17. "Trump's grandfather 'kicked out of Germany for avoiding military service,'" Angela Dewan and Madleen Schroeder, CNN, November 23, 2016.

18. "In 1927, Donald Trump's Father Was Arrested After a Klan Riot in Queens," Philip Bump, *Washington Post*, "The Fix," February 29, 2016.

19. "Inside the Government's Racial Bias Case Against Donald Trump's Company, and How He Fought It," Michael Kranish and Robert O'Harrow Jr., *Washington Post*, January 23, 2016.

20. "'No Vacancies' for Blacks: How Donald Trump Got His Start, and Was First Accused of Bias," Jonathan Mahler and Steve Eder, *New York Times*, August 27, 2016.

21. "5 Reasons Trump Will Win," Michael Moore, michaelmoore.com, July 2016.

22. Ibid.

23. "Trump on God: 'I Don't Like to Have to Ask for Forgiveness,'" Maxwell Tani, *Business Insider*, January 17, 2016.

24. "Trump Calls For 'Total and Complete Shutdown of Muslims Entering the United States,'" Jenna Johnson, *Washington Post*, December 7, 2015.

25. "Where the Idea for Donald Trump's Wall Came From," Stuart Anderson, *Forbes*, January 4, 2019.

26. "These Are the Biggest U.S. Trading Partners," Saray Grah, *Fortune*, April 2, 2018, originally published March 8, 2018.

27. "'They're Rapists.' President Trump's Campaign Launch Speech Two Years Later, Annotated," Amber Phillips, *Washington Post*, June 16, 2017.

28. "What Trump Has Said About Judge Curiel," Maureen Groppe, *Indianapolis Star*, June 11, 2016.

29. "Rep. Steve King Called Immigrants 'Dirt' in Recorded Conversation," Griffin Connolly, *Roll Call*, November 12, 2018.

30. "Steve King and the Case of the Cantaloupe Calves," Amy Davidson Sorkin, *The New Yorker*, July 25, 2013.

Chapter 2: Two Nations, Under Trump

1. "256 Women Won House and Senate Primaries, a Huge New Record," Grace Sparks and Annie Grayer, CNN, September 17, 2018.

2. "Women Legislative Candidates Jump 28 Percent Since 2016," Katie Ziegler, National Conference of State Legislatures blog, October 3, 2018.

3. National Conference of State Legislatures, October 3, 2018.

4. "Voting Rights Become a Flashpoint in Georgia Governor's Race," Associated Press, October 9, 2018.

5. "Georgia Cancels Fewer Voter Registrations After Surge Last Year," Mark Niesse, *Atlanta Journal-Constitution*, October 17, 2018.

6. "Georgia Republican Candidate for Governor Puts 53,000 Voter Registrations on Hold," Ben Nadler, Associated Press, October 12, 2018.

7. World Population Review.

8. "Judge Tosses Kansas' Proof-of-Citizenship Voter Law and Rebukes Sec. of State Kobach," Bill Chappell, NPR, June 19, 2018.

9. "Republican Gov. Larry Hogan Wins a Second Term in Deep-Blue Maryland," Erin Cox, Ovetta Wiggins, and Rachel Chason, *Washington Post*, November 7, 2018.

10. "Latest House Results Confirm 2018 Wasn't a Blue Wave. It Was a Blue Tsunami," Harry Enten, CNN.com, December 6, 2018.

11. "Hyde-Smith Attended All-White 'Seg Academy' to Avoid Integration," Ashton Pittman, *Jackson Free Press*, November 23, 2018.

12. "Diversity on Stark Display as House's Incoming Freshmen Gather in Washington," Elise Viebeck, *Washington Post*, November 13, 2018.

13. Tweet by Dave Wasserman, December 9, 2018.

14. Ballotpedia.

15. "Prisoners in 2016," E. Ann Carson, PhD, U.S. Department of Justice, Office of Justice Systems, August 7, 2018.

16. "GOP-Run Senate Backs End to Sanctions on Firms Tied to Putin Ally," Daniel Flatley and Laura Litvan, *Bloomberg*, January 16, 2019.

17. "Little Partisan Agreement on the Pressing Problems Facing the U.S.," Pew Research Center survey, October 15, 2018.

18. Ibid.

19. "Most Border Wall Opponents, Supporters Say Shutdown Concessions Are Unacceptable," Pew Research Center, January 16, 2019.

20. "The Demography of the Alt-Right," George Hawley, Institute for Family Studies, August 9, 2018.

21. "1 in 10 Say It's Acceptable to Hold Neo-Nazi Views," Gary Langer, ABCNews.com, August 21, 2017.

22. "I Became a Democrat a Year Ago and Found My Own Voice. It Changed Everything," Kurt Bardella, *USA Today*, December 16, 2018.

23. "Roy Moore Is the Last Straw, You Can Now Call Me a Democrat," Kurt Bardella, *USA Today*, December 8, 2017.

24. "The Real Origins of the Religious Right: They'll tell you it was abortion. Sorry, the historical record's clear: It was segregation," Randall Balmer, *Politico Magazine*, May 27, 2014.

25. Ballotpedia: California Proposition 187, Illegal Aliens Ineligible for Public Benefits (1994).

Chapter 3: The Trump Republican Party

1. "Here's What Happened the Last Time the Government Shut Down," Kirsten Appleton and Veronica Stracqualursi, ABCNews.com, November 18, 2014.

2. "Final Tax Bill Includes Huge Estate Tax Win for the Rich: The $22.4 Million Exemption," Ashlea Ebeling, *Forbes*, December 21, 2017.

3. "Donald Trump's Eminent Domain Love Nearly Cost a Widow Her House," David Boaz, *The Guardian*, August 19, 2015.

4. "Donald Trump's History of Eminent Domain Abuse," Ilya Somin, *Washington Post*, August 19, 2015.

5. "Neil Gorsuch Opposes the Kelo decision—A Terrible Supreme Court Property Rights Ruling that Donald Trump Loves," Ilya Somin, *Washington Post*, March 28, 2017.

6. "A 1970 U.S.-Mexico Treaty Shows Why Trump's Border Wall Is Absurd," Joe Romm, ThinkProgress, January 7, 2019.

7. Ibid.

8. "Pat Buchanan Axed by MSNBC," Tim Mak, *Politico Magazine*, February 17, 2912.

9. "Trump's Campaign Enlists Commentator He Once Slammed as a Bigot and Hitler 'Fan,'" David Corn, *Mother Jones*, October 11, 2016.

10. "David Duke: I Think Trump 'Knows Who I Am,'" Gideon Resnick, Betsy Woodruff, and Tara Wanda Merrigan, *The Daily Beast* (2016).

11. "Infamous neo-Nazi Website Praises Trump's Racist Remarks: The Nazis Think Trump Is 'More or Less on the Same Page as Us,'" Luke Barnes, ThinkProgress, January 13, 2018.

12. Ibid.

13. "Trump Is Pat Buchanan with Better Timing," Jeff Greenfield, *Politico Magazine*, September/October 2016.

14. In fact, studies showed that undocumented immigrants commit crimes at substantially lower rates than U.S. citizens.

15. "Trump Tweets Op-Ed by Pat Buchanan, Whom He Derided as a 'Hitler Lover' in 1999," William Cummings, *USA Today*, January 14, 2019.

16. "By Promoting Pat Buchanan's White Grievances, Trump Shows He Isn't Trying to Persuade on Border Wall," Philip Klein, *Washington Examiner*, posted online January 14, 2019.

17. "Before Trump, Steve King Set the Agenda for the Wall and Anti-Immigrant Politics," Trip Gabriel, *New York Times*, January 10, 2019.

18. Press release and posted statement from Rep. Steve King, January 10, 2019.

19. "Rep. Steve King Quotes a White Supremacist While Comparing 'Leftists' to Nazis," Jared Holt, Right Wing Watch, September 12, 2018.

20. "A GOP Congressman Retweeted a Self-Described 'Nazi Sympathizer.' His Party Did Not Rebuke Him." Eli Rosenberg, *Washington Post*, June 13, 2018.

21. "The 116th Congress Has More Women and People of Color Than Ever—But There's Still Room to Improve," Richie Zweigenhaft, Guilford College, The Conversation, November 8, 2018.

22. "Trump Organization to Go Budget Friendly with 'American Idea' Hotel Chain," Steve Eder and Ben Protess, *New York Times*, June 5, 2017.

23. "House Majority Whip Scalise Confirms He Spoke to White Supremacists in 2002," Robert Costa and Ed O'Keefe, *Washington Post*, December 29, 2014.

24. "What Scalise and Vitter Told *Roll Call* About David Duke in 1999," Niels Lesniewski, *Roll Call*, December 29, 2014.

25. "Exclusive: Lee Atwater's Infamous 1981 Interview on the Southern Strategy," Rick Perlstein, *The Nation*, November 13, 2012.

26. "Nixon's Southern Strategy: 'It's All in the Charts,' " James Boyd, *New York Times*, May 17, 1970.

27. Ibid.

28. Ibid.

29. Ibid.

30. "The Case of the Missing White Voters," Sean Trende, RealClearPolitics, November 8, 2012.

31. SOURCE TK?

32. "Lindsey Graham Praises Trump Over Shutdown: 'Glad He Picked This Fight,' " Amy Russo, *Huffington Post*, December 22, 2018.

33. "McConnell's Laser Focus on Transforming the Judiciary," Burgess Everett and Elana Schor, Politico.com, October 17, 2018.

34. "I Am Part of the Resistance Inside the Trump Administration," Anonymous, *New York Times,* September 5, 2018.

35. "Omarosa Says She Suspects Pence's Chief of Staff Wrote Anonymous *New York Times* Op-ed," Emily Heil, *Washington Post*, September 10, 2018.

36. "I Am Part of the Resistance Inside the Trump Administration," Anonymous, *New York Times*, September 5, 2018.

37. "Mitt Romney: The President Shapes the Public Character of the Nation. Trump's Character Falls Short," Mitt Romney, *Washington Post*, January 1, 2019.

Chapter 4: A New American Civil War

1. "The Year in Hate and Extremism," report of the Southern Poverty Law Center, edited by Mark Potok, February 15, 2017.

2. Ibid.

3. "Hillary Clinton on *Ralston Live*," transcript of interview by Jon Ralston, June 18, 2015.

4. "Trump Denies 'Nationalist' Has Racial Undertones: 'I've never even heard that,' " Brett Samuels, *The Hill*, October 23, 2018.

5. "After New Zealand shooting, Trump downplayed white nationalist threat.

But experts say it's growing," Linda Givetash and Geoff Bennett, NBC News, March 17, 2019.

6. "Here are some key differences between Trump's new trade deal and NAFTA," John W. Schoen, *The Hill*, October 1, 2018.

7. Snopes: "Is Stephen Miller a Descendant of Asylum Seekers Who Fled Anti-Semitic Violence?"

8. "Stephen Miller Is an Immigration Hypocrite. I Know Because I'm His Uncle," David S. Glosser, *Politico*, August 13, 2018.

9. "Meet the White Nationalist Trying to Ride the Trump Train to Lasting Power: Alt-Right Architect Richard Spencer Aims to Make Racism Cool Again," Josh Harkinson, *Mother Jones*, October 27, 2016.

10. Ibid.

11. "The Immigration Act That Inadvertently Changed America," Tom Gjelten, *The Atlantic*, October 2, 2015.

12. "Household Income Growth Under Four American Presidents," Elaine Kamarck, Brookings Institution, March 6, 2015.

13. "Obamacare Jacked Up Taxes on the 1 Percent, Gave $16 Billion Annually to Poor," Jeff Stein, *Washington Post*, Wonkblog, March 28, 2018.

14. "Ann Coulter: It's Not Just Illegal Immigration That's the Problem; It's All Immigration," *Dallas Morning News* interview with Ann Coulter.

15. "Liberals, You're Not as Smart as You Think," Gerard Alexander, *New York Times*, May 12, 2018.

16. Ibid.

17. "Apparently Only the Left Is Allowed to Satirize and Mock Their Political Opponents," Brandon Morse, Redstate.com, July 25, 2018.

18. Ibid.

19. "Transcript of "Hannity," Fox News, June 13, 2017.

20. "The Numbers from Louisiana Add Up Chillingly: Duke's Claim on White Vote Shows Depth of Discontent," Paul West, *Baltimore Sun*, November 18, 1991.

21. Ibid.

22. Ibid.

23. Ibid.

24. All three men would be the subjects of a 2018 lawsuit by people injured in the violence that followed.

25. Ibid.

26. Ibid.

27. "More CEOs Quit Trump Advisory Council After Merck Chief Resigns Over Charlottesville," Igor Bobic, Huffington Post, August 14, 2017.

28. "Wal-Mart CEO Criticizes Trump's Charlottesville Statement but Remains on Advisory Council," KATV.com, August 14, 2017.

29. "WH: No Mention of Jews on Holocaust Remembrance Day Because Others Were Killed Too," Jake Tapper, CNN.com, February 2, 2017.

30. "Stephen Miller Is an Immigration Hypocrite. I Know Because I'm His Uncle," Dr. David S. Glosser, *Politico Magazine*, August 13, 2018.

31. "'Stephen Actually Enjoys Seeing Those Pictures at the Border': The West Wing Is Fracturing Over Trump's Callous Migrant-Family Policy," Gabriel Sherman, *Vanity Fair*, June 20, 2018.

32. "Trump's sexual assault allegations: The full list of women who have accused the President", Clark Mindock, *The Independent* (UK), February 25, 2019.

33. *Black Reconstruction in America, 1860-1880*, W.E.B. DuBois, The Free Press, 1935.

34. Ibid.

Chapter 5: The Man Who Sold the World

1. "New England's Scarlet 'S' for Slavery," C. S. Manegold, *Boston Globe*, January 18, 2010.

2. Papers of John Winthrop: Letter from Israel Stoughton to John Winthrop, June 28, 1637. Winthrop Family Papers, Vol. 3, Massachusetts Historical Society.

3. "New England's Scarlet 'S' for Slavery," C. S. Manegold, *Boston Globe*, January 18, 2010.

4. United States House of Representatives, History Art & Archives: Blanche Kelso Bruce.

5. United States House of Representatives, History Art & Archives: Hiram Rhodes Revels.

6. "Mandrake the Magician," King Features Syndicate cartoon created by Lee Falk, Toonopedia.

7. Trump at various times in his life has been a Democrat, a Republican, and an ostensive member of the Reform Party, for whom he considered running as a presidential candidate in 2000.

8. "How Trump's Time Running a Doomed Football Team Fueled His Political Fight with the NFL," Jacob Pramuk, CNBC.com, September 16, 2018.

9. "A Time magazine with Trump on the cover hangs in his golf clubs. It's fake," David A. Fahrenthold, *Washington Post*, June 27, 2017.

10. "Trump Engaged in Suspect Tax Schemes as He Reaped Riches From His Father," David Barstow, Susanne Craig, and Russ Buettner, *New York Times*, October 2, 2018.

11. "In 1927, Donald Trump's father was arrested after a Klan riot in Queens," Philip Bump, *Washington Post*, February 29, 2016.

12. "2 Relocation Companies Accused of Harassment," Walter H. Waggoner, *New York Times*, July 7, 1972.

13. "Donald Trump Gets What He Wants," Graydon Carter, *GQ Magazine*, May 1, 1984.

14. Ibid.

15. "'Tiny hands,' the insult that's been driving Donald Trump bonkers since 1988, explained," Libby Nelson, Vox.com, June 17, 2016.

16. "Steel Traps and Short Fingers," Graydon Carter, *Vanity Fair*, November 2015.

17. "Donald Trump's Ghostwriter Tells All," Jane Mayer, *The New Yorker*, July 25, 2016.

18. *Trump: What's the Deal?* 1991 documentary by Jesse Kornbluth, produced by Libby Handros and Al Levin.

19. "Trump or Drumpf—What's in a Name?" Palash Ghosh, *International Business Times*, April 19, 2011.

20. "Donald Trump's Drive to Surpass His Father's Success," Matt Viser, *Boston Globe*, July 16, 2016.

21. "Donald Trump's Business Decisions in '80s Nearly Led Him to Ruin," Russ Buettner and Charles V. Bagli, *New York Times*, October 3, 2016.

22. "Trump, 'King of Debt,' The Debt Ceiling 'Crisis,' and the Politico-Media Complex," Ralph Benko, *Forbes*, August 27, 2017.

23. Michael Cohen Says He Arranged Payments to Women at Trump's Direction," William K. Rashbaum, Maggie Haberman, Ben Protess and Jim Rutenberg, *New York Times*, August 21, 2018.

24. "Cohen Describes Trump's Involvement in Hush-Money Payments," Joe Palazzolo, *Wall Street Journal*, December 14, 2018.

25. *Trump: The Greatest Show on Earth: The Deals, the Downfall, the Reinvention*, Wayne Barrett, New York: Simon and Schuster, 2016.

26. "The A-List Celebrities Who Used to Flock to Trump's Mar-a-Lago Estate in the 90s," Mitchell Sunderland, Broadly/Vice News, April 25, 2017.

27. "How Mark Burnett Resurrected Donald Trump as an Icon of American Success," Patrick Radden Keefe, *The New Yorker*, January 7, 2019.

28. Ibid.

29. "Exclusive photos: Donald Trump's Palm Beach Wedding," *Palm Beach Post*, August 13, 2018.

30. Ibid.

31. Ibid.

32. "Flashback: When Hillary and Bill Hit the Wedding of Donald and Melania," Michael Callahan, *The Hollywood Reporter*, April 7, 2016.

33. "Introducing Donald Trump, Diplomat," Maureen Dowd, *New York Times*, August 15, 2015.

34. "A 2Live Crew Boss Explains Trump," Joy-Ann Reid, *The Daily Beast*, October 13, 2015.

35. "The A-List Celebrities Who Used to Flock to Trump's Mar-a-Lago Estate in the 90s," Mitchell Sunderland, Broadley/Vice.com, April 25 2017.

36. "The Trump Files: Donald Weighs In on 'Ghetto Supastar,'" Tim Murphy, *Mother Jones*, September 13, 2016.

37. "A 2Live Crew Boss Explains Trump," Joy-Ann Reid, *The Daily Beast*, October 13, 2015.

38. "What Kanye West's Trump Phase Meant," Spencer Kornhaber, *The Atlantic*, October 31, 2018.

39. "Let's Talk About It: Why Did It Take Hip Hop So Long to Turn Away From Donald Trump?" Michael Arceneaux, *Essence*, March 16, 2018.

40. "Ivanka Trump Brand Saga: Which Department Stores Really Dropped the Label," Sheena Butler-Young, *Footwear News*, July 16, 2018.

41. "Donald Trump: All the Sexist Things He Said," Adam Lusher, *The Independent*, October 9, 2016.

42. Ibid.

43. "A Timeline of Donald Trump's Creepiness While He Owned Miss Universe," Tessa Stuart, *Rolling Stone*, October 12, 2016.

44. "Donald Trump: All the Sexist Things He Said," Adam Lusher, *The Independent*, October 9, 2016.

45. "Teen Beauty Queens Say Trump Walked in on Them Changing," Kendall Taggart, Jessica Garrison, and Jessica Testa, BuzzFeed News, October 13, 2016.

46. "Donald Trump to Howard Stern: It's okay to call my daughter a 'piece of ass,'" Andrew Kaczynski, Chris Massie, and Nate McDermott, CNN, October 9, 2016.

47. "Karen McDougal Says Donald Trump Told Her She Was 'Beautiful Like

Ivanka' During Alleged Affair," Tierney McAfee, *People*, March 23, 2018.

48. "Our Next President, the Godfather," Richard Cohen, *Washington Post*, November 23, 2019.

49. "Draft Washington Post Column Claimed Trump Said He Was 'Sexually Attracted' to His Teenage Daughter," Tamerra Griffin, BuzzFeed News, November 22, 2016.

50. "Trump Recorded Having Extremely Lewd Conversation About Women in 2005," David A. Fahrenthold, *Washington Post*, October 8, 2016.

51. "The 23 Women Who Have Accused Trump of Sexual Misconduct," Eliza Relman, *Business Insider*, February 25, 2019.

52. "John Wayne, Man and Myth," Pat Dowell, *Washington Post*, September 25, 1995.

53. "John Wayne: The *Playboy* Interview," *Playboy*, May 1971.

54. "The Whiskey Ring and America's First Special Prosecutor," History.com, May 18, 2017.

55. "Agnew Resigns the Vice Presidency and Admits He Evaded Taxes on 1967 Income," James M. Naughton, *New York Times*, October 11, 1973.

56. "Reagan's 'Worst' Speech," David Hoffman, *New York Times,* July 20, 1987.

57. "Warren Harding and 5 Other Presidents Who Have Faced 'Love Child' Questions," Amber Phillips, *Washington Post*, August 13, 2015.

58. "Shirley Temple Running for Congress in California," Associated Press, August 29, 1967.

59. "Making President Trump's Bed: A Housekeeper Without Papers," Miriam Jordan, *New York Times*, December 6, 2018.

60. "Trump's New Jersey Golf Club Employs Undocumented Immigrants, Women Say," Kate Snow, NBC News, December 6, 2018.

61. "'My Whole Town Practically Lived There': From Costa Rica to New Jersey, a Pipeline of Illegal Workers for Trump Goes Back Years," Joshua Partlow, Nick Miroff, and David A. Fahrenthold, *Washington Post*, February 8, 2018.

Chapter 6: American Strongman

1. "The Hidden History of Trump's First Trip to Moscow," Luke Harding, *Politico Magazine*, November 19, 2017.

2. Ibid.

3. "When a Young Trump Went to Russia," Craig Unger, *Politico Magazine*,

August 15, 2018, adapted from a section of the book *House of Trump, House of Putin* by Craig Unger (New York: Dutton Publishing, 2018).

4. Ibid.

5. Ibid.

6. Ibid.

7. "The Gorbachev Visit; Manhattan Goes Gorbachev, From Fish to Oreo Cookies," Maureen Dowd, *New York Times*, December 7, 1988.

8. "Chaos at airports as America introduces a travel ban," A.W., *The Economist*, January 30, 2017.

9. Source: PolitiFact.

10. "'We're Not Going to Turn On Our Own': Republicans Rally Around Trump as Threats Mount," Robert Costa, *Washington Post*, March 2, 2019.

11. "Trump Says He'll Sign Executive Order for Free Speech on College Campuses," Tal Axelrod, *The Hill*, March 2, 2019.

12. "All the times Trump has called for violence at his rallies," Kate Sommers Dawes, Mashable, March 12, 2016.

13. "Donald Trump Suggests 'Second Amendment People' Could Act Against Hillary Clinton," Nick Corasaniti and Maggie Haberman, *New York Times*, August 9, 2016.

14. "It Isn't Complicated: Trump Encourages Violence," David Leonhardt, *New York Times*, March 17, 2019.

15. "F.B.I. Opened Inquiry Into Whether Trump Was Secretly Working on Behalf of Russia," Adam Goldman, Michael S. Schmidt, and Nicholas Fandos, *New York Times*, January 11, 2019.

16. "China Grants Ivanka Trump Initial Approval for New Trademarks," Austin Ramzy, *New York Times*, November 6, 2018.

17. "Trump Ordered Officials to Give Jared Kushner a Security Clearance," Maggie Haberman, Michael S. Schmidt, Adam Goldman, and Annie Karni, *New York Times*, February 28, 2019.

18. "Watchdog: Secret Service for Eric, Donald Trump Jr. Trips Cost $230,000 in 1 Month," William Cummings, *USA Today*, July 18, 2018.

19. "Steven Mnuchin Draws Claims of Conflict of Interest in Decision on Russian Oligarch," Kenneth P. Vogel, *New York Times*, January 29, 2019.

20. Letter to Secretary of the Treasury Steven Mnuchin from the chairman of the House Oversight and Government Reform Committee and the Ranking Member of the Senate Finance Committee, January 29, 2019.

21. "Trump Discussed Pulling U.S. from NATO, Aides Say Amid New Con-

cerns Over Russia," Julian E. Barnes and Helene Cooper, *New York Times*, January 14, 2019.

22. "Macron Calls for 'True European Army' to Defend Against Russia, US, China," Euractiv and Agence France-Presse, November 7, 2018.

23. "'I Don't Believe He Knew About It.' Trump Defends Kim Jong Un on Otto Warmbier's Death," John Fritze, *USA Today*, February 28, 2019.

24. "Trump Applauds North Korea's 'Great Beaches,' Says They Would Be a Perfect Location for Condos and Hotels," Pat Ralph, *Business Insider*, June 12, 2018.

25. "Rating World Leaders: 2018; The U.S. vs. Germany, China and Russia," Gallup Organization, January 2019.

26. Ibid.

27. Gallup International End of Year Survey, 2018.

28. Ibid.

29. "The Rise and Fall of Soft Power," Eric X. Li, *Foreign Policy*, August 20, 2018.

30. "Defense Secretary Mattis' Resignation Letter Is a Must-Read Warning About the Future," Fred Kempe, CNBC.com, December 21, 2018.

31. "Revoke my security clearance, too, Mr. President," William H. McRaven, *Washington Post*, August 16, 2018.

32. "Trump Has Concealed Details of His Face-to-Face Encounters with Putin from Senior Officials in Administration," Greg Miller, *Washington Post*, January 13, 2019.

33. "Trump Cancels Meeting with Putin, Citing Naval Clash Between Russia and Ukraine," Peter Baker, *New York Times*, November 29, 2018.

34. "Trump and Putin Sat Down for Meeting in Buenos Aires with No U.S. Staff, Report Says," William Cummings, *USA Today,* January 30, 2019.

35. "The Madman and the Bomb," Garrett M. Graff, *Politico Magazine*, August 11, 2017.

Chapter 7: What America Can Learn from South Africa

1. King's letter to Claude Barnett, Martin Luther King, Jr. Research and Education Institute, Associated Negro Press, March 24, 1960.

2. Ibid.

3. World Population Review.

4. "The Myth of White Genocide," James Pogue, The Pulitzer Center, February 15, 2019.

5. "Will the US Follow South Africa Down the Path of White Decline?" Dan Roodt, *American Renaissance*, November 9, 2012.

6. "Trump Tweet Cheers White Supremacists," Matt Pearce, *Los Angeles Times*, August 24, 2018.

7. "No, Katie Hopkins, there is no white genocide in South Africa," Joe Walsh, *The New Statesman*, American Edition, May 22, 2018.

8. "Policemen Jailed for Racist Dog Attack," Chris McGreal, *The Guardian*, November 29, 2001.

Chapter 8. The Media in the Trump Age

1. "When I was on trial as one of the Central Park Five, Donald Trump didn't care that I might be innocent. And I was," Yusef Salaam, *Washington Post*, August 21, 2017.

2. "Is Trump-Whisperer Maggie Haberman Changing the New York Times?" Joe Pompeo, *Vanity Fair* "Hive," October 5, 2017.

3. "Donald Trump Ends 2018 with a Fox News Interview—His 41st Since Inauguration," Brian Stelter, CNN Business, January 1, 2019.

4. "The Times Publisher Asks Trump About 'Anti-Press Rhetoric,'" *New York Times*, February 1, 2019.

5. Ibid.

6. "Leslie Moonves on Donald Trump: 'It May Not Be Good for America, but It's Damn Good for CBS,'" Paul Bond, *The Hollywood Reporter*, February 29, 2019.

7. Ibid.

8. Ibid.

9. "Donald Trump Rode $5 Billion in Free Media to the White House," Emily Stewart, TheStreet, November 20, 2016.

10. "Final newspaper endorsement count: Clinton 57, Trump 2," Reid Wilson, *The Hill*, November 6, 2016.

11. "Editorial: Trump Is the Change Agent America Needs," *Florida Times Union* Editorial Board, November 4, 2016.

12. *The Negro Holocaust: Lynching and Race Riots in the United States, 1880–1950*, Robert A. Gibson, New Haven, Conn.: Yale–New Haven Teachers Institute.

13. "Busing and the Press," Philip Weiss, *The Harvard Crimson*, September 25, 1974.

14. Howard K. Smith, *Who Speaks for Birmingham*. CBS News Reports (1961).

15. "How Woodrow Wilson's Propaganda Machine Changed American Journalism," Christopher Daly, *Smithsonian*, April 28, 2017.

16. *The War*, Communication, News & Censorship; PBS.org.

17. Ibid.

18. Ibid.

19. "Trump, Clinton Voters Divided in Their Main Source for Election News," Amy Mitchell, Jeffrey Gottfried, and Michael Barthel, Pew Research Center, January 18, 2017.

20. *Washington Post* Fact Checker poll, November 30–December 10, 2018.

21. "John Dean: Nixon 'Might Have Survived If There'd Been a Fox News,'" Edward-Isaac Dovere, *Politico Magazine*, January 2, 2018.

22. "The Making of the Fox News White House," Jane Mayer, *The New Yorker*, March 11, 2019.

23. "Bill Shine, Ousted From Fox News in Scandal, Joins White House Communications Team," Maggie Haberman, *New York Times*, July 5, 2018.

24. "A comprehensive list of former Fox employees who have joined the Trump administration" By Matt Gertz, Media Matters for America, April 12, 2019.

25. "The Making of the Fox News White House," Jane Mayer, *The New Yorker*, March 11, 2019.

26. "Advertisers Recoil as Tucker Carlson Says Immigrants Make US 'Dirtier,'" Luke O'Neil, *The Guardian*, December 18, 2018.

27. "I've Studied the Trump-Fox Feedback Loop for Months. It's Crazier Than You Think," Matthew Gertz, *Politico Magazine*, January 5, 2018.

28. "'Enemy of the People': Trump's Phrase and Its Echoes of Totalitarianism," Emma Graham-Harrison, *The Guardian*, August 3, 2018.

29. *The Hunting of the President: The Ten-Year Campaign to Destroy Bill and Hillary Clinton*, Joe Conason and Gene Lyons, New York: Thomas Dunne Books, 2001.

30. "How the 'War on Christmas' Controversy Was Created," Liam Stack, *New York Times*, December 19, 2016.

31. "How Many People Actually Watch Fox News in America?" Eric Schaal, Entertainment Cheat Sheet (citing Nielsen data), January 8, 2019.

32. Ibid.

33. Ibid.

34. "Fox News's Audience Almost Exclusively White as Network Faces Backlash Over Immigration Coverage," Greg Price, *Newsweek*, August 10, 2018.

35. "Does Vladimir Putin Kill Journalists?" Linda Qiu, PolitiFact, January, 2016.

36. Ibid.

37. "Trump Praises GOP Congressman Who Assaulted Reporter: 'Any guy that can do a body slam—he's my guy,'" Christal Hayes, *USA Today*, October 18, 2018.

38. "Trump Inciting 'Violence': More Than 200 Retired Journalists Condemn President's 'Un-American' Attacks on Press," Meagan Flynn, *Washington Post*, October 25, 2018.

39. "Feds: Coast Guard Lieutenant Compiled Hit List of Lawmakers," Michael Balsamo, Associated Press, February 20, 2019.

40. "'You Ask a Lot of Stupid Questions': Trump Comments Draw Condemnation from Black Journalists Group," Noreen O'Donnell, NBC 5 Chicago online, November 9, 2018.

41. "President Trump Has Made 6,420 False or Misleading Claims over 649 days," Glenn Kessler, Salvador Rizzo, and Meg Kelly, *Washington Post* Fact Checker, November 2, 2018.

42. "News Media Hesitate to Use 'Lie' for Trump's Misstatements," Associated Press, August 29, 2018.

43. "The Production of Innocence and the Reporting of American Politics," Jay Rosen, PressThink, project of the Arthur L. Carter Journalism Institute at New York University, October 2, 2013.

44. Tweet by Ian Millhiser, January 20, 2019.

45. "Diversity in Newsrooms Has Been Bad for Decades and It Probably Won't Get Better: Study," Karen K. Ho, *Columbia Journalism Review*, August 16, 2017.

46. "The Production of Innocence and the Reporting of American Politics," Jay Rosen, PressThink, project of the Arthur L. Carter Journalism Institute at New York University, October 2, 2013.

47. "WHERE HITLER DREAMS AND PLANS; At the Berghof on a Bavarian Peak He Lives Simply, Yet His Retreat Is Closely Guarded; Hitler Has Transformed His Simple Chalet Into a Mansion and Impenetrable Fortress," Otto D. Tolischus, *New York Times*, May 30, 1937.

48. "*The New York Times*' First Article About Hitler's Rise Is Absolutely Stunning," Zack Beauchamp, Vox.com, March 3, 2016.

49. "How Many Times Does Trump Tweet a Day? The President Basically Lives on Twitter," Joseph D. Lyons, Bustle.com, May 21 2018.

50. "Activists Are Outing Hundreds of Twitter Users Believed to Be 4chan Trolls Posing as Feminists" By Ryan Broderick, BuzzFeed, June 17, 2014.

51. "Russia's Social Media Propaganda Was Hiding in Plain Sight," Sarah Kendzior, NBC News THINK, November 2, 2017.

52. *The Eugenicist Doctor and the Vast Fortune Behind Trump's Immigration Regime*, Brendan O'Connor, *Splinter News*, July 5, 2018.

53. *Anti-immigrant Groups Continue Greenwashing Campaign*, by Alexander Zaitchik, Southern Poverty Law Center, October 8, 2010.

54. "The shady group behind the African-American anti-immigration rally" by Michelle Cottle, *The Daily Beast*, July 2012, 2013.

55. Ibid.

Chapter 9. "Mr. Barr Goes to Town"

1. "Mueller Report Confirms Trump Runs the White House Like It's the Mafia," Eric Levitz, *New York Magazine*, April 18, 2019.

2. Letter to the chairmen and ranking members of the House and Senate Judiciary Committees from Attorney General William P. Barr, March 24, 2019.

3. Ibid.

4. "Obstruction Inquiry Shows Trump's Struggle to Keep Grip on Russia Investigation," Michael S. Schmidt, *New York Times*, January 4, 2018.

5. "President Trump Called For Roy Cohn, But Roy Cohn Was Gone," Ron Elving, NPR, January 7, 2018.

6. "How Donald Trump and Roy Cohn's Ruthless Symbiosis Changed America," Marie Brenner, *Vanity Fair*, August 2017 issue.

7. "Obstruction Inquiry Shows Trump's Struggle to Keep Grip on Russia Investigation," Michael S. Schmidt, *New York Times*, January 4, 2018.

8. Memo by William (Bill) Barr to Deputy Attorney General Rod Rosenstein and Assistant Attorney General Steve Engel, June 8, 2018.

9. "William Barr's Ahistorical View of the Constitution Would Give Donald Trump All the Power," Peter M. Shane, *Slate*, January 10, 2019.

10. "William Barr Has a Long History of Abusing Civil Rights and Liberties in the Name of 'National Security,'" Manar Waheed, Senior Legislative and Advocacy Counsel, ACLU, and Brian Tashman, Political Researcher and Strategist, ACLU, January 14, 2019.

11. Hearings before the Committee on the Judiciary, United States Senate, November 28, December 4, and December 6, 2001.

12. "Barr sent or discussed controversial memo with Trump lawyers," Ariane de Vogue, CNN, January 15, 2019.

13. "The real Whitewater shocker," Joshua Micah Marshall, Salon.com, March 22, 2002.

14. "Essay; The Patsy Prosecutor," William Safire, *New York Times*, October 19, 1992.

15. A 1995 report by Attorney General Janet Reno cleared the Bush administration of wrongdoing, "releasing an internal department report saying no evidence could be found of any criminal conduct beyond that of six U.S.-based employees of an Italian bank who have been convicted of illegal transactions." Source: "Bush Administration Cleared in Iraqgate Probe," *Los Angeles Times*, January 24, 1995.

16. "Bush Pardons 6 in Iran Affair, Aborting a Weinberger Trial; Prosecutor Assails 'Cover-Up,'" David Johnston, *New York Times*, December 25, 1992.

17. "William Barr Did What He Was Hired to Do," Charles P. Pierce, Esquire.com, March 24, 2019.

18. "William Barr Can't Exonerate Donald Trump," David R. Lurie, *Slate*, March 24, 2019.

19. Quote from John Dean appearing on *Don Lemon Tonight* on CNN, March 25, 2019.

20. "The Many Problems with the Barr Letter," Neal Katyal, *New York Times*, March 24, 2019.

21. "Joy Reid: 'It Feels Like the Seeds of a Cover-Up Are Here,'" Josh Feldman, Mediaite.com, March 23, 2019.

22. "Pelosi says Barr believes Trump is 'above the law,'" Manu Raju and Jeremy Herb, CNN, March 26, 2019.

23. "Nunes on Mueller report: 'We can just burn it up,'" Justin Wise, *The Hill*, March 24, 2019.

24. March 25, 2019 Tim Murtaugh Trump Campaign Memo to TV Producers.

25. Mueller report, p. 213.

26. Ibid.

27. Ibid, p. 157

28. "The 10 instances of possible obstruction in Mueller report," Mark Sherman, The Associated Press, April 18, 2019.

29. "Trump Tells Aides: 'Keep an Eye' on Fox News, Make Sure It Stays Loyal to Me," Asawin Suebesang and Andrew Kirell, The Daily Beast, April 17, 2019.

30. "White House Obamacare reversal made over Cabinet objections," Eliana Johnson and Burgess Everett, *Politico*, March 26, 2019.
31. "Will anyone leave the Trump administration with an intact reputation?" Paul Waldman, *Washington Post*, April 25, 2018.

Chapter 10. Un-Democratic America?

1. "Mitch McConnell: Making Election Day a Federal Holiday Is a Democratic 'Power Grab,'" Tara Golshan, Vox.com, January 30, 2019.
2. United States Elections Project. The voting-eligible population (VEP) represents an estimate of persons eligible to vote regardless of voter registration status in an election and is constructed by modifying the voting-age population (VAP), by components including non-citizenship, imprisonment, probation or parole, and ineligibility based on overseas residence.
3. "'This Is the Link Between Voting in Elections and Income," World Economic Forum, July 20, 2018.
4. "Does Your Wage Predict Your Vote?" Derek Thompson, *The Atlantic*, November 5, 2012.
5. The National Assessment of Educational Progress, which conducts a periodic assessment of U.S. student achievement versus children around the world, found in 2014 that fewer than one in four American eighth graders had a strong grasp of civics, a further indication of an eroding hold on democracy.
6. "U.S. Trails Most Developed Countries in Voter Turnout," Drew DeSilver, Pew Research Center, May 21, 2018.
7. "A History of 'Draining the Swamp,'" Eric Garcia, *Roll Call*, October 18, 2016.
8. "SECRET VIDEO: Romney Tells Millionaire Donors What He REALLY Thinks of Obama Voters When he doesn't know a camera's rolling, the GOP candidate shows his disdain for half of America," David Corn, *Mother Jones*, September 17, 2012.
9. Ibid.
10. "Global Wealth Inequality," Gabriel Zucman, National Bureau of Economic Research, Cambridge, Mass., January 2019.
11. "We did the math to calculate how much money Jeff Bezos makes in a year, month, week, day, hour, minute, and second," Hillary Hoffower, *Business Insider*, January 9, 2019.
12. "The 400 Richest Americans Own a Greater Share of Wealth Than the Bottom 150 Million," Natasha Bach, *Fortune*, February 8, 2019.

13. "Income Inequality Is Growing Across the US—Here's How Bad It Is in Every State," Mark Abadi, *Business Insider*, March 15, 2018.

14. "'Time for the Ku Klux Klan to Night Ride Again': An Alabama newspaper editor wants to bring back lynching," Antonia Noori Farzan and Michael Brice-Saddler, *Washington Post*, February 19, 2019.

15. "Alabama Newspaper Editor Wants to Bring Back the Ku Klux Klan," Nick Martin, Splinter News, February 19, 2019.

16. "Alabama Newspaper Editor Calls for Klan Return to 'Clean out D.C.,'" Melissa Brown, *Montgomery Advertiser*, February 18, 2019.

17. "Who Pays? A Distributional Analysis of the Tax System in All 50 States, Sixth Edition," Institute on Taxation and Economic Policy, October 2018.

18. "For Most U.S. Workers, Real Wages Have Barely Budged in Decades," Drew DeSilver, Pew Research Center, Fact Tank, August 7, 2018.

19. "America's Moral Malady," William J. Barber II, *The Atlantic* "King Issue," February 2018.

20. Ibid.

21. "Anger in Michigan Over Appointing Emergency Managers," Julie Bosman and Monica Davey, *New York Times*, January 22, 2016.

22. Ibid.

23. "3 Years Later, No One Is in Jail Over Flint Tainted Water," Ed White, Associated Press, January 18, 2019.

24. "Lawsuit: State's Emergency Manager Law Discriminates Against Black Communities," Virginia Gordan, Michigan Public Radio, December 6, 2017.

25. Transcript, "The Cost of Inequality," Davos World Economic Forum, January 25, 2019.

26. Ibid.

27. "The Real American Emergency Is Fascism," Umair Haque, Medium.com, February 14, 2019.

28. Ibid.

Epilogue: After Trump, Who Are We?

1. "Immigrant Detention Is a Profitable Business," Jackie Speier, *San Francisco Chronicle*, October 24, 2018.

2. "Nearly 6,000 Abuse Complaints at Migrant Children Shelters," Colleen Long, Associated Press, February 26, 2019

Afterword to the Paperback Edition: The Bell Tolls

1. President Richard Nixon resigned before he could face a House vote to impeach him in 1974. Therefore, the three impeached presidents have been Andrew Johnson (1868), William Jefferson Clinton (1998), and Donald J. Trump (2019).

2. Evan McMullin tweet, January 30, 2020.

3. "In Private, Republicans Admit They Acquitted Trump Out of Fear," Senator Sherrod Brown, *New York Times,* February 5, 2020.

4. *Frederick Douglass: Prophet of Freedom*, David W. Blight, New York: Simon & Schuster, 2018.

5. "Trial Memorandum of the United States House of Representatives in the Impeachment Trial of President Donald J. Trump," United States House of Representatives, January 18, 2020.

6. "Jeffrey Epstein Dead in Suicide at Jail, Spurring Inquiries," William K. Rashbaum, Benjamin Weiser, and Michael Gold, *New York Times*, August 10, 2019.

7. NBC News report, January 28, 2020.

8. Ibid.

9. "Trump's impeachment lawyer at center of disputed Bolton claims," Andrew Desiderio, Kyle Cheney, and Darren Samuelsohn, *Politico*, January 31, 2020.

10. "White House Reportedly Replaced Ukraine Policy Staff With '3 Amigos,'" Philip Ewing, NPR, October 15, 2019.

11. Declassified memorandum of telephone conversation: President Donald Trump and Ukrainian President Volodymyr Zelensky, July 25, 2019.

12. "The impeachment trial is a reminder: our democracy is fragile. Civil rights activists already know that," Reverend William Barber, *The Guardian* US, January 31, 2020.

13. "EXCLUSIVE: Trump cites lessons from Nixon, says he 'was never going to fire Mueller'" Quinn Scanlan, Kendall Karson, and Mitchell Alva, ABC News, June 16, 2019.

14. "Trump Fires Impeachment Witnesses Gordon Sondland and Alexander Vindman in Post-Acquittal Purge," Peter Baker, Maggie Haberman, Danny Hakim, and Michael S. Schmidt, *New York Times*, February 7, 2020 (updated February 14, 2020).

15. "Republican Senators Tried to Stop Trump From Firing Impeachment Witness," Peter Baker, Michael S. Schmidt, and Maggie Haberman, *New York Times*, February 8, 2020 (updated February 14, 2020).

16. "Kurt Volker, Trump's Envoy for Ukraine, Resigns," Peter Baker, *New York Times*, October 3, 2019.

17. "U.S. Ambassador to Ukraine Recalled in 'Political Hit Job,' Lawmakers Say," Robbie Gramer and Amy Mackinnon, Foreign Policy, May 7, 2019.

18. "Bolton Objected to Ukraine Pressure Campaign, Calling Giuliani 'a Hand Grenade,'" Peter Baker and Nicholas Fandos, *New York Times*, October 14, 2020 (updated November 26, 2019).

19. "Barr blasts Trump's tweets on Stone case: 'Impossible for me to do my job': ABC News Exclusive," interview with ABC News Chief Justice Correspondent Pierre Thomas, ABCNews.com story by Anne Flaherty, February 13, 2020.

20. "Bill Barr Must Resign," Donald Ayer, *The Atlantic*, February 17, 2020.

21. "More than 2,000 former DOJ officials call on Attorney General William Barr to resign," Luke Barr, ABC News, February 17, 2020.

22. "While Stained in History, Trump Will Emerge From Trial Triumphant and Unshackled," Peter Baker, *New York Times*, February 1, 2020.

23. Tweets by Donald J. Trump, February 15, 2020.

24. Vacancies in the Federal Judiciary, 116th Congress, updated February 14, 2020.

25. "Federal Judge Lashes White House 'Banana Republic' Influence In Andrew McCabe Case," Mary Papenfuss, HuffPost, February 14, 2020.

26. "Judge cites Barr's 'misleading' statements in ordering review of Mueller report redactions," Spencer S. Hsu and Devlin Barrett, *Washington Post*, March 5, 2020.

27. "Trump Administration Suspends New Yorkers From Trusted Traveler Programs," Joel Rose and Colin Dwyer, NPR, February 6, 2020.

28. "Masked White Nationalists March in Washington With Police Escort," Reuters report, *U.S. News & World Report*, February 8, 2020.

29. "'I Fully Intend to Outlast These People': 18 Federal Workers on What It's Really Like to Work for the Trump Administration," written by Rachel M. Cohen and photographed by Jeff Elkins, *Washingtonian*, April 7, 2019.

30. "Open for Business: The Trump Revolution on America's Public Lands," Jim Robbins, Yale Environment 360, October 8, 2019.

31. "For the first time in history, U.S. billionaires paid a lower tax rate than the working class last year," Christopher Ingraham, *Washington Post*, October 8, 2019.

32. "Trump's $28 Billion Bet That Rural America Will Stick With Him," Mario Parker and Mike Dorning, *Bloomberg Businessweek*, September 19, 2019.

33. "Trump Says Those On Grand Princess Cruise Ship Should Stay On Boat So U.S. Coronavirus Numbers Don't Go Up," Jeffrey Martin, *Newsweek*, March 6, 2020.

34. "'He's Definitely Melting Down Over This': Trump, Germaphobe in Chief, Struggles to Control the Covid-19 Story," Gabriel Sherman, *Vanity Fair*, March 9, 2020.

READ MORE FROM JOY-ANN REID

Fracture

Barack Obama's speech on the Edmund Pettus Bridge to mark the fiftieth anniversary of the Selma to Montgomery marches should have represented the culmination of Martin Luther King Jr.'s dream of racial unity. Yet, in *Fracture*, MSNBC national correspondent Joy-Ann Reid shows that, despite the progress we have made, we are still a nation divided—as seen recently in headline-making tragedies such as the killing of Trayvon Martin and the uprisings in Ferguson and Baltimore.

With President Obama's election, Americans expected an open dialogue about race but instead discovered the irony of an African American president who seemed hamstrung when addressing racial matters, leaving many of his supporters disillusioned and his political enemies sharpening their knives. To understand why that is so, Reid examines the complicated relationship between Barack Obama and Bill and Hillary Clinton, and how their varied approaches to the race issue parallel the challenges facing the Democratic party itself: the disparate parts of its base and the whirl of shifting allegiances among its power players—and how this shapes the party and its hopes of retaining the White House.

The Man Who Sold America

The *New York Times* Bestseller

"The host of AM Joy on MSNBC argues that President Trump's administration is characterized by grift and venality that demeans the office and diminishes America." —*New York Times Book Review*

MSNBC'S Joy-Ann Reid calculates the true price of the Trump presidency and charts the road to Congress's impeachment investigation, now updated with a new afterword.

Is Donald Trump running the "longest con" in U.S. history? How did we get here? What will be left of America when he leaves office?

Providing new context and depth to our understanding, *The Man Who Sold America* reveals the causes and consequences of the Trump presidency and contends with the future that awaits us.